BEYOND BELIEF

ELLE HARDY

Beyond Belief

*How Pentecostal Christianity
Is Taking Over the World*

HURST & COMPANY, LONDON

First published in the United Kingdom in 2021 by
C. Hurst & Co. (Publishers) Ltd.,
New Wing, Somerset House, Strand, London, WC2R 1LA
© Elle Hardy, 2021
All rights reserved.
Printed in the United Kingdom by Bell and Bain Ltd, Glasgow

The right of Elle Hardy to be identified as the author of
this publication is asserted by her in accordance with the
Copyright, Designs and Patents Act, 1988.

A Cataloguing-in-Publication data record for this book
is available from the British Library.

ISBN: 9781787385535

This book is printed using paper from registered sustainable
and managed sources.

www.hurstpublishers.com

For Aden

CONTENTS

ACKNOWLEDGEMENTS

Firstly, this book wouldn't have been possible without the wonderful folks at Hurst. Michael Dwyer got the project from the beginning, and gave me support and freedom to do my thing. My sainted editor Lara Weisweiller-Wu put up with a lot, and put this all together. I am forever in her debt for her guidance, meticulous attention to detail, and gentle way of beating my words into coherence.

Nor could I have embarked on something so ambitious without the help of some brilliant academics, who were beyond generous with their time, wisdom and friendship. To Professors André Gagné, Sung-gun Kim, Solomon Kgatle, Ebenezer Obadare and David Smith, I cannot thank you enough. Credit for the good things in this book belongs to you.

While this list is almost certainly incomplete, I also must give thanks to the contributions and kindness of José Mazaricgos, Grace Moon, Anne Nelson, Lívia Reis Santos, Gustavo Ribeiro, Ronda Snyder, Dr Jin-Heon Jung, Dr Steven Horne, Dr Michael Shively, and Professors Olufemi Vaughan, Richard Flory, Ryan Burge and Andrew Chesnut. Without their advice and assistance, many of these stories would not have come to light.

Writing is a solitary pursuit, and one I often struggle with. Four friends made it far less lonely, always available for bouncing ideas, advice, reading chapter drafts, and providing more emotional support than they bargained for. Thank you to my broth-

ACKNOWLEDGEMENTS

ers David Patrikarakos, Joseph S. Furey, Adam Wesselinoff and Jason Wilson. Throughout it all, I missed the company of my late friend and mentor Mark Colvin.

In my travels around America, a few friends put me up along the way, and not for the first time. A huge thank you to Tim Vaught, William Bedwell, Doug Lapierre, Jim Eaton, and Antonia Eliason and Tom Morley for their exceptional company and far, far too much southern hospitality.

And of course, my people. I can't thank everyone dear to me, but must take time to acknowledge the twenty-two members of The Thread, the world's premier group chat, who in spite of their best efforts keep me sane and make me smarter. Without Alice Knight, Jasmine McCarthy, Marika Clemow, Alexis Bergantz, Holly Yates and John Norris being their wonderful selves and supporting me from near and far, I never would have made it across the finish line.

Above all, this book is an ode to my family, for whom I am eternally grateful if not good at showing it: the extended Dignan clan, especially my late aunt Cec for showing me the worldly life, and Marie for her humour and being invested in everything I do. Nothing would be possible without the love and support of my sister Louise, who is with me daily; my dad Terry, for blessing me with his work ethic and timeless advice that 'people only want to know what happens next'; and my mum Kate, who gifted me her endless curiosity and ear for a great expression.

Finally, this is all for Aden, who is everything.

PREFACE

The video of Tata Domingo Choc Ché's execution had been sitting on my laptop for the best part of a year before I could bring myself to watch it.

Fortifying myself with a few beers, I sat in my hotel room in a small rural town in northern Guatemala, unable to put it off any longer. The next morning I would be meeting with witnesses to find out exactly what happened that day—and why.

My investigation into this murder was the culmination of several years spent researching the global Pentecostal Christian movement. In just over a century since its founding, Pentecostalism has grown from a spontaneous outpouring of faith at a small church in downtown Los Angeles to become possibly the fastest-growing religion on Earth.[1]

Spreading the word across the globe, from its historic heartland in the United States to countries on every continent—South Korea, the UK and Brazil, to name but a few—the faith has collected some 600 million followers and counting.[2] Of the world's 2 billion Christians, a quarter are now Pentecostal—that's up from just 6 per cent in 1980.[3] It's predicted that, by 2050, 1 billion people—or one in ten of us—will be part of the movement.[4]

Owing largely to birth rates, Islam and Hinduism are the great competitors in the global race for souls, but no single denomination is getting people in the tent quite like the Pentecostals—by some estimates, the movement is converting 35,000 new followers each day.[5] In 2018, more Americans reported having had a born-again experience than in any record since 1972—at the same time in which evangelicals as an overall percentage of the population have been declining.[6] It's not only the born-again, however: the Pentecostal faith is being handed down to new generations in some of the planet's fastest-growing populations, including the world leader, sub-Saharan Africa.[7] If demography is destiny, then this movement is the future of Christian belief.

A branch of evangelical Christianity, Pentecostalism is 'born-again plus'—after accepting Jesus as Lord and Saviour, believers need to be filled with the Holy Spirit, usually by speaking in tongues. Yet trying to capture the uniqueness of this religion is easier said than done: for starters, there's no Pentecostal Pope or Archbishop of Canterbury, and the movement contains churches by countless other names. It's also establishing itself as an official renewal movement within other denominations desperate to stem the tide, most notably Catholicism; at a local level, it is even influencing the style of worship among certain rival Jewish or Muslim communities.

Many Pentecostals don't refer to themselves as such. In Korea, they're generally 'Presbyterians'; in Brazil and Spanish-speaking Latin America, *evangélicos*, or members of the Catholic Charismatic Renewal movement. Nigerians tend to take the Pentecostal name, while believers in America and Australia will think of themselves as 'non-denominational' and identify with whatever branding their specific megachurch goes by. Some Pentecostals simply call themselves 'Spirit-filled', and then there's the 'third wave of the Holy Spirit', or the New Apostolic Reformation—terms used (or, as I have found, avoided) by particular groups today. Where possible, I've tried to use local lingo in referencing different communities of believers, but for the most part I refer to the wider movement as 'Pentecostalism' to avoid confusion.

While it's ever more difficult to identify a Pentecostal church by what it might call itself, this is very much in keeping with a faith that has, from its first days, been distinguished by actions more than rigid doctrine. A movement that took its first steps in makeshift American camps, hawking visions of salvation to small crowds in poor rural areas, has transformed itself into a commercial and multimedia leviathan. Churches, some the size of airports, are still central to its mission; but these days, they offer record labels, speed dating events and addiction cures.

'Holy Rollers', as they've been pejoratively called, might be best known for the practice of speaking in tongues, but the movement has long specialised in addressing the specific needs of its followers in any given society—who, from the outset, have been the downtrodden and discriminated against. And this uplift is offered not as a reward in the afterlife, but as an instant improvement in the here and now. What's more, Pentecostalism doesn't just mediate with God on its followers' behalf; it empowers them to feel the blessings of the Spirit within themselves. This ability to bring down healing and prosperity, by yourself and for yourself, is no small thing in communities where governments don't seem able to provide adequate healthcare, job opportunities or living conditions.

Equally, the idea that anyone who believes can feel the Spirit has been a powerful one for outcasts or minorities in search of belonging. Whereas traditional Christian ministries have teams of trusted leaders, today's Pentecostals have Prophets and Apostles, and any believer can be one. 'God's conduits', these individuals practise 'power evangelism', performing miracles and providing signs and gifts while they preach, and finding the Holy Spirit's ability to manifest material riches. At the same time, despite this 'direct line to God' among the congregation, the best way to spot a Pentecostal church is by the charismatic preacher standing at the pulpit, doing 'church' their way and often holding great sway over their flock—maybe paradoxically, the personalised nature of Pentecostal faith, plus the lack of a central authority or overarching structure, often makes the individual church leader a figure of unrivalled importance.

There's a reason why Pentecostalism tends to be referred to as a movement, more than simply a faith. Long blessed with the ability to tell two stories at once, it appeals equally to people interested in feel-good spiritual experiences and to hardcore biblical fundamentalists; to cultural conservatives and to social media entrepreneurs. But no matter what you call it, Pentecostalism remains focused on the Holy Spirit: on its believers' direct experience of and personal interaction with the presence of God, and all the miracles that come with it—success in matters of the mind, body, spirit, and wallet.

* * *

Part One of this book explores how the movement's astonishing flexibility has proven a powerful draw across very different societies, making Pentecostalism feel as relevant to people's lives today as it did in the late nineteenth century. Part Two unpacks what the movement's explosion means for the world, travelling from that brutal murder in a tiny Guatemalan village to the halls of global power and the trappings of the 1 per cent.

It was in a cowhide-clobbered converted warehouse in Texas that I first stumbled across the depth and breadth of this movement, its ambition and its influence. For six weeks in 2018, I lived in Waco, a town better known for another, though far more fringe, Christian sect (the Branch Davidians, whose 51-day standoff with law enforcement resulted in seventy-six deaths). I was there to report on Waco's little known, but rapidly growing, Pentecostal-led industry of reform schools for men caught soliciting prostitutes (see Chapter 9).

The couple who ran the school weren't ones for labels, and they certainly didn't court the fake news media I belonged to, but they agreed to let me take a front row seat for what they considered to be a social revolution. As they began to loosen their distrust, these Christian revolutionaries revealed why they had let me join them. The inspiration for their mission had come from watching YouTube videos by a female preacher who cut her teeth at the Hillsong church of my native Sydney. She has been leading a crusade in the United States—and now the world—to end 'sexual slavery'. And, as is often the case with the Pentecostal movement, the concept wasn't all that it seemed.

As this book will show, there's much more than religion at play here. The positive, inclusive, here-and-now message of Pentecostalism may be drawing millions of marginalised people to the faith—but increasingly, those at the top of the movement are powerful figures with their own agenda. Today's Pentecostalism has a lot in common with the global political shift towards a populist, right-wing movement railing against the liberal world order and its ideals of globalisation, feminism, mass migration, and mainstream science. It is no accident that the faith's popularity has coincided with a marked shift in the political, social and economic outlook in all corners of the world; and Pentecostalism has played a vital, direct role in raising to power a new brand of strongmen including Donald Trump, Jair Bolsonaro, Viktor Orbán and Rodrigo Duterte. As the final chapters of the book reveal, this convergence of intolerance, instability and a sense of existential crisis, when coupled with the movement's strength of self-belief, can lead rapidly 'Pentecostalising' societies to a darkly violent place.

Research for *Beyond Belief* began long before the pandemic, but like everything else in our lives, it has been undeniably shaped by it. I wasn't able to travel to places such as India and the Philippines to see those countries' local movements in action; but Pentecostalism's overall characteristics and effects seem to hold true no matter where we look. Visiting some twelve countries

PREFACE

and six US states, I wanted to take the Pentecostal movement out from under the glass: not to offer a theological examination of the faith—work that has been done by many brilliant academics—but to tell the story of *how* Pentecostalism has grown so quickly, and *why* it's so significant.

Most importantly, this book is a profile of these fascinating, heroic and flawed people who are profoundly shaping not just their own religion, but the world we are living in.

PART ONE

THE GOOD NEWS

THE UNSTOPPABLE RISE
OF PENTECOSTALISM

1

THE LAST VOMIT OF SATAN

The spiritual landscape of nineteenth-century America was among history's most fertile ground. Prophets and priests wandered the country mending bodies and souls, trading ideas and rancour, and debating the conditions and timetable on which Christ would return. In a nation still far from coming to terms with itself after a series of bloody wars, people were wondering how it would all end, and they were anxious about where they would end up.

Pentecostals have always been great storytellers, and storytellers want nothing more than an audience. Their ability to connect their stories meaningfully to our lives was critical to the movement's birth, and remains critical to its ongoing rise—personal storytelling has been as important in Pentecostalism as anything that can be read in the Good Book.

How this movement came into being is a tale best told through the cinematic biographies of three unlikely founding figures, who each in turn shaped and furthered the Pentecostal movement. Together, this trio was as significant in transforming Christianity as Martin Luther—but instead of nailing their theology to a door, they crashed straight through it.

3

There's Charles Fox Parham, the renegade Methodist whose quickness to judge others was turned back on him as the movement overtook him; then there's William J. Seymour, the intelligent, humble son of freed slaves who brought the movement's emerging ideas into one big bang; and Aimee Semple McPherson, the controversial celebrity evangelist who was able to take Pentecostalism to the masses.

The religion they founded, by accident as much as design, was long seen as a bastard child of Christianity. But while many other denominations had a habit of talking down to the dispossessed, from the beginning the Pentecostal faith uniquely empowered women, migrants, African-Americans and the poor. This approach is as important to the movement now as it was then, and goes a long way to explaining its mass appeal: in this life, as much as the next, people want to be lifted up.

* * *

Early Pentecostalism took in the orphans and belief systems of a smattering of people seeking salvation and hope, but it was largely an outgrowth of the Holiness movement, which itself emerged from the teachings of John Wesley and his eighteenth-century British Methodists. With an emphasis on personal liberty, as well as being emotional and expressive, American Methodism was, in the words of historian Allan Anderson, the "frontier religion par excellence".[1]

Harnessing the power of the Holy Spirit wasn't new or exclusive to Holiness Methodists—in seventeenth-century America, the early Quakers may have got their name from what we would call 'spiritual gifts', quaking and jerking with the power of the Holy Ghost. Some forms of Scottish and German Protestantism were heavily into gifts, and in the 1800s Joseph Smith and his Latter Day Saints probably indulged in these kinds of practices too. You can trace them through slivers of history and different faiths all the way back to biblical times. But before the Holiness movement, 'Spirit-filled' beliefs were fringe elements within fringe movements. It wasn't until the start of the nineteenth century that they really got going.

Holiness became particularly influential in the religious movement called the Second Great Awakening, between 1790 and 1840. At this time, Holiness was being democratised and decentralised, and Americanised—spreading through camps and revivals, the evangelical saloons that were a distinguishing feature of early-nineteenth-century America. One important early figure in this movement gave a hint of what was to come: Phoebe Palmer (1807–74), one of the first major female preachers in the United States, helped inspire the Higher Life movement, which would lay much of the theological groundwork for Pentecostalism.[2]

In this time of camp revivals, as the fledgling nation was chasing after the frontier while careering towards civil war, mainstream Protestant churches appeared to be becoming more liberal, and more disdainful of the working classes. By contrast, Holiness churches were both hell-bent on biblical literalism, and far more diverse and accepting. Long after Phoebe Palmer's death, our three lead actors, each in their own way, would discover that the social element of faith was as important as the theological.

One man clearly influenced by the radical ways of the Holiness movement was Charles Fox Parham. Born in Iowa in 1873, and raised in Kansas in the Methodist faith, his birth coincided with winds of change that were fanning flames across not only America, but the world. The 1875 Keswick Convention in Britain kicked off a series of Protestant tent revivals within the Higher Life movement; a year later at a camp in North Carolina, there were reports of 130 people babbling in strange voices. Ever bent on reform and renewal, by the turn of the century there were three distinct branches of the Holiness faith, all "figuring out how to catch lightning in a bottle."[3]

Parham began preaching to congregations as a teenager in the late 1880s, but by the age of 22 had become disillusioned with a Methodist hierarchy that wouldn't let him deliver by "direct inspiration". He struck out on his own, becoming a popular itinerant preacher whose silver tongue could clock 250 words per minute.[4]

Throughout his life, Parham's self-assuredness led people to love and loathe him in equal measure. Unlike many other evangelists of his time, he displayed the hallmarks that have become particular to the Pentecostal movement: addressing the needs of people from all walks of life, in the here and now, with the unerring certainty that Jesus and history were on his side. Lack of humility is a charge that could be levelled against many self-proclaimed men of God, but Parham had a particular knack of rubbing other religious authority figures the wrong way, while appealing to ordinary people. It was his focus on sickness and healing that set him apart from other preachers of his day—and meant that he was never without a desperate and dedicated following.

Say what you like about his character, but this was a time when the biggest theological questions were all up for consideration, and Parham always picked a position and argued for it forcefully. Those who encountered him were left with no doubt that he believed he understood God's will, and he made big bets on key interpretations of faith. (Unlike the other two members of Pentecostalism's founding trinity, he had the advantage of staking such claims with house money. For starters, he was a white man, and had married the daughter of a prominent Kansas figure.)

From the outset, the Holiness movement was particularly interested in the idea of a 'third blessing'. Followers already believed in two blessings—that *first* you were born again; *then* you were sanctified, made holy and free from sin and its consequences, such as sickness. But what if there could also be a further blessing, or act of grace, which saw an outpouring of the Spirit in action?

Parham was one of the preachers who not only believed in the third blessing, but actively sought it. As with almost every issue in this emerging faith, the precise steps to salvation were a matter of contention: some thought there were three stages (conversion, sanctification, Holy Spirit baptism); others said it could be done in two (conversion and sanctification both happening at once, before baptism in the Spirit).[5] Parham was a three-step kind of guy.[6]

While he never shied away from a theological quarrel, Parham had far more immediate concerns. Divine intervention had saved the preacher and his young son from serious illness, and the family resettled in Topeka, Kansas, to focus on supernatural healing and Bible study. On their arrival, at the dawn of the twentieth century, Parham founded the Bethel Healing Home. Needless to say, it wasn't a debate about second versus third blessings that got people through the door.

Parham also started a Bible college in a suburban mansion called Stone's Folly. A Catholic church purchased the grounds in the 1940s, and built its rectory over the sandstone foundations.[7] Today, the remnants of the college are barely a dust speck on the map—on visiting, I was told that I was one of few local or international pilgrims who come to see where it all began; where the first flock was born.

It was at Stone's Folly, during a prayer meeting on the eerily complete date of 1 January 1901, that a 30-year-old worshipper at Bethel named Agnes Ozman began speaking and writing in 'Chinese'; she was unable to return to her native English for three days.[8] We now call what happened to Ozman *glossolalia*, or speaking in tongues—fulfilling the prophecy of 1 Corinthians 14:2, where St Paul the Apostle writes, "For one who speaks in a tongue speaks not to men but to God; for no one understands him, but he utters mysteries in the Spirit."

Following the death of Jesus, tongues were widely spoken by the Apostles, in the hope of spreading the Gospel. Yet by the time of St Augustine in 400 CE, the practice was already dying out. Some in the Orthodox East continued it, but in time *glosso-lalia* became largely confined to monasteries.[9] By the Middle Ages, Catholics saw speaking in tongues as a sign of possession that required exorcism. But, written as it was in the New Testament, the practice never disappeared from Christian thought completely. The nine gifts of the Holy Spirit that St Paul described in Corinthians—including prophecy, healing, miracles, and tongues and their interpretation[10]—were precisely what Parham's congregation was seeking on that first day of 1901.

For Parham, Ozman's gift was confirmation that she had received the third blessing—baptism by the Holy Spirit. For a congregation that suspected the End Times were coming, and soon, "this mighty truth" was a sign that they had the power to convert people in strange lands, following in the footsteps of St Paul two millennia earlier. "And if I was willing to stand for it," Parham later wrote, "with all the persecutions, hardships, trials, slander, scandal that it would entail, He would give me the bless-ing." He asked God for the gift for himself, and two nights later was rewarded with a "slight twist in my throat", before "a glory fell over me and I began to worship God in a Swedish tongue, which later changed to other languages and continued so until the morning."[11]

The Bethel Bible College was derided in the local press as "the Tower of Babel".[12] But for Parham, Ozman and their small group of true believers in the mansion, lightning had struck their little congregation—and it was up to them to tell the world.

* * *

Merging his spiritual and silver tongues, Parham began preach-ing and publishing news of the blessing that had been bestowed upon his little congregation, throughout Kansas and into neigh-bouring Texas and Oklahoma. On one of these trips to Houston, in 1905, Parham found a fervent disciple in the form of a fellow travelling man who had recently lost an eye to smallpox.

In 1895, while Parham had been splitting with the Methodist Church, a son of emancipated Louisiana slaves named William J. Seymour had been fleeing the poverty of subsistence farming and growing racial persecution in the Deep South. As was typical of his time and place, Seymour had been raised in an African-American Catholic church infused with strong elements of the supernatural and special revelation.

He was also everything that Parham was not: the opposite of a zealous firebrand, Seymour was a quiet, somewhat austere man who had moved through a number of religious movements before deciding what was right. Reverend Glenn A. Cook, a white Los Angeles journalist who resigned his position to work with Seymour's fledgling congregation, described Seymour's "wonderful character", which drew believers to him. "No amount of confusion or accusation seemed to disturb him. He would sit quietly behind the make-shift pulpit and smile at us until we were all condemned by our own activities," Cook wrote.[13] Another important Pentecostal figure we'll come across later, William Howard Durham, wrote kindly and cruelly that "Seymour was the meekest man I ever met. He seems to maintain a helpless dependence on God and is as simple-hearted as a little child, and at the same time is so filled with God that you feel the love and power every time you get near him."[14]

Before Seymour became a revered figure, he was a young man who moved North many years before the Great Migration of Black Americans from the rural South. He was born again into the Methodist faith in Indianapolis, and introduced to the Holiness movement around the turn of the century. But it was during a smallpox outbreak in Cincinnati that he truly saw the Lord's hand. The virus cost Seymour his left eye—a punishment, he thought, for being too slow to answer the call to minister.

After they met in Houston, Parham welcomed the "humble" and "unassuming" William J. Seymour into his circle. The sense of the 'white man's burden' to impose himself on recently freed slaves remained strong; in spite, or perhaps because, of Parham's deeply unpleasant racial views, he invited Seymour to study at his newly formed Bible college in the Texan city, against the South's Jim Crow laws. Seymour had to take his instruction sitting in the hallway outside the classroom.

The two men began sharing pulpits and street corners together in early 1906, with Parham encouraging Seymour to bring the new Christian bent to the Black community—and only the Black community—while critiquing Seymour's preaching style. We don't know how Seymour felt about the indignity of this relationship, but we do know that he was praying fervently for the Holy Spirit to baptise him in the gifts that were so critical to his faith.

Parham's white disciples took his message to northern cities such as Chicago and New York, and into Canada. Within a month of Seymour's banishment to the hallway, on the other hand, this gifted orator headed west: to Los Angeles, where he had been invited by Black preacher Julia Hutchins to preach at her Santa Fe Street Holiness Mission.

In what seems to have been a rite of passage for our founding trio, Seymour fell out with the congregation leaders almost as soon as he had arrived. Despite not having received the gift of tongues himself, Seymour had taken on Parham's strident theology. This insistence that *glossolalia* was evidence of having received the Holy Spirit saw Santa Fe Street's church doors padlocked to him. William J. Seymour was no longer welcome.

Undeterred, he began preaching to a group of friends. They planned a 10-day fast and spent several days studying the Bible verse in Acts 2:2–4, which describes the day of Pentecost:

> And suddenly there came a sound from heaven as of a rushing mighty wind, and it filled all the house where they were sitting.

And there appeared unto them cloven tongues like as of fire, and it sat upon each of them. And they were all filled with the Holy Ghost, and began to speak with other tongues, as the Spirit gave them utterance.

Eventually, this came true for Seymour's study group. Some present began speaking in tongues, yet it took the truest believer of them all three days of intense fasting and prayer to receive the gifts. On 12 April 1906, the Holy Spirit finally came to Seymour himself, baptising the preacher in the long-awaited blessing that had already so defined his 35 years.

Word that a revival was underway moved through Holiness circles across the US, and a crowd of the faithful flocked to bear witness. The spiritual weight of the moment soon became physical reality, with the front porch of Seymour's makeshift church collapsing in the outpouring of exuberance. What became known as the Apostolic Faith Mission moved into an empty African Methodist Episcopal church at 312 Azusa Street, downtown Los Angeles. Today, we call what happened in those momentous days 'the Azusa Street Revival', for it is considered the birth of Pentecostalism.

You wouldn't know it to see the place today, however. That original Pentecostal stomping ground is now an abandoned, graffitied shopfront where Little Tokyo meets Skid Row, surrounded by the homeless camps that line the streets of the inner city. A small sign marks the significance of the site, but it's far from a tourist attraction. Indeed, within the modern movement, references to Azusa Street and to Seymour himself are strikingly uncommon. Humble to the end, Seymour would have said that it was never about him, anyway. But the question of how a Black man's revival became so much more powerful than his white mentor's had been, only five years earlier, is an interesting one.

Based in a cosmopolitan, fast-growing city of internal and international migrants, Seymour welcomed all comers. Azusa Street encouraged Blacks, whites and immigrants to pray side by side, and promoted women to leadership positions, in defiance of the established evangelical order of the day. The fact that it was located in Los Angeles also meant that Seymour's church was able to draw in a far greater crowd of curious believers than the Bethel Healing Home in Topeka, Kansas. And there was something intangible—Heaven-sent, if you will—about this Revival. Accounts from the time describe a phenomenal energy, all overseen by a man who can only be described, in temperament at least, as a Jesus-like figure.

But there is another critical explanation for why Seymour's movement, and not Parham's, is considered the origin of Pentecostalism—a more disheartening one. The hand of history gave those first days crucial meaning. "The weird Babel of tongues", the headline that first reported the Azusa Street Revival, appeared on the front page of the *Los Angeles Daily Times* on 18 April 1906. It was also the morning of the great San Francisco earthquake.[15] This was a sign for many believers inside and outside of the building.

Sensational newspaper reports like this first one would become as important to Azusa Street's success as any Bible passage. Steeped in the yellow journalism that was the colour of the day, they reported the outpouring at Seymour's church, which lasted night after night for three years. Believers might have seen the hand of God, but the press treated the revival with disdain: "With the blare of trumpets out of tune and harmony, but lustily blown with all the power of human or inhuman lungs; they shine with phosphorescent gleam," one article read, carrying the scornful report of a local preacher.

> Strangely like that of brimstone, and with odor more or less tainted; they distract the affrighted atmosphere with a bewildering jargon of babbling tongues of all grades—dried, boiled, and smoked; they rant and dance and roll in a disgusting amalgamation of African voudou superstition and Caucasian insanity, and will pass away like the hysterical nightmares that they are.[16]

Historian Cecil M. Robeck Jr says that members of Seymour's congregation "were subjected to regular and frequent ridicule, both public and private." Not only were they viewed as fanatics, but a regular police presence saw many worshippers arrested "on grounds that they were 'insane.'"[17]

The coverage was far from favourable, but the press might have helped bring the movement into the popular imagination. Without all these scornful, seething, vicious and gleeful reports of the Revival, Azusa Street may have been lost to history. The papers mocked, but their regular reports saw an endless flow of both curious onlookers and the sincerely faithful, desperate to receive the Spirit. In time, these vivid descriptions and chaotic scenes would become the Mission's—and Seymour's—downfall. But for three glorious years, his house of "Love, Faith, Unity" would have daily meetings from mid-morning until midnight, with up to 1,500 people cramming the pews as the movement grew at "unparalleled speed".[18]

The popular preacher might have been a compassionate man, and socially radical for his day; but he was also a biblical literalist to his core. Seymour saw "impure doctrine" as a form of "spiritual fornication", and this particular approach—reaching out to the downtrodden, but with an absolutist belief system—is as much a part of the legacy he bequeathed to Pentecostalism as receiving the gifts of the Holy Spirit.[19]

* * *

Azusa Street attracted preachers from all over the country, and Seymour invited his former mentor to speak at the church. Parham was not impressed by the fervent egalitarian revival that greeted him, and muscled his way to the pulpit to tell the congregation that God was disgusted by what they were doing, described by another observer as "the last vomit of Satan".[20] The Revival's tearing down of social barriers appeared to be what chiefly offended opponents of the movement.

Never one to back away from a fight, Parham established a rival congregation just blocks away from Seymour's. This was, after all, the very limit of the American frontier that his Methodist forebears had long craved to conquer, and it was being led by Black people the Kansas preacher considered less than equal. Six years later, Parham would blast Seymour's movement as bringing forth "the worst prostitution of Christianity I ever witnessed." He described the missionaries who went out into the world from Azusa as "fanatics and fools" and "a monkey chattering"; "Seymour, drunken with power and swollen to bursting", had brought "justified criticism and condemnation from the Christian press and public" down on what Parham still regarded as his movement.[21]

Only, by then, the Kansas preacher himself had come to know a lot about condemnation and the power of the media. The man who had long been obsessed with social purity found the gun turned on him. In 1907, Parham was arrested in San Antonio, accused of sodomy. By the time the case was dropped, he had already been tried by the court of public opinion in newspapers and leaflets, his supposed confession distributed in towns along his preaching trail. Parham would maintain his innocence to the end, claiming that he had been set up by rival Holiness evangelist and prominent flat earther Wilbur Glenn Voliva, who would also come into conflict with Aimee Semple McPherson, the last of Pentecostalism's founding trinity.[22]

Whatever the truth, the scandal was his undoing, especially after it was closely followed by an incident at a 'Parhamite' church in Illinois, where Parham's followers began to believe that the End Times were drawing near. There was a frenzy as accusations of demonic possession and financial scandal led to a riot in his congregation, resulting in a spate of brutal exorcisms that saw three people tortured to death.[23] If the energy of the movement hadn't already shifted from Parham to

Seymour before these controversies, the national media attention the Kansas preacher had so long craved now ruined what was left of his name.

Parham faded back to Kansas, but the Holy Spirit's stay at Azusa Street was equally short in the cosmic scheme of things. Only three years after the Revival sparked to life in Los Angeles and the Christian world, the congregation itself receded.

As much as anything, historical reasons are to blame: revivals tend to have a lifespan of around three years. The kind of frenzied worship that comes with trying to bring on gifts of the Spirit can only last for so long, particularly considering Azusa's daily fasting and prayer rituals. New converts had slowed to a trickle as the secular press tired of printing their spectacular accounts. Seymour's star didn't flame out like Parham's, and he remained pastor at what settled into a small, Black congregation until his death in 1922. As the revival dispersed, however, he did come into conflict with William Durham, one of the early witnesses to Azusa Street; Seymour invited him back to lead the congregation while he went on tour in 1911. Durham's stay didn't last long, the congregation urgently recalling Seymour and padlocking the guest preacher out of the church—just as Seymour had been shut out five years earlier at Julia Hutchins' mission, the event that had led to the foundation of his own congregation.

By now, though, it didn't especially matter. The Pentecostal movement had expanded well beyond Azusa Street and the city of Los Angeles. Spirit-filled people moved up and down the Californian coast, through the Midwest and over to the East Coast.

The outpouring that had taken place at Azusa Street spoke more loudly to believers than any lurid stories in the printed press. The "negroes, poor, lowly, ignorant and despised" who made up the church's earliest days were now rapidly spreading the word about the possibilities in this life, and the imminence of the next—and the message was resonating not only across the United States, but throughout the world.

* * *

The word 'Pentecostal' might not have come into use until the 1910s (and wasn't popularised until the 1920s), but in a few short years, the nascent movement was already looking like what we recognise today.[24] Yet, in the process of becoming a formal church, it discarded the radical inclusion of Seymour's movement.

Before Azusa Street had brought it all together, there had already been congregations of the nascent movement gathering outside of Los Angeles. The Holiness-inspired Church of God in Christ (COGIC) had formed at the close of the nineteenth century, and by 1906—the year of Seymour's revival—it had some 100 congregations across the Deep South. In fact, it's thought that, a year or two before that great moment, COGIC's African-American founders had met William Seymour in Jackson, Mississippi.[25] Once Azusa Street started up, these leaders travelled to see the revival making all the noise in California, and they liked what they saw. The next year, the Church of God in Christ became the first legally incorporated Pentecostal body in the United States.

But there were bigger things going on in the South at the time, namely the peak of the Jim Crow segregation laws—and they would continue to affect Pentecostalism long after Seymour was forced to take his instruction from Parham in the hallway. In 1914, a group of white ministers split with the multiracial COGIC to start a new Pentecostal church, the Assemblies of God. Another group would later splinter off to form the United Pentecostal Church, and these two congregations would become America's two main white Pentecostal churches. Today the Assemblies of God, no longer a segregated church, remains the largest Pentecostal branch in the world.

Dividing and conquering the American spiritual map was a nice idea, but domestic 'church-planting' was far from the early Pentecostals' only calling. With the gift of tongues and God's blessing to go forth, foreign lands offered even greater bounties of souls to be saved. One of the earliest missionaries out into those 'strange lands' was a young Canadian woman called Aimee Kennedy. The once-rebellious child of a Salvation Army stage mum, she became the protégée of influential Chicago preacher William Durham—that friend-turned-foe of William J. Seymour.

After Aimee married Irish Pentecostal missionary Robert James Semple in 1908, the young couple moved to Chicago to join Durham's Full Gospel Assembly, whose overcrowded, raucous, all-night meetings reflected those he had witnessed at Azusa Street. In addition to these outpourings and personal experiences of healing, the Semples encountered a missionary movement that wasn't new or unique to the fledgling faith, but which had a zeal unlike the missions of other Christian denominations. The couple felt called to China—an exotic, 'godless' place that has long captured the Pentecostal imagination, from Agnes Ozman's first experience speaking tongues at Bethel Healing Home to believers in the present day. The Semples set off to Asia, their enthusiasm only matched by their ill-preparedness: James died of dysentery in Hong Kong before they'd even made it to the mainland.

Returning to the United States, the widowed Aimee Semple married Harold McPherson in 1912. But she had little interest in the role of a traditional wife—she was being called to the pulpit herself. By now, Mrs Semple McPherson was a locked and loaded Holiness Pentecostal, part of a growing movement that one observer described as "either insane over religion, or drunk on some glorious dream."[26]

It can be argued that the phenomenon of American women preachers had begun out of necessity, the sheer death toll of men in the Civil War of the 1860s bringing forth the likes of Phoebe Palmer. By the time Pentecostalism was a 'thing', the Holiness movement was uniquely comfortable in accepting female leaders. Still, none so far had been quite like Mrs Semple McPherson, who took to the so-called sawdust trail, where preachers evangelised on dust-scattered floors that dampened both noise and smell. Under her mother's gaze, Sister Aimee, as she became known, was blazing a trail of her own, taking her message—and that of Pentecostals—into the mainstream.

Combining Parham's loud confidence with Seymour's intuition for what people want and need, Semple McPherson began to temper some of the frenzied style that had been characteristic of the movement under her forebears, moving the screamers and tremblers filled with 'signs and wonders' into side tents at her revivals. Sister Aimee was the main event, and as word of her popularity grew, she took her travelling roadshow and message on tour in a "Gospel Car"; painted on its side were the words "Jesus is Coming Soon—Get Ready."[27]

A star had been born again. Semple McPherson took the best of her predecessors and made the whole package into a compelling show for the roaring '20s, stamped with her own brand of panache and eternal eye for publicity. This was an early incarnation of what we now recognise as televangelism, weaponising the advent of radio to grow faithful audiences. Grant Wacker, one of the great historians of the Pentecostal movement, says that Sister Aimee's followers "knew what they liked and rewarded it accordingly."

She knew what she liked, too. Separated from her second husband Harold (for what he would describe in the divorce papers as "abandonment"), Semple McPherson left for Los Angeles in 1918, and the press she courted there duly picked up on the fervour of her faith-healing demonstrations. The doctrine of direct experience with the Spirit, introduced by Parham and Seymour, opened up the movement to anyone sitting in the pews—but it also placed great weight on the person at the pulpit. Like many of the movement's leaders today, Sister Aimee discarded the Pentecostal label due to its stigma, recognising the power of an individual charismatic leader over that of encouraging the experience of her congregation alone.

The final cog in the wheel of a burgeoning faith that didn't much care for history or expertise, in 1920s America this 30-something widow-turned-divorcee shaped the Pentecostal movement's unmistakable way of 'doing God', laying the path for a style of practice that has become almost as important as the practice itself. When it comes to miracles, prophecy, and direct experience of God, Aimee Semple McPherson shaped the modern conception of a Pentecostal preacher, presiding over a world where it's often said that if you can name it, you can claim it.

Of course, this style of preaching requires as much faith in the self as in the Lord. Wacker describes Semple McPherson's ministry as "rollicking self-promotion" that, among other things, saw her trying to sell burial plots near her own in Los Angeles, marketed to her followers with the slogan "Go Up With Aimee!" Both the white-only Assemblies of God and the Black-founded Church of God in Christ might have been gathering followers at their growing number of congregations, but Sister Aimee was establishing herself as the face of the movement. Her Hollywood persona was equal parts preaching and performance, playing the emotions of a willing audience as though they were scales on a pipe organ, with an "uncanny" ability to sense and revive the waning attention of a congregation.

She may have cultivated a celebrity brand, but 'Sister' was far from an empty vessel. In starting America's fifth religious radio station, she became one of the first women to enter the radio business anywhere in the world.[28] Just as her radio shows were a forerunner to today's televangelism, she also built what we would probably recognise as the first megachurch. Her International

Church of the Foursquare Gospel, believed to be the largest church in the world at the time, could seat up to 10,000 and claims to have had 40 million visitors in its first 10 years.

Best remembered for her media savvy and knack for not only embracing the times, but staying ahead of them, Semple McPherson set the tone for her successors both culturally and ideologically. As in most other American evangelical sects, the Holiness preachers and early Pentecostals who went before her had been children of God with little care for day-to-day politics, other than preaching First World War pacifism. Christ was coming, and so long as there was religious freedom, they had little time for the burgeoning American state; they wanted to set religious life apart from it. As always, Semple McPherson stood up and stood out, and was not afraid to launch herself into the issues of the day. Most notably, she was an ardent creationist and public supporter of William Jennings Bryan throughout the 1925 Scopes Monkey Trial, which tested the legality of teaching evolution in public schools.

Sister Aimee might have ditched the label of Pentecostalism, but she was always happy to reap the benefits of its growing brand recognition. A willing recipient of the opportunities that the movement afforded to both women and minorities, she and Black preachers like Seymour still required a strength of personality to overcome society's hurdles—and perhaps she never truly did. For all of her charisma, Semple McPherson's inner life was far from charmed. She struggled with obsessive compulsive disorder, seems to have engaged in numerous affairs, and had a strained relationship with her mother, the towering figure in her life.

And then, one day, she vanished. Reported missing after swimming at a Los Angeles beach in May 1926, Aimee Semple McPherson's disappearance was headline news across the country. But another version of events quickly emerged: that she had run off with her married lover.[29]

Charles Parham's sex scandal had ended his public career; but, if anything, Sister Aimee's boosted hers. What unfolded served as an 'uncautionary' tale that has haunted so many of the Pentecostal leaders who have followed in her footsteps: the power and value of Semple McPherson's mass media reach, combined with her charismatic leadership, meant that she could never be lost in the public imagination. Emerging in a Mexico desert five weeks later with a sordid tale of capture and escape, Sister's 'abduction', and her subsequent trial for conspiracy and obstruction of justice, raised significant funds, and publicity.[30] The not-so-holy roller resumed life back in California—perhaps appropriately, drifting through Hollywood circles and capitalising on her infamy with speakeasy tours.

This might sound like a fitting tragic end for Pentecostalism's first showbiz figure, but there was another act left in her. Semple McPherson became known for her church's charitable aid during the Great Depression, and she even tinkered in politics. Supporting Herbert Hoover before publicly clashing with him when her interests were at stake, she turned her support to Franklin D. Roosevelt after he won the 1932 election. Ever looking beyond the horizon, she travelled overseas, meeting with Gandhi and witnessing a speech by Mussolini. Returning home to vehemently oppose both communism and fascism, Semple McPherson broke with the Pentecostal movement's historical anti-war stance to ardently support America's involvement in World War II, and was among the first prominent American Christian figures to support the idea of a Jewish homeland.

With a seemingly endless ability to raise money and a flair for self-promotion, Aimee Semple McPherson wrote the script for the public evangelicalism that can be seen in her many heirs today: combining political expediency with biblical literalism, and blurring genuine charity with a charismatic leader's self-enrichment. Add to this her ability to thrive in the face of scandal, and you have the quintessential modern Pentecostal preacher.

But, unlike today's Prophets, Sister Aimee didn't have social media. She might have survived scandals similar to those that had brought down Charles Parham, but much like William J. Seymour—although he didn't court fame—her relevance was largely dependent on newspapers. The International Church of the Foursquare Gospel that she founded now claims more than 6 million members in more than 50,000 congregations world-wide.[31] But following her 'kidnapping', Semple McPherson's own star power gradually waned. She embarked on various national tours, but slowly became a figure of self-parody.

The tragedy that she seemed destined for finally arrived in 1944, when she died from an overdose of barbiturates. And, as seems fitting, by the time of her death, 'Pentecostalism' had become a word for hushed circles.

* * *

By the end of the Second World War, the Pentecostal move-ment's brand of raucous, revivals-based faith had fallen out of favour in the United States, but its three founding figures—the fire-and-brimstone father, his inclusive protégé, and the mod-ernising free spirit—had already left an indelible mark on the material world. Wacker says that the genius of Pentecostalism is its ability "to hold two seemingly incompatible impulses in pro-ductive tension." We might associate Pentecostalism with intense spirituality, but it has never wavered from its beginnings as a salve for people trying to negotiate their everyday problems.

At the same time, it has always spoken to people who think that time is about to be called on everyday life. A hellfire passage from Acts might provide the biblical inspiration, but the move-ment has always tilted to the final book of the New Testament, the Book of Revelation. God has given Pentecostals the tools to prepare the earth for Christ to return and reclaim the church—to fix everything that's wrong with society and culture.

THE LAST VOMIT OF SATAN

With the uncanny ability to be all things to all people, the 'liquid smile' of a preacher, Prophet or Apostle—who might not have had fancy theological training, but can speak to ordinary people, especially in times of change and uncertainty—has never been more relevant. The heirs to those European Protestant upheavals centuries earlier, the first Pentecostals had not only unshackled religious doctrine, but spawned a movement that unshackled believers from religion's traditional gatekeepers. Parham, Seymour and Semple McPherson were touchingly human, condemned to sin, and forever repeating it. For all their many flaws, they created a movement that perfectly weighted the spiritual with the practical.

Speaking in tongues is closely associated with Pentecostal believers—both to their minds and in the minds of others—and the opportunity to experience the miraculous personally and for oneself, particularly through healing, remains as important now as it was in the earliest days. All Christian faiths allow a direct line to God—but what if He doesn't simply speak to you, but *through* you?

With the confidence and media savvy of Semple McPherson, Pentecostals were inspired to set out from the ramshackle pews of Parham and Seymour, and spread the good news across the globe. Only a few years after Azusa Street, they were sparking revivals in places from Johannesburg to Pyongyang. It was already plain that Pentecostalism was much more than a religion—it was a social, political and cultural force.

2

I JUST SING LIKE THEY DO BACK HOME

The opening song of the church service rolled over and over for 45 minutes, but I didn't want it to end. It was pure rock'n'roll, a sound that danced up and down the guitar frets, along the drum beats, and through the congregation. "*One, one, one,*" went the only lyrics, "*one way to God.*"

Worshippers moved like they were conjuring tricks, and my eyes instinctively looked for a hand at work. A teenage girl took hold of a guitar, put down by a man who had been moved to pick up a rattlesnake from a glass cage on the altar; other worshippers fanned out from their places to lay hands on an elderly man who had fallen backwards 'slain in the Spirit'; two women in veils held a flaming plastic bottle to their throat and spun around and around and around.

The Rock House Holiness Church in Section, Alabama is one of the few remaining 'snake-handling' churches in the country. The ecstatic outpourings of its services are probably the closest thing we might see in America today to Azusa Street. But this congregation couldn't be more different from Seymour's people.

Section is located on Sand Mountain, the tail of the Appala-chians that reach into northern Alabama. In living memory, the plateau was a 'sundown town'—a place that had a sign posted at the foot of the mountain telling Black people to get out before dark or face the consequences. Sundown towns were generally a weapon of the North until the civil rights era: after all, the South had the more discriminatory Jim Crow laws in full effect. But, for the avoidance of doubt, this was sundown country, and locals told me that the sign was only taken down in the 1990s.

The Holiness movement, a precursor to Pentecostalism, found this "strange land and peculiar people" in the late nineteenth century. The Rock House is a 'with signs' Holiness church—the most literal end of the Pentecostal spectrum, unique to the Appalachians. They take their cues from Mark 16:17–18:

> And these signs shall follow them that believe; In my name shall they cast out devils; they shall speak with new tongues; They shall take up serpents; and if they drink any deadly thing, it shall not hurt them; they shall lay hands on the sick, and they shall recover.

Most Pentecostals interpret the snakes and poison as metaphorical, but 'with signs' followers believe that the word "shall" in the Scripture is a command. Snakes are considered a demonic presence, so handling them demonstrates your power over the darkness. Drinking poison is a sign of faith: the sufficiently godly will be fortified against its effects.

Cylus Crawford lives next door to the church, and has been a member for over 20 years. He doesn't care for the Pentecostal label—"I just consider myself a Christian, ma'am"—but the way he and his people practise is as important as what they believe. Cylus and most of the thirty or so members of the Rock House were raised in the snake-handling tradition. "I got family members on both sides going back 100 years doin' it," he said.

While belief for Cylus is completely tied up in the signs, he claims that the tradition is a little less biblical than we may be led to believe. Back when the faith was roaring through the

Appalachians, "the moonshiners were losin' customers as people started receivin' the Holy Ghost, so they started puttin' snakes in lard cans and everything else to harm us."

Cylus and a cousin regularly travelled to snake-handling congregations throughout the region to sample—and at times, be sampled by—the devil's emissaries. "I've been bitten pretty bad," he said to my inevitable question, fiddling with his overalls. "They got me on the hand, on the leg, on the chest." When I asked what he did when he was bitten, he looked offended I even had to ask. "Pray."

The pain only lasted "two or three days, in terms of body functions", but the actual bites from the rattlesnakes, copperheads and cottonmouths the Rock House keeps "can hurt for months—one of my bites, it's been years." But snakes, they're predictable in their own way. What really makes Cylus mad is the authorities messing with his faith. After one of his bad bites, an ambulance that happened to be in the area took him to hospital—and in the state of Alabama, when you pass out, "you have no say, they have full control." You also have to be alert for unwanted medical assistance when drinking strychnine, because "it messes with your nervous system" and the body can involuntarily spasm. The medical people interfering mucks up the whole point: if you've been a good enough Christian, the snake bites and failing organs will heal through prayer.

Hospitals interfering with their faith is one thing, but it's never been the same in Alabama since 1991, when the authorities stopped looking the other way when it came to 'with signs' churches, after they came to unwelcome, worldwide prominence. In a drunken rage, Pastor Glenn Summerford, cousin of the Rock House's lead pastor Billy Summerford, stuck a gun to his wife Darlene's head and dragged her by the hair to a shed where he kept his seventeen poisonous snakes. As the court heard, after rattling and banging the cages to get them mad, he made her put her hand in the cage—if she didn't, he would shove her face in there. This horrific scene in Scottsboro, next door to Section, wasn't an exercise in faith—after recovering from her life-threatening bites, Darlene testified that her husband had tried to kill her because he wanted to marry another woman. A court found Summerford guilty of attempted murder and sentenced him to 129 years in prison.[1]

Needless to say, my presence as an outsider back at the Rock House was more tolerated than welcomed. Billy Summerford gave a sermon about the perils of breaking with tradition. About the people who, once they cut their sleeves or their hair, stop going to church. "Then you can't take that back," he warned, in an accent as thick as the Sand Mountain woodlands, "because you're a transgressor." But, once the consequences of losing faith had been established, it was time to worship in full glory. And with that, the bass drum thundered and the music began. A man jumped up onto the front pew to a rising beat of cheering and stomping. Father's Day was coming up, he said, and the day used to be a hard time for him "because o' my upbringing." But now, his voice only just audible above the banging and clapping, he knew "no other Father," he screamed, and the band exploded into another song.

I feel like dancin' my own way was its commandment, and the congregation obliged in full frenzy. A beautiful woman with hair down to her hips was the only one who could sing loud enough to be heard over the music. But the song went on for about an hour; what had gone before was only a warm-up act. A plump man with black suspenders holding up his jeans yelled over the music, "Brothers doing the signs!" At the altar, Billy pulled up snakes like they were rope and held them aloft; people began falling to the floor shaking in ecstasy; the beautiful woman kept singing and bashing her tambourine. It felt as though we were the only people left on Earth; and if this were it, I could think of no better way to go out.

They may be in a euphoric place, but it is clear that Cylus and the Rock House worshippers define themselves in opposition to the rest of society. And yet, they are so much a part of it. More than the ambulances coming to give them modern medicine, Billy Summerford's sermons were about holding on to how the members dress, and what they put in their bodies. Global capitalism and everything that comes along with it is moving in a way, and at a speed, that this congregation hasn't agreed to.

This, I came to discover, is a huge part of the appeal of the Pentecostal faith. A powerful and globally connected religious movement, its resurgence in the twenty-first century also represents a crisis of spirituality in today's world—one founded on consumption and individualism that replicates the social and political chaos of our time.

Since Aimee Semple McPherson—the proto-charismatic leader of the interwar years who understood the power of burgeoning consumer culture, and harnessed it into a celebrity following—the movement's torchbearers have all been creatures of their age. The trend continued throughout the twentieth century, embracing the American counterculture through figures we'll meet in this chapter, such as Lonnie Frisbee and John Wimber; and finally morphed into a global, digital corporate culture at the turn of the millennium, led by Brian Houston's Hillsong churches in Australia.

The commandment to pick up a rattlesnake in the name of faith has a lot in common with the way Spirit-led churches have felt compelled to adopt popular culture for their own ends. When it comes to holding belief in the modern world, the poison is part of the cure.

* * *

It feels fitting that, as the children of Azusa Street dispersed across the country in the early twentieth century, the energy of the movement drifted to the Deep South, a place the author

Flannery O'Connor noted was "hardly Christ-centered", but "most certainly Christ-haunted." The Ghost had already been working its way through places like Section even before it had reached Los Angeles. Now, the Church of God in Christ (COGIC)—the Black Southern Pentecostal church whose leaders had been influenced by William J. Seymour and Azusa Street—was about to change the culture of the United States, both secular and holy.

It all started when a little African-American girl in the Arkansas COGIC picked up a guitar. This musical prodigy came to be known as Sister Rosetta Tharpe, and by the early 1920s the young star and her mother were touring the South with an evangelist troupe. With her heavily distorted electric guitar backing, and her sweet voice singing first gospel and in time very unholy lyrics, she found admirers and imitators in Chicago and New York City.[2]

She wasn't alone. The Great Migration from the South was in full swing, and the "foot-stomping, boogie-woogie pianists, jazz trumpeters, and jug bands" that led Southern Pentecostal worship began to move their way around the country. The white churches that had split from Rosetta's people had also been infusing particularly Southern strains of music into their worship, with things like flatpicking guitars and washboards lighting up their gospel.[3] The thing we now call rock'n'roll was the record-friendly version of the music being played in the South's Pentecostal churches; as Sister Rosetta put it, "Oh, these kids and rock and roll—this is just sped up rhythm and blues. I've been doing that forever."[4] It wasn't only the music, but the style: the whooping, stomping, frenetic, ecstatic manner in which it was played, and the way it built an emotional bond between the person on stage and the audience. Preacher or performer could reach out and touch you in a way that would give you goosebumps.

After Rosetta Tharpe, who became known as the 'Godmother of Rock'n'Roll', a whole host of stars emerged from the

Pentecostal churches of the South. Little Richard's first public performance outside of his church was at age 14, opening for Sister Rosetta, who had seen him playing her songs.[5] In Mississippi, Tammy Wynette's stuffy Baptist church wouldn't allow itself to stoop to that kind of worship, but the local Pentecostal church "would let you bring in guitars and play rockin' gospel more like black gospel music."[6] B.B. King had a similar experience, while Jerry Lee Lewis and Johnny Cash didn't have to fight to play like that—they were born into Pentecostal churches.

Roaring through the congregations and denominations of the Deep South, a teenage Elvis Presley in Memphis, Tennessee, himself born into a family of devout Pentecostals, began sneaking down to a Black church to hear the style of his idol, Sister Rosetta. After he had translated it to secular radio, Presley had been labelled 'The King', and his music rock'n'roll. But, when asked about his distinctive sound and way of performing, Presley simply said, "I just sing like they do back home."[7]

As hip-thrusting, ecstatic, energetic rock'n'roll provided the soundtrack to a country on the up and up, a profound theological shift was also taking place that would have an equally seismic effect on the evangelical faith—albeit far from Dixie.

Starting in Saskatchewan, Canada, in 1947, two populist revivals took place, speaking to the age in a very different way from Elvis' music. The North American movement that grew out of events in Saskatchewan was countering the 'spiritual dryness' of the previous decade, and is generally known as the Latter Rain movement—the 'former rain' being the Holy Spirit's visitation of the disciples on Pentecost, establishing the Church; the 'latter rain' being the current focus for Pentecostals: the expectation that the Church would now complete its work, ahead of the Second Coming. In line with the American triumphalism of the postwar years, Latter Rain moved away from the thundering warnings that the End of Days were coming, and into this victorious outlook. Just as the Allies' enemies had been defeated by what was good and just, the Pentecostals' biblical adversaries could also be overcome.

Culturally, Latter Rain marked a change in temperament for the movement. Instead of 'tarrying'—that is, waiting for the blessings of the Spirit to fall upon them, as with Parham and Seymour's prayer and fasting rituals—this revival asserted that the laying of hands could deliver God's grace 'on demand'.[8] Christ's return to Earth would be achieved by emphasising the nine gifts of the Holy Spirit (healing, miracles, prophecy, tongues, and so on), as well as restoring the five-fold ministry of leadership, an idea that would become key to Pentecostalism's current, third wave (see below). In short, the Latter Rain revivalists wanted to make things mirror the early Church—the time of St Paul, when Christianity was established following the crucifixion. Latter Rain might have been relatively small, largely white, and rejected by many in Pentecostalism; but, as we'll see in Part Two, its influence would be substantial in the decades to come.

By that time, many traditional evangelists were condemning the "inverted Pentecostalism" that was rock'n'roll. But something else was happening in American culture: the first faultlines of the New Age movement of mind, body and spirit were beginning to show, arising within the 1960s counterculture. Countless young souls had been sold to "the devil's music", and it now became apparent that there might be an opportunity to use popular music to bring people back the other way.

After the Summer of Love, growing out of San Francisco's Haight-Ashbury neighbourhood in 1967, a young man named Lonnie Frisbee made his way to Southern California. Relying on his extreme charisma and musical talent, this original 'Jesus Freak' came to God through a troubled childhood and experimentation with LSD. It's unclear if Frisbee was one of the disaffected people who saw failure and hypocrisy among all of the good vibes, but he certainly found success as a 'hippie preacher'—a Pentecostal celebrity, the likes of which hadn't been seen since Sister Aimee. In one of Frisbee's many visions, he saw "thousands and thousands of young people at the ocean, lined up in huge crowds along the coast, and they were going out into the water to be baptised."

Strains of Frisbee's own life can be heard in his preaching. "When I first turned on to drugs, I thought that was the truth, so I turned everybody on to drugs," Frisbee said. "I lost everybody. I lost my parents and my brothers and friends, all my friends, they just left me, they marked me off as a fanatic ... Except [being born again] lasted, and it was real, and it was solid and it changed my life. And I immediately started to grow my hair a little bit longer than it was."[9] Frisbee seemed an eternally restless soul, and perhaps this helped him connect with his audiences, at a time of great cultural change and social upheaval.

Lonnie's 'lifestyle' was a don't-ask-don't-tell affair for many in the movement. It is said that people in charismatic circles knew that he would "party on Saturday night and preach on Sunday morning." Friends would mention later on that he considered homosexuality a sin. It doesn't matter, of course—but it did to the man he most greatly influenced, and who went on to write Frisbee out of Pentecostal history.

In the early '60s, a rock'n'roll band called the Paramours were beginning to find success in Los Angeles. The band soon split up and morphed into the Righteous Brothers, with one of the original Paramours, John Wimber, as their manager. Wimber was, in the words of *Christianity Today*, a "beer-guzzling, drug-abusing pop musician, who was converted at the age of 29 while chain-smoking his way through a Quaker-led Bible study."[10] In his own words, he was "just a fat man trying to get to heaven."[11]

Unlike many in the movement he would come to lead, Wimber wasn't a prodigal son returning to the faith, but what he called "a fourth-generation unbeliever". He had turned to God in his late twenties when his life was "in shambles" and he was "told a personal relationship with Jesus Christ offered hope from the despair."[12] This wasn't an intellectual conversion, but a metaphysical one.

Fire in his soul, and showbiz in his veins, Wimber quickly came into the orbit of 'kindred spirit' Lonnie Frisbee. He became enchanted by what the mystic called 'power evangelism'—that is, directly experiencing the signs, wonders and miracles of the Spirit through touching, trembling, screaming, healing, brought on through a "spontaneous, Spirit-inspired, empowered presentation of the gospel."[13] A bit like rock'n'roll, Frisbee's was a white, sanitised version of what had long been going on in Black churches like Azusa Street; but power evangelism—doing good, any way that made you feel good—was also a lot like a spiritual version of the Summer of Love.

Power evangelism is a proof of concept, showing God's power in action. Or, as Wimber liked to call it, "doin' the stuff." "When I worked for the devil, he let me do his stuff," he once famously said. "But when I came to work for Jesus they didn't want to let me do His stuff. To tell you the truth, I joined up to do the stuff!"[14]

Whatever you call it, the idea would propel Wimber to fame and glory, while Frisbee would be forgotten, and deliberately so. When it got back to their church in the early '80s that a young man had confessed to an affair with Frisbee, Wimber confronted the hippie preacher. Frisbee was effectively excommunicated, and became an independent missionary overseas. He began trying to deal with his personal demons, including the sexual abuse he had been subjected to as a child.[15]

But the band played on without him, and it seems as though they preferred it that way. As a friend of Frisbee's later noted, many in the movement that owed so much to him were "willing to rip pages out of a history book". Not only is Frisbee absent from the histories of his church and of the 'hippie Jesus' movement, but in John Wimber's six own published works, the man who had transformed Pentecostalism with his New Age power evangelism is only briefly mentioned as "the young man".[16] When Frisbee passed away from AIDS in 1993, not all of his former friends and disciples maintained this vow of silence. Some said that he was a figure akin to the biblical Samson, a leader with divine gifts brought low by temptation. Chuck Smith, the pastor who first 'discovered' Frisbee, described him as someone who failed to live up to his potential, saying, "I often wonder just what it could have been."

Frisbee was always a free spirit with a feel for a crowd, but Wimber brought to his hippie-infused movement a business acumen that helped him expand the reach of, and also balance out, "doin' the stuff". A former colleague said that Wimber "delivered new respectability to a congregation that had long been viewed as a bunch of holy rollers, babbling in tongues, rolling on the ground."[17] The era of Wimber and Frisbee that began in 1968 and lasted for around a decade is what is now called the second, charismatic wave of Pentecostalism—the time of "kinder, gentler Pentecostals" who opened up the faith to a new set of believers.[18]

Wimber argued that one of the reasons why old-school Pentecostal churches didn't experience signs and wonders was because they weren't banking on seeing the miraculous. To him and his growing followers, the themes of expectation and promise were important. As anthropologist T.M. Luhrmann put it, "the hippies changed what it meant to be Christian in America ... The radical innovation of the Jesus movement was the claim that Jesus is a person—not only historically, but now—and that he has a personal relationship with you in particular."[19] Their churches were places for surfers in flip-flops to get their *other* spiritual fix;

for students wearing big flares and bigger beards to continue their search for 'something more'; for hippies to swap their LSD for speaking in tongues, without losing the transcendental; for young people to participate in the changing culture through the folk and rock music that was so essential to the time.

In many ways, the LSD to 'Jesus Freak' pipeline resembled what I saw Cylus and his friends doing at the Rock House in Alabama, with their snakes and strychnine: grabbing hold of their poisons and adapting them into a virtue.

* * *

The square old preachers who benefited greatly from the New Age Jesus were never entirely comfortable with it. Wimber came into conflict with some in his small, Southern Californian church for his "experimental approach" to the Holy Spirit. As one former leader described the meeting that led to Wimber leaving the Calvary Chapel and striking out on his own, "Look, when you go to a McDonald's, you know you can order a Big Mac. If someone walks into a Calvary Chapel, they should be able to know what's there."[20]

Wimber moved on to the Vineyard Movement, which was bringing together the elements of the second wave: power evangelism; missions to establish new churches, known as church-planting; and popular music as part of worship. At one point, Vineyard counted Bob Dylan as a Bible school student, after the singer felt Jesus as a "physical thing" and began to tremble in a Tucson hotel room in 1978. "The glory of the Lord knocked me down and picked me up," he later said.[21] But Dylan was a late adopter, and by then, Charismatic Pentecostalism was indeed beginning to look more like McDonald's than McCartney.

Wimber might have fallen out with the guys who wanted to ensure spiritual customers knew what they were getting, but a movement intent on living up to people's expectations also looks a lot like consumer culture. Wimber, the music man who thought that the people who bought tickets deserved to see a show, had become the businessman, who believes that the customer is always right. These contradictions never sat easily with him, however, and after his time with Vineyard he became frustrated with the bureaucratic responsibilities that he felt were making him distant to his flock.

As we already saw in the way Frisbee was discarded, the Charismatic, New Age twist of Pentecostal faith wasn't all peace and love. Nor was it the final rebirth of the movement. In the 1970s, Wimber paired up with C. Peter Wagner, a missionary who had just returned to the United States after working in South America. Two of the great thinkers of Western Pentecostalism, they began to synthesise their ideas on how to combine evangelism with healing and prophecy for the next revolution.

Nowhere was this 'new turn' seen more than in the 1994 Toronto Blessing, a revival that brought together many of the 'mystics of Main Street' we know today, such as 'Mama' Heidi Baker of Iris Global, who we'll meet in Chapter 5, and Bill Johnson of Bethel Redding, who we'll meet in Chapter 7. At this modern-day Azusa Street, Wimber had to step in after secular media reported on believers under 'the power' practising hysterical "holy laughter" and making raucous animal noises.[22] Toronto marked the emergence of a new generation of media-conscious preachers, who had learnt the lessons of revelling in this kind of Spirit-filled experience. Today, overt shows of signs and wonders are still seen at some churches, like the Rock House in Alabama—but they are generally confined to the margins. Even though the 'hippiefication' of Pentecostalism changed the way the faith was practised, Wimber and his contemporaries still wanted it to be taken seriously as a fundamentalist religion with broad appeal.

In his later years, Wimber became invested in the idea that we're living in Satan's house, but the Kingdom of God is coming—in other words, distinguishing between the 'now' and the 'not yet'. While we're waiting for Jesus to return, the Devil's goods must be "plundered"—saving souls and casting out demons; we have to do the stuff, you could say. But in time Wimber found Wagner's emphasis on demonic spirits to be too much. The two men fell out over it and, after Wimber's death in 1997, Wagner went on to become the key theological figure in the third wave of the Holy Spirit, also known as Neo-Charismatic Pentecostalism (or, more recently, the New Apostolic Reformation).

Wagner helped a new crop of dynamic leaders steer their churches in a more corporate direction. One pillar of his movement was restoring the 'five-fold ministry'. Described by St Paul in Ephesians 4:11, this identifies Church leadership as Apostles, Prophets, evangelists, pastors and teachers—all working to get the world in order for Christ's return. It might not sound important—the closest most people will come to encountering this idea is the shift that has led many Pentecostal leaders and thinkers since the '90s to call themselves 'Prophet' or 'Apostle'. But it is all part of the movement's current, alarming shift towards an all-encompassing holy war, led by an army of believers striving to impose a dictatorship of the faithful. But this army is not an ancient, biblical one: it has taken the theology of Wagner and funnelled it into a monetised, globalised and digitised revolution for the age of Spotify and Instagram.

* * *

By the early 1980s, globalisation as we know it was really beginning to kick off, and the charismatic wave rolled across the Pacific Ocean to a place that looks a lot like California: Sydney, Australia.

My hometown was not a place for the born-again when I was growing up. Australia's Christian lines were fairly evenly divided between a vanilla Church of England, and Catholics from Irish or continental European backgrounds. If anything, Australians were actively hostile to the people we called 'happy clappers'. So much so that my parents were deeply uncomfortable with a high school friend's family asking me to a Christian spectacular with them in 1999—but there are worse things that teenagers can get up to on a Saturday night. It didn't carry any weight with me at the time, but I joined tens of thousands of others at a Hillsong event in Sydney's burgeoning western suburbs.

Hillsong has risen to become one of the most influential Churches in the Western world, best known as the Church of celebrities like Justin Bieber and various Kardashian-Jenners.[23] It has been called Australia's most powerful brand, a money machine, and even a cult. Since its humble beginnings of forty-five people, gathered at a school hall in Western Sydney, it has expanded to thirty countries on six continents, and now claims 150,000 weekly worshippers.[24]

Bricks-and-mortar churches are still central to the Pentecostal mission, but the successful third-wave church typified by Hillsong is much more than a building: it's a conglomerate. The megachurch's message is broadcast by a variety of means, not all of them by the book—at least, not the Good Book. Hillsong and their third-generation ilk have spawned a style that encompasses living-room congregations crowded around screens to watch YouTube preachers; a multilevel marketing industry selling products from miracle oils to self-education; and, importantly, the Holy Spirit's ability to manifest everything from private jets to Covid cures. Collection plates and tithes once accounted for most of a church's income, but these corporate churches can bring in up to 80 per cent of their revenue through music and other merchandise sales.[25]

Critics have held that the 'fast faith' practices of the third wave pander to the instant gratification culture that has given us social media 'likes' and shorter attention spans; but whatever the reality, it has proven a good fit for people who increasingly see themselves as time-poor. Personal experience—individualism—plays a greater role in determining 'truth' than Scripture or doctrine; and with its culture of innovation, leader worship and commitment to customer satisfaction, the Pentecostal third wave often feels like the spiritual incarnation of a Silicon Valley start-up.

Long before it was the house of worship of choice for twenty-first-century stars, with megachurches in New York City, London and Moscow, Hillsong was known as the Hills Christian Life Centre. Founded by Brian Houston and his wife Bobbie in 1983, within three years the church hosted its first worship music conference, called Hillsong. In 1988, the church's music group—known by the same name—released their debut album, *Spirit and Truth*. Building on the musical culture of the California Charismatic churches during the New Age, Hillsong has become the Grammy-winning world leader in mass-produced worship, and one of the most successful music brands in the world today. An estimated 50 million people around the world sing their songs each week. Hillsong UNITED's 2019 album *People* was the top-selling album across all genres in the United States in its debut week.[26] Hillsong's online streaming numbers are comparable to those of its most famous alumnus, Justin Bieber.[27]

The Houstons shed the Pentecostal label in favour of personal branding: it's simply Hillsong; at a push, a 'contemporary' Church. Structurally, it calls itself "one house with many rooms", and its mission statement is to be a "global movement positioned at the intersection of Christianity and culture". Brian Houston and his fellow Hillsong pastors like to repeat the idea that "the best is yet to come", meaning not only the fulfilment of biblical prophecy on Judgment Day, but in terms of our regular aspirations here on Earth.

Known for its uplifting style more than its substance, Hillsong fuses the basics of Christianity with general notions of spirituality and positive psychology. A social media clip of a Brian Houston sermon is illustrative of the mesmerising, circular wordplay that marks his preaching: "The Bible talks about self-control, and yet so often our self is *out* of control. It's ruling our emotions, it's controlling our spirit, it's choosing our actions ... I wonder if you are controlling yourself, or your *self* is controlling *you*?"[28]

But for all of these profundities on the self and the soul, Hillsong and the Houstons are very much of the material world. Like John Wimber before them, the Houstons have an incredible knack for feeling the pulse of popular and consumer culture. The couple have over 1.2 million Instagram followers combined; Brian has authored fourteen books, including *You Need More Money: Discovering God's Amazing Financial Plan for Your Life*; and together they oversee a vast business empire that generates around £50 million in annual revenue from tithing, merchandise, stadium tours and music.[29] Believers are enjoined to live their best lives as both disciples and consumers. By offering a personal connection with a distant pastor on social media, or the grandeur of being part of something big when you cross through turnstiles to enter a megachurch, Hillsong emphasises look and feel. Researchers have found that two thirds of megachurch attendees are under 50—and the pandemic is only likely to concentrate young worshippers further, in the hands of churches that already had the online infrastructure set up.[30]

For those outside of experiential megachurches, the trend of multimillion-dollar Christian record labels is a bizarre phenomenon that challenges the idea of devotional music as sombre and humbling. Some see the Church's cultural influence as serious and complex. One music scholar says that, while most musical styles "last for two generations", he has seen "three major shifts" in Hillsong's style in the space of just 15 years.[31] Others say that Hillsong and its ilk are becoming just another form of entertainment. At one point, the Church had so many members appearing on *Australian Idol* that in 2007 a whistleblower producer contacted the media to express his fears that Hillsong was manipulating the vote. A news programme on Channel Seven claimed that five of the nine finalists were from Hillsong; though this has been disputed, the report also interviewed two ex-Hillsong followers who said that Church members (who now number in excess of 40,000 in Australia) had been "pressured" to vote for Christian contestants in the past.[32] Hillsong's hit "Shout To The Lord" also featured twice in one season of *American Idol*.[33]

Hillsong's tidy indie-pop fusion could roll in at the end of your Spotify playlist without you noticing. A handy thing about devotional music is that it sounds a lot like love songs. A Hillsong hit such as "Oceans (Where Feet May Fail)" would sound at home in any commercial radio rotation. The Church's singers and sounds aren't as distinctive as a highly stylised pop starlet, but that's part of the point. Most importantly, it doesn't feel anything like Mum dragging you ear-first into Sunday school.

But make no mistake—for all of the emphasis on feeling good, you're still very much intended to feel God. After all, the Bible says that music is a tool to "teach and admonish" one another.[34] In the Book of Revelation, the only people who learn a new song in the End Times are those who are "redeemed from the earth".[35] Houston and his fellow pastors are biblical literalists, only they don't talk like them. Instead of delivering a thundering sermon against gay marriage, a Hillsong preacher is more likely to tell you that you must love yourself first and then find love—albeit with the coda that you should find love in the way God tells us to in the Bible.

In this regard, the Church's foray into Australia's same-sex marriage plebiscite in 2017 was instructive. "I urge all Christians to be a part of the upcoming postal plebiscite on same sex marriage," Brian Houston reportedly said in a statement ahead of the vote, since removed from Hillsong's website. He made use of many conservative political talking points:

> I believe God's Word is clear that marriage is between a man and a woman. The writings of the apostle Paul in scripture on the subject of homosexuality are also clear ... I believe that many Australians who are often referred to as the "silent majority" feel strongly on this subject but allow louder and often more aggressive voices to control the public dialogue.[36]

As much as it's known for its music, then, Hillsong has shown how a modern Pentecostal church can roll up its sleeves for a culture war without getting its hands dirty. The brand has been tarnished by a series of alleged sexual indiscretions on the part of Carl Lentz, famously Justin Bieber's former pastor and friend. But, just as the movement stepped over the fallen Lonnie Frisbee, Houston was quick to fire Lentz for his "moral failures".[37] In August 2021, Houston himself was charged with allegedly covering up child sex abuse by his father in the 1970s: according to *The Sydney Morning Herald*, "Frank Houston, who died in 2004, has been accused of abusing nine boys while a Pentecostal preacher." (Houston Jr denies the charges.)[38] Even in the unlikely event that the Church entirely succumbs to scandal, Hillsong's music, at least, will live on. An entertainment powerhouse, it is simply too popular—largely because it has shown that worship can be just another thing in our busy lives, and it can be fun and uplifting, too. In the end, it's hard to tell if modern Christian music—coming so far from the unbridled style of Sister Rosetta and even the Rock House, through defiant rock'n'roll and the emotive hippies of the counterculture—is secularising the sacred, or sacralising the secular.

Contemporary Pentecostal worship via neatly packaged, catchy devotional music is not always the antidote it promises to be. Thanks to the obvious wealth of megachurches like Hillsong, and the moral failings of some of their pastors, third-wave churches are often charged by the media with charlatanism; with encouraging vulnerable dupes to empty their wallets to buy 'Brian' another leather jacket—an insulting idea, to say the least. Whatever their flaws, third-wave churches have only absorbed an idea from the secular world that affects believers and non-believers alike: we've learned to conflate valuing something with paying for it. In today's way of "doin' the stuff", direct experience with God can be bought at a one-click checkout.

For all of its revolutionary potential, the Pentecostal faith has succumbed to the same forces as everything else in today's globalised, capitalised world. Instead of confessing to a pastor as we might have done in previous times, we're buying Hillsong Ministry School's seven-week short course on how to remedy our sins and improve ourselves from the comfort of our own homes. And while this model may have come out of the rich, consumer West, it's now selling across the world: with spiralling inequality everywhere, the new Pentecostal package of aspiration and belonging is compelling more seekers than ever before.

IF GOD MESSES WITH ME, HE'S DEAD

The morning sunlight was blinding, like a photographic flash in the eyes—only it wasn't a moment Chanyang Ju had expected to savour. To her, the car rolling up out of the light was a coffin on wheels, taking her from a Chinese prison cell to certain execution in North Korea, the homeland she had recently escaped.

Weeks earlier, the then 20-year-old had swum across the Tumen River that forms a natural border between North Korea and China. Arrested as soon as she scrambled onto the Chinese riverbank, and sent to a prison cell with twenty other defectors, she knew her fate. Upon repatriation, she would be executed, as she was the last of her family to have fled.

Years earlier, Chanyang's family had made a 10-year plan. First, her father had escaped, followed by her mother and younger brother and sister. Her mother was ill and would have died if she'd stayed; they thought that she could get treatment in South Korea. Chanyang had been interrogated by the authorities after her mother left, three years earlier. This time, she knew she wouldn't make it out the other side. "We were in an extremely dangerous situation," she told me, instinctively lowering her voice. "We would die if we were repatriated, because our family members had [already] gone to the South."[1]

On that tormenting last night in jail, Chanyang was prepared to roll all of the dice: "I might as well try praying before I die." The little she knew of God had been told to her in whispers by her grandparents, educated people who knew about life before the shutters had come down in the North. When she was 9, her father had got hold of a radio. The strongest signal they could receive was an American-funded Korean Christian broadcast, and she learned a little more; but honestly, it never made much sense. "And so I prayed in the jail, even though I didn't know how to pray. I prayed to myself, 'God if you save me, I will believe that you are real.'"

The next morning, the door of the prison closed and she prepared to begin the journey to her death. Stepping into the car, the driver asked her to confirm her name. When she did, he revealed his true identity: an undercover South Korean Pentecostal. "God had covered the eyes of the Chinese guards," she said. "The driver said that he had come to rescue me."

* * *

For North Koreans, the path to physical salvation has become intimately connected with spiritual deliverance; but arrival in the South is often not all that it promises to be. The idea of souls being up for grabs—and, indeed, for sale—is haunting the Korean faith. While escape to South Korea is idealised by people who haven't had to undertake the journey, this quest for redemption, both religious and literal, is a complicated, at times ugly affair.

There was a time when Pentecostalism in Korea was far more romantic. Before the communist revolution, the North's capital Pyongyang was known as 'the Jerusalem of the East', thanks in large part to the Pyongyang Great Revival, which took place in

1907—five years before the birth of Kim Il-sung, the 'Great Leader' and founder of the Democratic People's Republic of Korea. Chanyang's grandparents weren't the only North Koreans immersed in Christianity growing up. The grandson of a preacher, Kim Il-sung himself was raised as Christian as a collection plate.

Coming only a year after Azusa Street, the Pyongyang Revival reportedly saw 100,000 people converted to Christianity; within three years, a further 50,000 Koreans had been saved, out of a total population of around 17 million—not bad for a new, foreign faith.[3] It's uncertain whether any missionaries from California were at the revival; but, as we saw with Aimee and Robert Semple, many of the early believers did set sail for Asia with a particular zeal. Thinking they had been blessed with the gift to speak Chinese and other languages, American missionaries arrived in Asian cities utterly unequipped, unable to communicate with locals and ripe for illnesses such as dysentery, smallpox and cholera.[4]

In Korean Christian folklore, the timing of the Pyongyang Revival was significant, coming three years before the Japanese colonisation of the Korean Peninsula (1910–45). The fledgling country of Korea had been beginning to imagine itself as a nation, but Japan's brutal colonisation never allowed it to blossom into greatness, either as a country or as the centre of Christian life in Asia. Churches, however, remained a source of resistance throughout the occupation.[5]

When the Japanese left Korea after their World War II defeat, the Peninsula was divided into two states. Christians saw the writing on the wall as communists moved into the newly created North Korea, and many believers fled to the South, as church leaders were arrested, imprisoned and often killed.[6] After the Korean War, Kim Il-sung banned the Bible and closed churches. He appropriated both Christian imagery and Japanese imperial fascism to create a national ideology and personality cult. North Korea expert B.R. Myers sums up the messaging this way: "The Korean people are too pure blooded, and therefore too virtuous, to survive in this evil world without a great parental leader." Kim's son and successor, Kim Jong-il, advanced the Bible-inflected mythology of the dynasty: "For Kim Jong Il so loved the Korean people that he gave them his only parent."[7]

The North–South border became not only a division between communism and anti-communism, but a clear demarcation between the old and the new. America was the South's saviour and the strong new global power, with none of the imperial baggage of traditional regional powers China and Japan (to this day, US military bases in the South are broadly popular). Christianity became an important part of South Korean nationalism, and the American way of doing both church and state a symbol of strength and wealth.[8]

By the 1970s, the South's capital Seoul was transforming into a global metropolis. Standards of living were on the rise, and people were flocking to the city from the villages and provinces for a better life. Korean religious scholar Sung-gun Kim, himself the son of Christians who fled Pyongyang, believes that there's a "special connection" between the market revolution and the spiritual evolution that took place in Seoul; that each required the other in order for them both to flourish.

And flourish they did. American-inspired megachurches—congregations with more than 2,000 members attending each week—began sprouting across the city, which is now home to seventeen of them, making Seoul the megachurch capital of the world.[9] Korean Protestant churches tend to label themselves Presbyterian, though around 85 per cent of them are Pentecostal. The Peninsula's shamanistic culture has made Pentecostalism's Spirit-led worship more of a natural fit.

And, of course, stoking fires is part of the business model: it's not unusual to hear sermons railing against the North and praying for reunification on a weekly basis. For better and for worse, a population of defectors is also baked into this noise, with some on both sides seeing these Northern refugees as pawns in a bigger game. Believing defectors are considered a blessing from God bestowed upon the congregation—one that confirms that it is spiritually and politically correct.

So, when the megachurch Chanyang's father attended saw one of their own—a man with not a lot, but one who worked hard and was a good Christian—in despair about the fate of his daughter, they moved beyond just prayer. God didn't cover the eyes of the Chinese guards—the church had passed the hat around and paid a significant bribe to allow Chanyang to escape.

Foreigners at this American church in South Korea were praying for her—a confusing thing to find out after receiving a typical Northern education. Chanyang had been taught that people in capitalist societies are too busy carving out their own lives to help others, so how would they have had time to pray for hers? But the story of her rescue had another moral, too: time wasn't the only thing these Christians had used to free her. "If you have money," Chanyang smiled, "you can execute anything."

* * *

Well, almost anything. There are tiny networks of Christians inside North Korea itself, though most worshippers are islands, quietly praying on their own. "We don't proselytise," I was told by a director of an international organisation that has placed Christians in the North, but "when people are interested, we do share." The director boasted that in China, he had once personally baptised a North Korean. A joyous occasion "in the sense that they saw the light," but also sobering, "because that person had to go back to North Korea and keep their faith to themselves."

Most of the interest—and money—from such groups is not about plucking ordinary people from inside the country; it's in reaching North Korean businesspeople and officials while they are in China. But divine entrepreneurs, usually Korean-Americans, can still do good business raising money for exotic missions. Church networks in South Korea and across America raise money to fund broadcasts that pipe Korean sermons into the North, like the ones that Chanyang sometimes heard as a child; or the even more popular programmes to send balloons carrying Bible messages across the demilitarised zone between the two Koreas. It's a practice that particularly enrages Pyongyang, to the point where the South Korean government recently banned balloon launches as a gesture of goodwill.[10]

Defectors, of which there are around 1,000 per year to the South,[11] tend to learn quickly after joining South Korean life that certain people like to hear certain things. Escape stories often change depending on their audience. Inside North Korea, there is a general understanding that the cousins below the 38th parallel are prospering. But the Kim regime maintains relative stability in the North, and appears to enjoy a significant degree of popular support, as Myers points out. The country isn't just a giant prison camp, as the West often believes: most North Koreans leave not to escape political oppression, but "because of hungry", as Chanyang said in self-mocking English—for material reasons.[12] And their stories of flight are not usually as dramatic or decisive as hers. More often, it's a case of those who cross the border regularly to work in China and Russia seizing the opportunity to stay; and around half of the defectors to China voluntarily return to their homeland.[13] There is also a population that makes it to the South, but *then* defects back, or at least wishes to. But these realities often end up being replaced in the retelling with soundbites for eager foreign ears: abstract ideas such as defecting for the sake of freedom of speech.

Serious money and organisation goes into the co-ordinated network of smugglers and safehouses, predominantly in China, but also Russia and other parts of Asia. Christians run most, or are connected with most, of the underground that helps people escape North Korea.[14] Resettlement payments given to arriving defectors by the South Korean government have been slashed in recent years: originally, they were unofficially designed, with room for brokers' fees. Today it is more of a package deal: housing, incentives for training, and so on. But smugglers know what refugees receive on landing, and the going rate is usually half of the government payout. It usually gets paid, too, because defectors tend to want smugglers to go back and help their family members.

If finding help to leave isn't the hardest part about defecting, nor is the physical escape from North Korea—the problem is where you escape *to*. There's no 'Defector Express' you can catch straight to Seoul. Although today it's more of a tourist zone on both sides than any kind of Cold War battlefront, crossing the demilitarised zone is near impossible unless you're a soldier with access. On the other hand, most of North Korea's 850-mile border with China is formed by natural rivers. Depending on where you live, the physical act of crossing can be pretty easy.[15] Foreign ears seeking cinematic stories of escape from North Korea—and there's a particularly strong market for those among conservative Christians in the United States—would find it implausible, yet it's one of the least fearsome natural borders anyone could imagine. I've seen part of it first-hand: in the Chinese city of Dandong, part of the Yalu or Amnok River that forms the border is at best 4 metres wide, and freezes over in winter.

Chinese authorities are aware of how easy it is to make it over, and will set up stings to catch refugees like Chanyang crossing at night; enforcement along the border is deliberately severe, to head off a humanitarian crisis of 20 million people on China's doorstep. But Beijing's most important policy is to maintain diplomatic and financial support for the Kim regime, not ultra-aggressive border policing. The hardest part of defecting from the North isn't getting across, but the onward travel afterward; it's what happens to you once you make it to the far bank of the river. The hardships endured in China are what break many defectors—and make many Pentecostals. In some ways, Chanyang was lucky she was thrown into prison. More than 70 per cent of North Korean defectors are female,[16] a fact that is well known on the other side. If they're not nabbed by the military, there's a chance they will be caught by human traffickers and sold into sex or labour slavery, or into the booming bridal market for rural Chinese bachelors.

Of course, operating a Christian people-smuggling network isn't much easier in China than in North Korea. Religious organisations are required to register with the state, and Korean churches are kept on an especially tight leash. Chinese 'house churches', a movement to circumvent state control of worship, are more easily disguised and able to take in defectors. Members of these informal congregations, which meet in private properties, then operate clandestine safehouses in apartment buildings.

In the pay-to-play system of defecting to South Korea, money bellows. Chanyang's rescue mission was well funded, so she was spared the worst of it as she was quickly spirited across China and through Laos and Thailand, before flying to Seoul. Even with this relatively smooth passage, it was a spiritual experience for her, where "the people I'd meet in my dreams the night before would appear the next day and help us."[17]

Without Chinese language or identity cards, North Koreans are easily ratted out. Smugglers—or missionaries, as they prefer to be called—can create and enforce rigid rules, where the discipline is often physical. Given that most safehouses are in residential buildings, to avoid alerting neighbours their charges must live quietly and follow the strict routines. Cooped-up teenage boys getting frustrated and aggressive is a notorious problem.

One person familiar with the networks says that he has personally witnessed missionaries being "brutal, decisive, and violent."
These are "desperate conditions," he told me, which refugees
must simply "manage and endure."

For those undertaking a budget defection, Christianity
becomes the only thing to *do*. One refugee who was stuck for
three years in China claims to have read the Bible 100 times.[18]
In the long wait for passage to South Korea, that expression you
hear from the imperialist Americans, *have you been saved*, takes
on both a personal and a literal meaning. Christians want to
make it possible for the defectors to embrace God—but for the
refugees, accepting the Lord is both a spiritual and a strategic
decision. Christians are 'Saving' them, but also *saving* them, and
conversion for many is seen as part of the process into a new life.
In theory, conversion to Christianity is not something humans
can do themselves—Koreans will say that it's up to God—but, at
the same time, a person must accept Jesus as Saviour. Refusal to
do so while in a Pentecostal safehouse would likely see you cut
adrift. After all, being part of a smuggling network is a dangerous business that would see members jailed if caught—even
though they feel they've been divinely called to the mission,
smugglers aren't going to risk *this* life on someone who insists on
remaining a nonbeliever.

However, it's not accurate to say that these are gunpoint conversions, either. For the refugees, it's a process partly forced,
partly blessed, partly experienced.[19] Nor will they have been
totally estranged from ideas of faith, or ignorant of how these
can cement belonging and identity, before their defection.
North Korea has a rich spiritual tradition. Kim Il-sung derived
many ideas for the national ideology from his Christian
upbringing, for starters. And a closer reading highlights how
the figures of 'The Sun' and his son, the 'Shining Star of Paektu
Mountain', owe just as much to blood-and-soil nationalism and

Korean shamanism: the dynasty's mythology puts an emphasis on natural landscapes to symbolise racial purity, and consulting fortune-tellers is a widely accepted practice among ordinary people in the North.[20]

It shouldn't be a surprise, then, that the Bible put into many defectors' hands during their journey often ends up helping them to interpret their ordeal and put their suffering into context.[21] In time, this may well develop a deeper, spiritual meaning, as it did for Chanyang, if not an ideological one. Outsiders often crudely paint this transition as swapping one regime for another, a military power for a celestial one. Some defectors do become forever wary of missionaries after their experience, but many more testimonies speak to receiving a special spiritual moment of divine power that helped them to escape North Korea—a sense that God selected them personally for this divine journey. For many, coming to Jesus is simply part of the process of fleeing North Korea and settling in the South.

* * *

When it comes to escaping, there's making it to Seoul, and then there's making it *in* Seoul. After the interrogations to ensure they're not a spy, and a three-month integration course, defectors are launched out into one of the world's most high-tech megacities with a £250 monthly stipend. Workers tend to lack transferable skills for the modern workforce, and they carry thick Northern accents and antiquated vocabularies that mark them out immediately. "It's not like we could work at a cafe and make espressos—we even had a hard time reading the menus," Chanyang explained. "And while we could read, we couldn't understand things, like what a latte is." Defectors also tend to have residual health problems from Northern hardships such as the 'Arduous March' famine from 1994 to 1998 that killed up to a million people.[22]

The stark differences of South Korean society present a new set of challenges. Crushing competitiveness is a hallmark of life in Seoul. Pentecostal Christianity is the faith of the educated and ambitious. Believers study select verses each month from 'one-a-day' calendar books, or even write out the text of the Bible from Genesis to Revelation over and over again—sometimes in English, to illustrate how Americanised they are. But it is hard for defectors to integrate into this social and cultural milieu.

Northerners face widespread and increasing discrimination in the job market—Southerners, particularly young people, rail against affirmative action programmes and modest benefits bestowed on new arrivals. School dropout rates are about six times higher for North Korean students than for 'native' Southerners, unemployment around four times higher, and monthly wages around half the pay of other Seoulites. Tragically, the suicide rate for defectors is three times higher than for their Southern counterparts.[23]

When she reached Seoul in her early 20s, Chanyang adjusted better than many of her compatriots. Like a lot of defectors, she's taken on a 'Southern' name—*chanyang* means praise, and *ju* means Lord. Knowing a little about the city from the radio her father kept in the house, she knew that she wanted to go to nightclubs, get a manicure, "drink all the alcohol I could, and meet a boyfriend." God might have helped her escape, but if she "followed only God wholeheartedly", she would have to give it all up. "So instead, I turned my back and just lived the way I wanted to."

As a defector, your story is your most valuable asset, and Chanyang confided in me that telling it out loud still gives her chills. Defecting and converting each have their own set of rewards, and not long after she arrived in Seoul, she was invited to appear on a television programme called *Now on My Way to Meet You*. It's a chat show where North Korean 'beauties' share stories about life under the regime to a soundtrack of gunshots, before they are given assistance to track down relatives in the South.[24] The wild success of Chanyang's appearance sparked numerous others on the 'defector circuit', including *DefectorTV*, which propelled her to minor celebrity and Instagram influencer status. She turned her life towards nightclubs and fame and material things, as she'd hoped for; but "I felt like I was in a living hell, not accepting what God had given me and instead making my own decisions," she said. By the time she divorced her husband in 2018, He was there waiting, like an impatient friend looking at their watch.

"The way He answered my calls, the dimension of it was different. It wasn't a picture or movie this time—it was just fire. *Fire.* I closed my eyes, and it wasn't merely red fire. It was shiny, blinding like the sun and it felt like my sins were being showered away," she remembered. "It felt like I had cleaned all the dirtiness off of me. My health soared, I'd never felt so good even after taking medicine. Everything was so clear and perfect."

This baptism of fire gave her the gift of tongues. "People pray with their lips, but God showed me the light and my emotions were not human," Chanyang told me. "My voice is usually not very high, but it shot up so high and I couldn't speak. I couldn't speak in Korean. And I began speaking so fast in this unrecognisably high pitch. I communicated with God, He forgave me, washed me and loved me ... I ended up just going up to the cross and laying down next to it. And then God began delivering to me messages from the Bible."

There might be something in common between these two highly charged, seemingly opposite experiences after defecting to the South. Neuroscience has found that the same reward-based neural systems associated with drug-taking are activated when individuals are "feeling the spirit".[25] But after 'feeling the fire', there was only one direction Chanyang was going to take. God told her that there's a global spiritual war underway, but she need not feel the burden of saving all North Koreans. The important thing was that she could recognise evil forces, not only in her former homeland, but all around her. God gave her the gift of *fighting*, a word that, in the Korean, carries a sense of working hard and persevering.

For a new convert, Pentecostalism provides immediate signs, and some wonders too. This physical experience becomes a clear demarcation between two lives, closing one door and opening another. Since the earliest days of Azusa Street, Pentecostals have pioneered salvation narratives of a personal relationship (*He* died for *me*) with a first-name-basis friend (Jesus, minus the Christ). The faith has rejected ideas of living a virtuous life and waiting for God to choose you—if anything, *you* have to choose *Him*, as Chanyang did. The bright lights of the big city may have distracted her for a while, but ultimately, the 'underground railway' to Seoul, a modern-day Road to Damascus, led her to make this choice.[26]

* * *

A conversion narrative is a currency in South Korea, and one that's readily accepted. Not only that, but it is a tool for believers to help navigate their new world; for people adrift in big urban societies that didn't grow up under the yoke of the Kim dynasty. It's also a way to meet the social pressure to prove that they can integrate, assimilation of defectors being seen as a kind of test run for the popular and widely expected eventual reunification of the Peninsula.[27] North Korean defectors are more religious than their Southern counterparts, and in the wake of a series of devastating scandals in the megachurches, South Korean Christians are using the conversion of refugees in order to revitalise weakened churches.[28]

Megachurches provide significant and ongoing support, but the price of admission is clear: what defectors call their "face being sold". Like marquee drawcards, they are expected to attend fundraising events and put their story in the shop window.[29] In return for participating in this spectacle—which brings the churches prestige and money—they receive 'scholarships' for attending churches, sometimes to the tune of several hundred US dollars a month; not to mention other perks such as free dentistry and medical services from members of the congregation, and donations of clothes and homewares.

So-called 'church-hopping' is a regular, if humiliating, custom. Given that megachurches have many services across a Sunday, a defector can attend three or four in a day, showing their face and picking up money to supplement their meagre government benefits and low-income jobs. Some, like Chanyang, refuse the scholarships as a matter of pride—"there's a mainstream narrative of having to automatically 'care for' defectors in South Korea"—but for many who haven't had the good fortune and income generated by media success, it's a matter of necessity, albeit a deeply uncomfortable one.

"A lot of defectors hurt each other, and they wind up getting hurt," she continued. "Life becomes feigned and drenched in envy. If a person at church was once caring and attentive to you, then one day stops being so, there will be jealousy and anger." The unedifying spectacle of selling your face means that defectors often shun each other. Paranoia is rife, as they are desperate to be accepted, or fear Kim regime spies within their communities. Overwhelmingly, they do not accept the political and spiritual leadership of fellow defectors.

Yoseb Shin is one of those people—but it's not only the refugee community that he's struggling with. Defecting to the South, even when you embrace Pentecostalism and become the best possible refugee, won't necessarily make you happy.

The 52-year-old had left Pyongyang three years before I met him, adamant that "God came to me."[30] He was working as a driver for North Korean labourers in Vladivostok, the far-eastern Russian city, when he made a split-second decision to escape. Yoseb—Joseph in Korean, the Christian name he would adopt for his new life—hid for eight days before being transferred along a secret route that had been newly opened to defectors. "After spending time in a country where the Internet worked, I began to see the world for what it is," he said, in a North Korean accent so thick that my translator Grace had trouble understanding him. ("Sometimes he uses entirely different words to South Koreans," she explained, "and he speaks in an incredibly poetic, almost outdated manner.")

Making friends with Russian coworkers was his first awakening. They showed him South Korean news on their smartphones, and taught him about Russian politics. He came to realise that the Kim dynasty had people trapped "in a closed state with our ears covered", and came to understand "that a lot of what I knew was wrong." During those five years of back and forth between Russia and his home in Pyongyang, he began doubting everything he thought he knew, as though marbles had been rolled under his feet.

Around the time that Yoseb was first agonising about defection, I had arrived in Pyongyang on a small tour for Westerners who were shown the best of the country. We weren't allowed to interact with locals—other than the odd drunken man crashing through the barriers on the Metro, or the hour we spent at a beerhall. "North Koreans are wearing shackles," Yoseb would tell me, with a seriousness that I've learnt never breaks. "After living on and off in a free country, I had to go back to being monitored by others, to suppress my thoughts."

What stayed with me about Pyongyang was the sensory deprivation. The audible sound of footsteps during peak hours, because public conversation is avoided; the sight of entirely carless highways that cut across the city; the complete darkness at night without the purity of a canopy of stars; the bland food, only offset by copious booze. To be overwhelmed is something we have all probably experienced, but to be entirely under-whelmed and dislocated for a sustained period is a strange feel-ing. Time had not forgotten Pyongyang; it was ticking along in the only way it knew how.

It's not hard to understand how Yoseb felt increasingly out of place after five years of living between two entirely different worlds. It's an anxiety that defecting hasn't quelled; making it South isn't always the salve it's made out to be. American jour-nalist Barbara Demick, who spent years interviewing Northern refugees in Seoul, came to a dispiriting conclusion. "The sad truth is that North Korean defectors are often difficult people," she writes in her book *Nothing to Envy*. "Many were pushed into leaving not only because they were starving, but because they couldn't fit in at home. And often their problems trailed after them, even after they crossed the border."[31]

Faith is Yoseb's consolation for the decision he made—it feels as though belief is all he has. And, after leaving his family behind, belief is what he needs. God tells him that they're alive. "It doesn't matter what other people believe," he said to me, unprompted. He's holding up his end of the bargain: God prom-ised Yoseb that if he left, He would protect his family. He is protecting them now, so "I'm just believing and waiting."

While he waits, Yoseb is plotting an escape of a different kind—trying to leave his megachurch. "These big churches can be overwhelming to me," he confessed. "You have to adhere to the mould of the church. In faith, you [should] have the free-dom that God gives you." He's grappling with understandable questions: why does a believer have to follow the strict com-mandments of a pastor, and why must he listen to their sermons along with 10,000 other people when he can hear God himself? Why does Pentecostalism have these dominating institutions, when the whole point of it is that the Spirit moves through you as an individual?'

Broadly speaking, Korean megachurches have a three-fold quest: saving local souls, conducting missions abroad, and restoring Pyongyang to its former glory as the Jerusalem of the East. The stakes of leaving his church are a lot lower than those of escaping North Korea, but Yoseb's unease is part of a wider trend facing believers trying to navigate Seoul's civil and spiritual worlds. His bad experiences of paranoia, interchurch rivalry and oppressive leadership within Seoulite Pentecostalism are representative of a possible decline of the movement itself, with churches turning on each other, and the alternative represented by breakaway cults enjoying growing popularity.

It might be that Pentecostalism has always meant more to South Korea than to other countries, where the faith can be more individualised and inwardly focused, and ultimately protected from broader instability. But Korean Pentecostalism has recently been in institutional crisis, with these megachurches fighting amongst themselves over the bounty represented by defectors; between the infamous Covid superspreader events in February 2020 and the ongoing fallout from pastor impropriety, this much instability could bring the whole edifice crumbling down.

* * *

Since the 2010s, South Korean megachurches have been beset by a series of scandals. Unlike the case of Aimee Semple McPherson, and of a number of other scandal-plagued preachers we will come to meet, in South Korea these falls from grace have stuck, more like Parham's or Frisbee's experience—provoking a crisis that has rocked the faith of a nation.

In 2014, Yoido Full Gospel Church founder David Yonggi Cho—grandson of a Pyongyang preacher—was convicted and given a three-year suspended sentence for embezzling £9 million in church funds.[32] Around the same time as Yoido's legal woes, a competitor, the Myungsung Presbyterian Church, saw the church elder in charge of finances jump to his death off the roof of his building, having been accused by investigative reporters of setting up a slush fund for the founding pastor. His suicide note "described more than $70 million in bank accounts managed solely by himself and [the founder]".[33] More recently, in 2018, Lee Jae-rock, pastor to some 130,000 members of Manmin Central Church, was given a 15-year jail sentence for raping eight members of his flock.[34] Other churches have seen succession crises, with megachurches often likened to a *chaebol*, a family-owned conglomerate such as Samsung, with leaders wanting to pass on the family business to the son rather than more popular preachers.

David Yonggi Cho is now an emeritus pastor of Yoido, which claims to be the largest Christian congregation on Earth—though, having visited some of the Nigerian megachurch campgrounds (see Chapter 8), I would suggest that this is untrue. Still, the numbers are impressive: around 200,000 regular attendees in Korea, and over 800,000 worldwide members—and an orchestra that draws faithful and secular tourists alike.[35]

By Seoul's architectural standards, the Church's headquarters are unimposing: a dated, multistorey brick building on Yeouido Island in the Han River, which cleaves Seoul in two. The church's location opposite the National Assembly speaks louder than its facade. Inside, tiered seating caters to 12,000 worshippers at a time, with overflow segments in nearby buildings; on Sundays, seven services are held from 7am to 7pm. Large screens and roving cameras make it feel something like an NBA area with an orchestra pit.

Just past the section reserved for North Korean defectors, a slice of balcony is reserved for foreigners, with live translations in a range of languages available via headphones. I put mine on, and Pastor Lee got straight to the point. "We all know about Coronavirus, but there's a worse virus out there, and that's fake news," he said, before moving on to the North. "Lord, send Gospel up there and let them give up their nuclear weapons. The Holy Spirit is our counsellor, our lawyer. We can have victory."

After church, I met Dr Hankyung Kim, director of the International Theological Seminary of YFGC. "When you succeed, people are automatically jealous," he said of the Church's controversies, before moving on to his preferred subject. Yoido has an NGO which is one of the largest in North Korea; owns a convenience store chain that employs recent defectors; boasts a 'Free Citizen' college to help them adjust to life in the South; and offers a training programme to prepare young leaders for reunification.

Kim believes that, beyond their borders, Koreans "have a sense of being God's elected country for world mission." Since 9/11, Korean churches have been particularly active in Asia and the Middle East, believing that America can't fulfil its missionary potential there because of the loathing many in the region harbour for US global dominance. Indeed, Pastor Cho has long desired to re-evangelise the United States itself, holding up Korean Pentecostalism as a more pure and experiential expression of Christianity. Korean megachurches are particularly interested in prayer mountains, all-night prayer vigils, exorcisms and healing. The church's "dream" is mission success, though Cho is disappointed by the fruits of its Middle Eastern operations—one couple spent two decades in a Muslim country and only managed to convert their maid.

With megachurch corporations so on the nose, they are facing calls themselves to be born again—ushering in the next phase of Korean society. Only, the form this would take is a matter of contention. Millennial churchgoers in particular have been fleeing to 'microchurches' in cafes and hotel rooms; others are leaving organised religion altogether and practising their faith privately. Meanwhile, descendants of Pyongyang's Christian refugees continue to form a hard-right political bloc—fervently anti-communist and pro-America, akin to Florida's Cuban population—that wants to set the South on a collision course with the godless communists in the North.

As the coronavirus was spreading through church groups in South Korea without our knowledge, I attended one of the Korean religious right's weekly rallies outside the US embassy, watching tens of thousands of mostly elderly Christians waving American and Israeli flags, awaiting a sermon from the firebrand pastor Jun Kwang-hoon, who once declared, "If God messes with me, He's dead."[36]

Pastor Jun is leading a modern-day revival, but in many ways, he's very much a man of yesteryear, and so are his disciples. In the face of the megachurch scandals, his focused and fiery rhetoric might just have been the kind of force needed to coalesce a wavering movement. Since his appointment as the chairman of the Christian Council of Korea in 2019, he has mastered stirring political passions through religious rhetoric, lambasting anyone not on the hard right of politics, at every opportunity. Sounding an awful lot like the American religious right, he has declared, "Homosexuality, Islam, and anti-discrimination laws are Satan."[37] (The Islamophobia, at least, is very much an imported concern: the religion is barely a force in South Korea, with some 100,000 believers, mostly born outside of the country.)[38] In 2020, Pastor Jun was jailed for continuing to hold his political rallies in defiance of Covid restrictions, events that have been linked to hundreds of infections.[39]

The faith crisis in Seoul that has followed all these scandals is now leading to a resurgence in the practice of 'flock-stealing'; the early days of the pandemic brought this issue back into focus. The first major breakout beyond China occurred in Daegu, at the southern city's branch of Shincheonji, Church of Jesus, the Temple of the Tabernacle of the Testimony—commonly known as Shincheonji, an extreme South Korean Christian sect sometimes referred to as a doomsday cult. At the time, I was days away from meeting Shincheonji's reclusive leader Lee Man-hee, having been warned by a contact in Seoul that the church is "obsessed" with foreigners and might try to use me for "propaganda". Because of the virus, the meeting never happened; but another outbreak soon emerged at Myungsung Church in eastern Seoul, with a pastor as the apparent patient zero.[40]

Dr Kim alleges that this pastor brought the virus directly from the Shincheonji outbreak in Daegu. "There is a suspicion that the pastor belongs to Shincheonji," he told me at Yoido, something Myungsung subsequently denied. "They have a lot of agents in churches. We know that they have agents here." The operation was so complex, he said, that there were even Shincheonji "sleeper cells" within megachurches, ready to be activated. Even before the Covid controversy, this suspicion led other megachurches to put up signs saying "Shincheonji Out!" or "Shincheonji cannot come into our church." I learned that someone at Yoido had confessed to being an agent just days ago, right as panic was setting in about the virus spreading through church gatherings.

Shincheonji's leader, Chairman Lee, built his theological career on jumping from church to church, learning his trade with the 'Moonies'—the cult-like Unification Church of the United States, known for its mass weddings and its missions to East Asia. He is only the most famous example of a phenomenon that dates back decades: in the 1960s, it was estimated that there were at least seventy "self-Christs" in Korea, Prophets who have broken away from Pentecostalism to say that they are God or His reincarnation.[41] Lee's primary goal is to lure Christians from other churches to Shincheonji, which calls itself the true church and justifies flock-stealing by citing its goal of achieving 144,000 members—the prophetic number in the Book of Revelation who will go to Heaven after Judgment Day. (This defence ignores the fact that Shincheonji already claims 200,000 members world-wide.)[42] At a time of squeeze in the number of Korean believers, Lee's church is working overtime for Northern refugees.

A friend of Yoseb's recently fell in with Shincheonji after a 'fishing' operation, and Yoseb "went through the educational training" to try to find him. The church is particularly effective in Gayang-dong, a suburb on the outskirts of Seoul where many Northerners are assigned government housing; they target lonely men with honeytraps, and elderly people in need with money. They make generous offers to get people through the door, and many defectors "bite and take the bait". Members are expected to bring in one new person each month, and those who don't will pay recruiters up to £800—for whom the easiest catches are North Koreans. "It's like selling a person," Yoseb said. "In North Korea, we grew up practising idolisation, performing rites—Kim Il-sung, Kim Jong-il and now Kim Jong-un. We unconsciously grew accustomed to it. No matter how hard we deny it, the desire to idolise resides within us. I chased away those ghosts—not by myself but through God."

Believing that the South Korean government is riddled with spies, Yoseb's defector friends "are on edge" and some have "defected again" to Western countries. They ask him to go too, but he refuses. "God will be victorious and I will witness that here," he told me. Throughout our conversation, Yoseb was tense and terse, but talking politics seems to bring him to life. In his journey through Seoul's churches, God has taught him three things: do not idolise people, do not idolise money, do not idolise lust. He has recently created a "defector ministry" to bring together youth from North and South "to prepare our-selves for reunification."

"I've found peace, because reunification is approaching," he repeated—as though Korean reunification were tied to prophecy, and the end of a divided Peninsula would usher in God's Kingdom for the end of days. He added, "We are nearing destruction." And, just like getting over the border, every man must look out for his own salvation.

"I'd rather just pray and communicate directly with God myself."

4

THE FATHER, THE SONS
AND THE HOLY MESS

Like any good love story, Anderson do Carmo de Souza and Flordelis dos Santos de Souza were more than the sum of their parts. Their displays of public affection left you in no doubt that the attractive faces of Brazil's blooming evangelical movement were wildly in love. They loved their growing family—fifty-five children, all but four adopted out of poverty. They loved God, with their Rio de Janeiro megachurch franchise a testament to His glory. And, judging by their lifestyle, God really, really loved them.

Flordelis, as she was simply known, was a Madonna figure in more ways than one. Instantly recognisable by her halo of long, pale red hair, she sang the Gospel with a husky voice and frenzied stage presence. Anderson, with slicked, black hair and a playful curl of a smile, was the charismatic pastor who kept people coming through the doors of their growing congregation.

"She was like a star, she was always on the altar," a former member of the couple's church told me. "Pastor Anderson was blessed, always very friendly and attentive. He passed among everyone, talked to everyone. His preaching was so strong and impactful. He was an intelligent man, and always attentive to what was happening within his church."

They were also increasingly attentive to life outside of it. Prolific Instagrammers, Flordelis and Anderson used social media to show the benefits of 'seeding', part of the controversial form of worship known as 'prosperity gospel', whereby true faith will lead to riches—not just in the Kingdom of Heaven, but right here on Earth. This *teologia da prosperidade* is as meaningful to believers as it is derided by outsiders. Prosperity theology is central to the Pentecostal faith, and especially so in countries where prosperity is hard to come by. The idea is that God rewards you for giving money to your church and pastor: in 'seeding' these donations, followers plant an act of faith that then grows a material harvest. In Flordelis and Anderson's case, the fruits reaped included expensive cars, designer clothes, and a jet-setting lifestyle.[1]

This is fairly par for the course for Brazilian preachers, but what had catapulted the happy couple to national fame was far more extraordinary: adopting fifty-one street children, raised alongside four biological children (three from Flordelis' first marriage, and one together) in the ever-growing family home.[2] It all began one night in the 1990s, when the newlyweds heard a loud noise outside their home in the Jacarezinho favela, on the north side of the rapidly growing city. "When my husband and I opened the door," Flordelis later explained, "we were surprised by thirty-seven desperate youngsters, running from a mass murder scene in Rio's central train station. That's how my story with adoption started."[3] She was a lesson to us all: this is how you pull yourself up by your stiletto-straps, with values and hard work and God. "If I had to do it all over again, I would do it, because it was worth it," Flordelis would say about the adoptions.[4] "It was a time of harmony in our home."[5]

Flordelis used her growing celebrity to enter politics, running for election to Brazil's national parliament in 2018. Part of a rising movement of evangelicals in the capital Brasília, she received one of the highest vote tallies in all of Rio de Janeiro state, running on a platform of getting tough on crime and defending families. Not that Anderson was taking a back seat. Having masterminded his wife's political career, he was keen to make the most of it, planning a monument to their success—a new headquarters for their church that would house 5,000 worshippers.[6]

"He loved his flock," remembered Alexandre Macedo, who helped the couple start their first church. "Unfortunately, in the past few years, he was obsessed with growing it." Of course, with great power comes great paranoia. Anderson was eternally worried about the family finances, and had become wary of his and his wife's growing fame. And understandably so. A lot of unusual things had been happening lately.

Over the course of the last year, there had been several attacks on Anderson. He and various members of the family had been hospitalised with suspected arsenic poisoning—even the dog hadn't been spared. Alongside the poisonings, there had been a number of failed robberies—all in all, Anderson counted at least six botched attempts on his life. He had fallen away from some of the friends he'd known on the way up, and drifted away from others, like Alexandre, who told me that Anderson started to change with the growth in the couple's stature.

On the night of 15 June 2019, Anderson and Flordelis went to the famous Copacabana Beach. "We walked on the boardwalk, we played, we walked on the beach," Flordelis later said. "I know he arrived in a place that had many cars parked ... He kissed me a lot, I sat on the hood of the car and we had intercourse. I said 'love, tomorrow we'll wake up early, right?'"[7] They drove home; Flordelis would later say that she'd thought they were being followed by a motorcycle. Anderson pulled into the front drive, and she went in, while he sat in the car finishing some emails.[8]

At around 3am, Anderson was met with gunfire. Hearing six shots, Flordelis came running down the stairs, but it was already too late—Anderson died almost instantly. For Brazil's wealthy, such garage robberies are not uncommon; for the politically connected, assassinations are all too thinkable.

Flordelis was reportedly too distraught to make any public comment, but the family released a statement. "At this moment, we hold the hand of God and beg for his comfort. Pastor Anderson was fulfilling a marvelous ministry, redeeming souls in the fight against hate due to an absence of God."[9] The murder left his flock in a state of disbelief. Who would do this to a man of God? "It was a great loss, in spite of our spiritual preparation," a former congregant told me. "It shook everyone's faith."

Before the first arrests were made in connection with Anderson's killing, the Brazilian press, grimly energised by the shocking turn of events, put the couple's faith on trial, subjecting it to minute scrutiny—even calling into question their adoptions, as some, it was alleged, didn't have the right paperwork to have passed through Brazil's heavily bureaucratic system, which isn't exactly geared towards helping people from the favela.

Anderson and Flordelis were prime tabloid fodder because they were preachers of the controversial prosperity gospel, which their own backstories seemed to prove to their congregations. Though there was a 16-year age gap between them, both had grown up in Jacarezinho at a time when it was the largest and roughest slum in the city, a place where murders, gangs, drugs were all a part of life. There is little information about Flordelis' meteoric rise from slum kid to gospel goddess, but on her way to becoming a singer and favela preacher, she claims to have been a mediator between the two ways of life: the law of God and the law of the streets.[10] It's all part of the de Souzas' mystique—what matters is that God brought them together, and then paved a road of gold for them.

Now, the couple had it all: money, power, and a legion of adoring fans. There was even a biopic made about Flordelis' life, in which many respected actors worked for free to tell the story of this homegrown Mother Teresa. Anderson believed fervently in the almighty dollar, showing his people a way of life that promoted giving to receive, and holding himself up as an example of how to profit handsomely from the practice. The couple's unique household meant that things weren't always easy, but they were testament to the belief system: after all, God had promoted them from the favela to the favoured.

* * *

Once considered the most Catholic nation on earth, Brazil is now the most Pentecostal. In 1980, Pentecostals comprised just 3 per cent of the population.[11] As of 2020, over 30 per cent of Brazilians are evangelicals—the vast majority of them Pentecostal—and it's now predicted that they'll outnumber Catholics in the country by 2032.[12]

Prosperity theology has been critical to the movement's rise here. The Bible is a contract between God and man like any other, the thinking goes: if you fulfil your end, He will bestow riches on you. The more you give, the more you will receive—but your faith in the idea must be unwavering.

If this sounds similar to the soft-focus televangelists of 1980s America, it's because the idea trickled down the Atlantic. As gifts from the United States to Latin America go, it's up there with the military coup. But what started off as spiritual colonialism is now as Brazilian as *carnaval*, having been adapted to local tastes by local adherents. The theology behind prosperity gospel is simple, and like any other part of Pentecostal faith: after being baptised in the Spirit (in this case, by giving to God's representatives on Earth), the redeemed soul will receive His gifts (in this case, the blessings of health and wealth). It's an idea that appealed to the rapturous congregation of Azusa Street as much as it does to faith healers in Johannesburg (see Chapter 5)—or telegenic couples in Rio de Janeiro.

The godfather of Brazilian prosperity gospel, who we'll meet later, is famous for holding December 'Holy Bonfires' to make the most of believers' Christmas bonuses. Pastors would implore the faithful to surprise God and, in a frenzy of giving, surprise everyone including themselves, by giving over their cars and the deeds to their houses. This became so successful that it started causing logistical problems, so pastors have more recently been advising believers to sell their items first, then give over the money.[13]

Christianity has never been shy of the good things in life—Catholics allowed indulgences, which was usually a monetary way to be excused from sin or receive blessings in general. What's different about prosperity gospel is the explicit idea that it's perfectly acceptable, even desirable, to give to the Church in order to get rich—for Pentecostals, wealth is a sign of the strength of your faith. The more cynical might call it a spiritual Ponzi scheme: it seems convenient that giving a homeless person a fiver might not put you on the path to riches and God's favour, but handing it to a Rolexed preacher will.

But within the logic of Pentecostalism's here-and-now, direct and personalised faith, it seems like common sense. For people of the Spirit, the contents of your wallet are as Heaven-sent as the thoughts in your head. This God isn't talking to them through prayers or priests, but through His Ghost moving inside of them. Some of these ideas pre-date the Azusa Street Revival, but they weren't foretold in Jerusalem—they were thoroughly made in America, bolted together along a production line of ideas that helped form a nation.

Kate Bowler, a historian of the prosperity gospel, says that this began with New Thought, an 1830s movement led by Ralph Waldo Emerson and others, who thought that illness was all in the mind and could be healed with the right way of thinking. To Bowler, this idea then mixed with Protestantism to form the "American gospel of pragmatism, individualism, and upward mobility."[14] Like most great American ideas, it really got going after the Second World War. The United States' sudden elevation to global superpower brought forward a flood of optimism; yet, for many leaders of both faith and industry, it was a time for vigilance. Business leaders were scarred by the redistribution of wealth under FDR's New Deal. Christian leaders were terrified of the godless 'reds' who were, to their mind at least, sweeping Europe. In fearing the slippery slope towards communism, these interests found common cause.

While they were busy merging the languages of business and Bible, the Pentecostals, often looked down on by their evangelical counterparts, were stoking new revivalist fires across the country. Out of the spirit of this patriotic, muscular postwar nation emerged a new type of Christianity. Pentecostals embraced the resurgent idea of 'mind power', and added the miracles of healing and prosperity to what Bowler calls an "electrified view of faith".[15]

If this way of 'doing Jesus' had just been plugged in, then the 1952 publication of Norman Vincent Peale's *The Power of Positive Thinking* turned the volume up to max. The New York–based preacher, born Methodist then born again Reformed, invented a simple formula—picturise, prayerise and actualise—that self-help gurus have been peddling ever since; this was a precursor to the 'mind, body, spirit' trend that would run through Pentecostalism in the '60s and '70s. Peale's message was a huge hit with the faithful, spreading rapidly from coast to coast. Marble Collegiate Church on Fifth Avenue, where Peale was pastor, was regularly packed. We know that at least one of the flock took the message to heart, making it a personal credo: his name was Donald J. Trump.

Just as Peale blended emerging (and dubious) strands of psychology and faith in his teachings, evangelical denominations were learning from each other. But no one embraced these ideas in postwar America quite like the Pentecostals, who were not only more focused on positive, immediate aspects of faith, but were starting to come into the tent of mainstream American life for the first time, after so long living outside of it.[16] In God they trusted, and the rewards could be apparent for all to see. Once again, the Pentecostals—who had been ahead of the game when it came to spreading the word—were at the cutting edge of culture. Just as Aimee Semple McPherson had used radio, the game-changing technology of her day, men of God in the postwar consumer boom harnessed theirs, recording sermons on audio cassettes for wide distribution.

Owning a TV soon became a blessing for a good Christian American. Faith programmes were a boon for hungry television producers, who could syndicate them across the country. They found a growing audience for modern preachers spouting all things positive and patriotic. Equally eager were the Pat Robertsons and Jim and Tammy Faye Bakkers, a new brand of televangelist preachers who felt they had outgrown their small-town beginnings.

By 1971, a small group of televangelists were behind 42 per cent of the top syndicated religious programmes on television; by 1981, they totalled 83 per cent. Good American men with good American wives, these preachers were independent, but of one mind. And that mind was for enrichment. Bowler says that their television dominance gave them a "theological monopoly" over the hearts and minds of the nation.[17]

The problem of independence has long beset branches of Protestantism—there isn't one decree, let alone one voice as with Catholicism's papacy—but by this time prosperity theology had fomented into one coherent line of thought. If television was the medium, then kitchen-table ideas about money were the message. In these years of social mobility and consumerism, God cared about how much money was left in your pocket at the end of the week, and about how an ordinary person could get ahead.

It's little wonder, then, that it was in the 1980s, with the movie-star president and the glamour and greed of Wall Street, that the prosperity gospel really hit its stride. The gospel was bastardised into taglines from the mouth of God. Jesus was wealthy, they claimed. A donkey was the equivalent of a Cadillac back then; Baby Jesus was famously bestowed with gifts; His guards at the crucifixion were like living in a gated community today—a sign that you've made it. At the same time as big-box stores were killing Mom and Pop on Main Street, so too the structure of places of worship was up for renewal. The mega-church—a church in excess of 2,000 members attending each week—was taking off. In 1970, the United States had fifty of them; by 1990, there were 310.[18]

Megachurches catered to a rapidly changing country, where people were moving in and around large cities; more women were entering the workforce; steps forward and backward were being taken in the struggle for civil rights. Though most prosperity preachers were focused on conquering local territory before moving to the bright lights of terrestrial television, some had that classically Pentecostal expansive impulse. It didn't take long for prosperity preachers to start looking beyond their own pews.

* * *

From the churches of Main Street, I arrived in Brazil to see *la teologia da prosperidade* in action. My first stop wasn't the sexiness of Rio, abuzz with a breakthrough in the investigation of Anderson's murder, but rambunctious São Paulo, South America's largest city, which sits to Rio's south-west along the narrowing South Atlantic coastline.

I left my hotel in the city centre as dawn broke, the first light not yet shining on the cathedral that kept the darkness for thousands sleeping rough at its feet. It was a Monday morning, and a city that can't afford to sleep was quickly rising. I walked with workers across the highway bridges to the suburb of Brás. Power lines overhead came together like bundles of twigs; apartment buildings clustered closer together.

Then, as if we were crossing a border, church signs appeared. They began with a cheeky cross in the title, then started giving way to Israeli flags. Well-dressed young people handed out pamphlets and motioned you towards a makeshift coffee table, set up for those who'd slept rough, or not at all. But, with the sun rising, this whole scene would soon be in the shadow of Solomon's Temple, the $300 million shrine to the god of health and wealth. With its jarring, gold-plated, big-box modernism, it is supposed to be an exact replica of the ancient Temple of Solomon in Jerusalem. It was built by the Universal Church of the Kingdom of God, which may just be Brazil's largest cultural export after its footballers.

The temple's claim to fame is no less ostentatious: at 55 metres tall, Universal Church claims it is twice the height of the Christ the Redeemer statue that towers over Rio. The building's muscular presence has cast a shadow longer than its physical structure, with the staunchly left-wing Dilma Rousseff, then Brazil's president, attending the opening in 2014 to praise it to the heavens. "It catches people's attention from far away. It's very beautiful," she said.[19] The man who built it was Edir Macedo, the founder of Universal Church and the man who brought the gospel of health and wealth to the masses. "If I leave this world today, I will be happy. I have nothing to lose," he said at the ceremony. But Rousseff had more to lose than he did: the following year, a poll of Brazilians would find that Universal Church was considered the fifth most influential institution in Brazil—above the presidency.[20]

My fellow congregants were impeccably dressed before work. Vivid music lifted the room as a ceremonial coffin, resembling an oversized moneybox, was brought in by six robed men. A young, attractive pastor who looked eerily like Anderson do Carmo de Souza ratcheted up the tension over the score, and worshippers began almost gyrating, with their hands in the air. A short man in front of me, in his mid-40s, opened up a huge tattered Bible and placed his wallet on top, holding it up to the sky and communicating to the heavens in tongues.

God, like money, never sleeps. The temple seats 10,000, though on a Monday morning at 7am it was only at a quarter of its capacity: Sunday is still nominally prime time for worship. Even so, for modern believers, before the working day starts is when it counts. The great innovation of the man who popularised the prosperity gospel in Brazil was opening churches first thing in the morning and last thing at night—the times when people who work in factories or as maids are on their way to and from their jobs. And he thought of this because Edir Macedo, one of Brazil's richest men and a powerful media mogul, was once like them, like Flordelis and Anderson: trying to escape the crushing poverty of Brazil's favelas.

While America was on the up, Brazil was in the midst of its own Great Migration. Between the 1930s and the 1980s, millions began moving to the more central cities from the poor north-east, displaced by ranchers who could make use of poor farming land for grazing. The practice of slavery had nominally ended in 1888, but indentured servitude continued in some areas of the north-east right into the 1990s. The cities offered rural northerners economic opportunities beyond tilling the fields for those who could only generously be described as their bosses. In 1960, São Paulo had a population of 4 million; today, the wider urban area has grown to five times that.[21]

This urbanisation brought with it mass social upheaval. Many saw their communities and families broken up, as people moved to the concrete jungles of São Paulo, Rio de Janeiro and the

freshly built capital Brasília. One of the families uprooting themselves were the Macedos, who moved from a small town to Rio
in the 1950s. They were very poor—ten of their seventeen children didn't make it out of childhood. One who did, Edir, wasn't
thanked for it. His father beat him for his deformed fingers.
Like most families, the Macedos were nominally Catholic, but
that God didn't seem to have given them much grace.

The secular prophecy of American greatness had come into
being, and the superpower's postwar cultural ascendancy was
relentless. The two great nations of slavery have long regarded
each other as neither too distant nor too close. Brazil might not
have been as much of a concern as closer neighbours like Cuba,
but US soft power flowed quickly downstream. On a continent
so spiritually defined by Rome, a wave of *Americanos* saw an
opportunity to introduce competition to this grand religious
marketplace. The great not-so-secret is that believers tend to
convert not from atheism, but across from denominations or
other places of belief; Pope John Paul II once called the
Pentecostals "ravenous wolves", charging into existing communities to feast on whatever they can catch.[22] This pattern of 'defection' to Spirit-led belief made Latin America a happy hunting
ground for the grandchildren of Azusa Street. A new mass
migration was about to take off in Brazil—this time, from
Catholicism to Pentecostalism.

In the early '60s, at the age of 18, Edir witnessed his sister's
asthma being cured by this muscular take on faith, and he was
baptised in the Spirit "as if a light turned on inside of me,
illuminating my whole body."[23] From his early adulthood, he
undertook street preaching with no great success. Then, his
daughter was born with a cleft palate, and in his despair he quit
his job. The man who became known as "the bossa nova pastor" began preaching the exuberant joy of the Spirit in a public
park. No soul was not worth saving, and his zeal was tireless.

THE FATHER, THE SONS AND THE HOLY MESS

In 1977, when he was 32, he formed the Universal Church of the Kingdom of God.

It was to these people, his people, that Macedo introduced the idea of a God and Ghost that people could work with directly, without the intervention of priests or popes. This was an upgrade on the God you thought you knew, for He spoke to your everyday needs—health and wealth—and He opened for business at an hour that suited you. The churches of *Espirito Santo* began to cram into the shopfronts of the nation's favelas and working-class neighbourhoods, becoming tangible, familiar institutions that were instantly, markedly different from the distant Sunday cathedrals.

Around the time Macedo was opening his first Universal Church, a teenage girl in Jacarezinho, the largest favela in Rio at the time, had just lost her father and brother in a car accident. We don't know if Flordelis dos Santos de Souza was personally moved by Edir or his Church, but the Spirit was very much in the air.

A police operation (not related to Anderson's murder) meant that it wasn't wise for me to go rubbernecking where Flordelis grew up, but Antonio, a friend who grew up in what is now Brazil's largest favela, offered to take me for a walk through its winding streets to see faith sprouting for myself. So we headed to Rochina, in the south of Rio.

At some points, every turn of the vertiginous main street had a little shopfront *igreja* of the Holy Ghost. Antonio was a second-generation Pentecostal; not a feverish believer, but someone who believed in the power of faith, and a keen student of history. "The difference between Pentecostalism and Catholicism is that Pentecostalism says that you can be happy in *this* life," he explained. He'd never heard of William Seymour; many of the American faithful probably don't know his name either. But every Brazilian knows of Edir Macedo, 'The Bishop', for better or for worse.

As Macedo's following grew, he used funds from his flock to buy a television station, Record, in 1989. Today, he is a self-made billionaire who has received everything he owns from believers—up to and including his only son, Moyses, given to Macedo in the street as a baby by his birth mother. Along the way he's been investigated for embezzlement and fraud,[24] and faced allegations, denied by the Church, of involvement in a dodgy adoption ring[25]—an accusation that has also been levelled against Flordelis by the Brazilian courts, concerning her adoption of those fifty-one street kids.[26] Macedo has also criticised interracial marriage by saying that it's unfair to children; and published a book, initially banned for hate speech, calling Afro-Brazilian religions like Candomblé "demonic sects".[27]

But his true legacy is having almost single-handedly removed the Catholic Church's monopoly on the nation's souls, through a combination of fate, faith and hard work—the very model of prosperity theology that sealed his personal destiny, and that of the couple who would become his ideological heirs.

As with the United States, Macedo saw that the key to prosperity gospel really taking off in Brazil would be the magic of television. From the 1950s, many middle-class Brazilians believed that American culture spoke to a glittering sense of progress that they ought to emulate. Television took a bit longer to arrive, but owning a set was to become a way of showing that you'd made it. The influence of the box in Brazil can't be understated: this is the land of the telenovela, with half the country's 200 million people regularly glued to those dramatic twists and turns.[28] *Novelas*, which tend to focus on the lives of the rich, are so popular that they run for short stints and are written almost daily to respond to the world—and, more importantly, to audiences' reactions to the characters and plotlines in the media and online.

Macedo's colossal Solomon's Temple in São Paulo is the power of television brought to life, just as the story of Flordelis and

THE FATHER, THE SONS AND THE HOLY MESS

Anderson was a telenovela brought to life. As a saying from those early days of the medium goes, "In Brazil, television isn't a concession of the state; the state is a concession of television."[29] Rather than creating Heaven on Earth, Brazil's Pentecostals have created television in real life: rags-to-riches stories where the children of the slums can rise up above everything and become something, armed with nothing but belief in their hearts.

Brazilians are nothing if not good for an expression. Another one that has emerged: "If God is the way, then Universal Church is the tollbooth."

Or, as Anderson would often tell the children, "In heaven it is God, on Earth it is Flordelis."

* * *

Down here on Earth, Flordelis dos Santos de Souza is a force of nature. Though she was born in 1961, she could pass for a woman half her age.

Her personal history is somewhat mysterious, and probably deliberately so, but the most widely told story goes like this. After the car accident that killed her father and brother when she was a teenager, Flordelis began preaching outside of funk dance halls and becoming a gospel singer of some renown.[30] She got married and had three kids, but after she separated from her husband at the age of 30, she turned her home in the favela into a shelter for up to a hundred kids escaping a life of drug-running or homelessness.

Among them was a 16-year-old Anderson do Carmo.[31] The charming and articulate boy was different from the other kids: still living with his parents as he completed his schooling, and with a traineeship at a bank awaiting him. He was also the boyfriend of Simone, Flordelis' biological daughter, and soon moved into the family home.

Not long after, he joined four other regulars at the house in becoming one of Flordelis' adopted children. He led the youth group at the pieced-together church that Flordelis had started.[32] At some point during all this mess, according to his biological mother, Anderson began an affair with Flordelis. The next year, he split up with Simone and made their mother his wife.

Anderson was the very model of the prosperity gospel. He worked hard from a young age, and God repaid him many times over. The strictness of his vision was imposed on all of the children. Flordelis was the spiritual and emotional leader of the family; he was the authoritarian who kept everything together. "Anderson was fair," I heard from Alexandre Macedo, the friend who helped the couple set up their first church (no relation to Bishop Edir). "But some of the children were bums who didn't do their fair share. If they did the right thing, they were rewarded."

* * *

They may have captured the hearts, minds and wallets of Brazil, but life at *casa do Flordelis* wasn't as blessed as it was depicted.

The Monday morning I was visiting Solomon's Temple, just over a year after Anderson's murder, "Operation Luke 12" was closing in on the perpetrators.[33] The police operation was named after the New Testament chapter in which Jesus tells his disciples: "There is nothing concealed that will not be disclosed, or hidden that will not be made known. What you have said in the dark will be heard in the daylight, and what you have whispered in the ear in the inner rooms will be proclaimed from the roofs." These days, the roofs of Brazil are all crowned with satellite dishes, and television stations—including Bishop Macedo's Record—were reporting the salacious details of Anderson's death round the clock. A lot didn't add up about that night.

You see, robbers, even when startled, don't usually shoot someone over thirty times—five times the number of shots Flordelis said she had heard[34]—and they definitely don't tend to aim so many of them in the groin. And guard dogs, like the two the family owned, don't tend to stay quiet when there are intruders in the dark hours. While home shootings are a common feature of garage robberies in Brazil, the only thing that appeared to have been stolen was the pastor's phone, taken from his blood-soaked and bullet-ridden body. Investigators also uncovered the multiple poisoning attempts against Anderson in the year leading up to his death. Anderson himself had even learned of one of the plots, but refused to believe that the people accused could have been behind it.

The police were less in credulous. At first they arrested five of Flordelis and Anderson's children, and one granddaughter, for involvement in the crime. Flordelis' son from her first marriage, Flávio, who had an outstanding warrant for domestic violence, admitted to having shot his stepfather six times. Lucas, one of the children of the mass adoption, was brought in on an old drug charge; he admitted to having bought the gun. Anderson's phone, a crucial piece of evidence, was not found, but investigators were able to track it through the hands of at least two family members before it disappeared from sight.

"They killed the goose that laid the golden eggs," remarked one politician who had frequent contact with the family.[35] Flordelis herself was less circumspect. "If it is proven that it was my children, I want them to be punished, I want justice," she said. "Whoever committed that act. I want justice for what happened to my husband."[36]

According to investigators, in the lead-up to the murder, there had been an intense internal conflict brewing within the family. Anderson was in charge of the prosperity, and had a lot of say in the gospel that was Flordelis' political career, too. From the time of his promotion from adopted son to young husband, he had controlled the money and the running of the household; but that was the least of it. The couple had moved up in the world, but money was tight. New kids arrived with conditions like lice and scabies and, at the start at least, there were never enough basics to go around. After the adoptions started, two of Flordelis' biological children—Flávio the self-confessed shooter, and Simone, Anderson's ex-girlfriend—couldn't cope with the arrival of so many new siblings.

There was a limit to the children's salvation. The adoptees lived on junk in a communal area on the first floor, and slept in shared rooms on the third floor. The second floor was restricted, featuring Flordelis and Anderson's room, and a separate fridge and pantry for the chosen ones: Flávio, Simone and five of the 'first generation' of adoptees, who were given superior status, and who communicated amongst themselves in a made-up language.[37]

But being chosen by the golden couple wasn't exactly easy. One man came forward and told detectives that he had met Flordelis at a prayer group in the 1990s and had been invited into their home, first as a guest, and then to live. He said that when he arrived at the house, he had to undergo a "purification ritual", forcibly isolated in a room for seven days. During that period, he had to wear white clothes, and only ate rice and vegetables. He reported that he kept a Bible, prayed, and received visits from some of the elite tier of the household, who participated in secret rituals.[38]

The man also told the police that he had witnessed a ritual in which Flordelis asked some children to cut their hands with a small knife and write Psalms from the Bible in blood. In another ritual, he said, one of the favoured sons placed a photo of a businessman—a benefactor to the family—on top of an apple with coloured ribbons, and threw honey over it, apparently "enlightening" the man to give the household more coin. The 'whistleblower' told police that he had recently been treated and medicated for mental illness, which he said hadn't arisen before his time at the de Souza house.

Anderson declared a select group in the family "fallen angels", and said that Flordelis was there to save them. Lucas, the son who allegedly bought the murder weapon, said that his adopted mother had a baseball bat that she hit misbehaving children with. Simone, the biological daughter, remained her favourite and spy within the house.[39] One of the 'lower-tier' adoptees, Roberta, said that Flordelis did not show any form of motherly affection towards her. Another, Daiane, said that the adopted children felt that they were "being used" by Flordelis and Anderson.[40]

In the end, detectives concluded that Anderson's old refrain was right: on Earth it is Flordelis. In a sensational series of further arrests in August 2020, police accused her of being the real mastermind behind the hit on her husband. She couldn't be prosecuted while enjoying parliamentary immunity, but she took down with her another ten members of the clan, across two generations—20 per cent of the family, as the homicide chief put it.[41] Simone was found to have googled information such as "poison that kills" and "assassin where to find"; Lucas, the kid who had been in trouble over drugs, said that he had been offered around US$850 by some of his siblings to arrange the killing.

One year later, in August 2021, Flordelis was finally kicked out of Congress; stripped of her immunity, she was charged with the murder.[42]

The officers of Operation Luke 12 proclaimed an ungodly motive. Flordelis, they said when they first pointed the finger at her, had been "unhappy with the way the victim controlled the finances" of the household.[43] "The investigation demonstrated that [Flordelis'] image of altruism and decency was merely a ploy to gain wealth and political power," Police Commissioner Allan Duarte had announced, on naming her as the ringleader of the murder plot.[44]

I spoke to some former members of Flordelis and Anderson's church after the 2020 arrests. "I feel disappointed. Deceived," said Ana Kelem Fischer, a social media influencer who was devoted to Anderson. "I was very blessed in that church," she added, before accusing the Flordelis tribe of "dating out of interest", because they knew "who had money at that church".

* * *

A viral Facebook post from playwright and actor Vinícius Soares spoke to what this Pentecostal power couple had represented in a country that was becoming obsessed with their fate. "Stop, just stop, saying that she does not represent the evangelical church. She is the very figure of the Brazilian evangelical church," he wrote. "She is an excellent representative of prosperity theology ... Do not come to me with 'she is not a true believer'. She is. YES."[45]

Brazilians know all too well that abusers can hide behind the cloth; indeed, such crises in the Catholic Church have undoubtedly contributed to the mass conversion taking place in the country. The Flordelis scandal was a betrayal to those who have come to the gospel of health and wealth in good faith. Sure, plenty of pastors were getting rich, but a rising tide was supposed to lift all boats. Pentecostalism in Latin America is an important rejection of the elite represented by the Catholic Church—the same elite that politicians such as President Jair Bolsonaro, and Flordelis' evangelical caucus, rail against.

In São Paulo, I met up with Gustavo Ribeiro, a journalist who founded the Brazilian Report website—which has been reporting on every twist and turn in the Flordelis saga. For him, the figure of the prosperity preacher is a lot like that of the populist politician taking over Brazil and the world. "They're fighting for the stuff you care about, like lowering street crime, that elites have always told them is stupid to care about," he said. "In Brazil, only 8 per cent of people are considered to be literate to a high degree. Half of the country doesn't have basic sanitation. People don't have access to education, or healthcare. Elite politics has marginalised people, and they pretend that this is not obvious."

But it also goes deeper than that. In a country where more than half the population identify as Black or mixed-race, and where poverty is still endemic, most Brazilians' local Catholic priest or bishop is likely to be far whiter and better-educated than the people visiting his church. He's essentially a bureaucrat who has been dropped into your favela, or your small town on the edge of the Amazon rainforest.[46] The appeal of the Pentecostal pastor is that they have bubbled up from below, just as you aspire to. He, or occasionally she, looks and talks like you. As with Macedo, Flordelis and Anderson, they grew up navigating the same streets you did. They hear on those streets that your mother is sick, and they can drop around to give her comfort before you've even gotten home from work. They encourage you to start that small street-vending business you've been dreaming about and to make it on your own. They're the first person to come around to give your idiot husband a talking to when he's been drinking and gambling and womanising again.

Sure, they're also pressuring you into tithing at least 10 per cent of your hard-earned money, but we live in a world where everything has a market value, so it makes sense. In the end, you're buying in—into a community in the gigantic city you've moved to; into a faith that you've seen turn around the lives of those around you; into an accountability system where someone is actually looking out for you.

For believers, the devil isn't in the detail. Faith is something that makes them feel good, and Pentecostals offer a straightforward narrative that anyone can plug their ambitions into. Prosperity theology is all about the idea of winning, with true faith reflected by victoriousness in all areas of life: spiritual, physical and financial. Raising yourself out of the favela, but never forgetting where you came from. After 500 years under the yoke of the Catholic Church, Pentecostalism is working-class and authentically Brazilian. Followers have absorbed ideas from their

Prophets such as anti-elitism and the importance of self-sufficiency. By throwing their lot in with miracles, they are altering Christian ideas of suffering and submission, and aligning them with some of the most antagonistic political forces of our time.

In the case of Flordelis, that narrative turned out to be a tale straight from the Old Testament: a familial fight for money and power that ended in bloody murder. And yet, the whole sorry story hasn't altered the faith of anyone I spoke to from Anderson and Flordelis' church. Most simply returned to the religious marketplace, looking for a new charismatic leader to help carry their hopes and dreams. "Prosperity theology works," Ana Kelem Fischer told me, with a shoulder-shrugging certainty. And, as a minor social media influencer, she's probably right in her case. "The bad thing is that people use it to their own advantage, and hide behind the name of God. But yes, it is possible to be prosperous through the Bible."

The gospel of money is far more than simply the greed it's so often dismissed as. It is an uncomfortable answer to a world that worships money every day, but usually without all of the ceremony. Prosperity gospel becomes a fortification simultaneously against and within the material world. For everything that the Pentecostal faith offers people like Ana, it is clear that the Lord helps those who help themselves. After all, there's a political system that depends on it, and it arrived down the Atlantic along with the brothers and sisters of the Spirit. Prosperity gospel is not only succeeding where states fail; it is offering an incentive for them to fail. This is because, as Ana said, prosperity theology works.

Research has found that people who come from poverty, or cycles of violence and addiction, have more chances of escaping that world if they join an evangelical church—the so-called "self-fulfilling prophecy" of God's favour being shown in material wellbeing.[47] And, for things well beyond the control of the average person, the Church wins there, too: countries in economic distress see a surge in faith. For every 1 per cent reduction in a country's GDP, Brazilian researchers found a 0.8 per cent increase in the number of evangelicals. Overall, the study found that "economic downturns lead to religious conversions to Pentecostalism from other Christian denominations", and

> that the expansion of Pentecostalism in society, triggered by economic downturns in the 1990s, was accompanied by a shift both in electoral outcomes and in legislative production towards a religious-oriented political agenda ... Once elected, these politicians carried out an agenda with greater emphasis on issues that are sensitive to fundamental religious principles.[48]

In other words, as one of the study's authors put it, "these churches give vulnerable populations a solidarity network the state has failed to." In turn, the religious start voting for faith-based political candidates.[49] But it's not the needs of the poor that drive policy once those politicians are in office—it's the priorities of Pentecostalism.

5

THE BIGGER THE PROPHECY,
THE BIGGER THE POCKET

Prophet Sithole beckoned me into his 24-hour 'medical clinic' and placed the broken door back over the doorway. He was still preparing his theatre, only it looked quite different from what you might expect: candles jammed into the tops of several 2-litre soft drink bottles, multiple mobile phones running hot, a blue satin boxer's robe with a taped-on cross pinned to the back wall, and two live chickens. Two *gigantic* live chickens, who looked as startled to see me as I was to see them.

"*Errrgghhh*"—he belched, and motioned for me to sit on a wicker mat on the floor. "My ancestors."

In addition to our streams of text messages, this was my second consultation with the Prophet—and he'd not once mentioned anything about chickens. Prophet Sithole's practice is in an abandoned church in Marshalltown, inner-city Johannesburg, which just might be the faith-healing capital of the world. A financial scandal had run the previous tenants out of town, and in the meantime, Sithole and his mates were using the rooms for various matters of God—though other neighbours with less pious intentions had also recently moved in.

Jozi, as locals call South Africa's largest city, is the religious centre of a country that wrestles demons for a living. The inner city, a reminder that unofficial Apartheid still exists, attracts self-proclaimed spiritual saviours from all over sub-Saharan Africa. Here, people put extra store in prophets and men of God from the bush, for they possess a purity that most city folk do not, thanks to their access to sites for traditional rituals and their perceived lack of the taint of mammon—a biblical term meaning greed, or weakness for material wealth. Prophet Sithole is from Chipinge in rural Zimbabwe, and puts a great deal of stock in that, despite having plied his trade in Johannesburg for the best part of two decades.

At a time when other diviners have become notorious for their social media antics, it's the way the Prophet advertises his services that really sets him apart. Posters bearing the legend "PROPHET SITHOLE FROM CHIPINGE—SEE YOUR ENEMY ON MIRROR" are plastered all over the city, stuck to telegraph poles and bins, even to the outer walls of churches and synagogues, invariably beside ads for abortion pills and penis enlargements.

Texting the number on the sign to enquire about seeing my enemy in the mirror was an admission of defeat on my part. I'd spent months crisscrossing Southern Africa trying to sample the local Pentecostal speciality—raising people from the dead— without success. Certainly, I felt a degree of guilt about my quest, as my desire to see such a spectacle probably said more about me than it did about the people promoting it. But my curiosity wasn't just sensational. Southern Africa's faith healing is a movement largely led by men, but fuelled by the faith of young women; many upwardly mobile young women I met at South African churches would leave work on Friday and attend all-night prayer vigils. I envied their belief and commitment. What was I missing?

Many of the same things as them, it turned out: women of my age usually see Prophet Sithole because of miscarriages or matters of the heart. While I'd sold myself on a journalistic adventure to find out how miracle men can pull off what seemed like a magic trick while keeping their faithful in the long run, really this was just a distraction from my own pain. What I was truly looking for was no less of a Hail Mary. I had come to South Africa to run away from a bad relationship, but so far in my trip nothing of tears, booze or climbing mountains had given much relief. I began to wonder if a bit of the spiritual might mend my broken soul.

Looking for miracle on demand felt embarrassingly Netflix, not to mention terribly selfish; but it was a time when I could only move about the world to look inside myself. It wasn't entertainment I was after, but the cheap convenience of knowing the answer to the big question once and for all. But, really, this approach to faith was quintessentially Pentecostal. Still, of course, a number of Prophets I engaged with saw right through me. For many, miracles aren't a way of determining your belief—faith is a prerequisite for miracles to occur. And, today, sub-Saharan Africans are among the most faithful people in the world.

In 1900, 77 per cent of the world's Christian population was in Europe and North America. By 2025, it's estimated that this number will fall to 29 per cent, and Africa is doing much of the demographic heavy lifting. More than half of Zimbabwe's population belong to African Pentecostal churches, along with 40 per cent of South Africans and over a third of Kenyans. The DRC, Nigeria, Ghana, Zambia—all have a population that's over a quarter Pentecostal.[1]

Lately, that faith has been tested, however. A series of scandals in South Africa—congregations sprayed with Doom Super Multi Insect Killer, fed live snakes, and encouraged to masturbate en masse until they reach orgasm—have led to a reining in, with spiritual entrepreneurs less keen to offer such *à la carte* forms of healing as resurrection. The outrageous promises that had come to dominate established traditions were being taken off the miracle menu.

Prophet Sithole wanted to push back against the men in shiny suits who were corrupting his vocation. Recognised to have gifts at a young age, he was trained in the mountains of Zimbabwe before passing tests administered by tribal elders to prove that his powers were genuine. But explaining my original quest for a resurrection ritual brought out a loud tut. The ultimate miracle "hasn't been done since the time of Jesus." But the Prophet, in his dressed-down holiness, knew a pained soul when he saw one. Sticking by his claim that he would help me see my enemy in the mirror, he knew that I would be able to sort out the issues in my heart.

Sithole slugged the second half of a 500ml ultra-can of Dragon energy drink, which *helps you not only keep up with your fast-paced life, but stay ahead of it!* The chickens and I jumped in unison as his ancestors suddenly made their presence felt once again.

The Prophet advised that they take a specific amount of pleasing: I was to slip the fee under the wicker mat for them. He wasn't interested in such worldly matters—I was laden with bad spirits, and he urgently needed to cleanse me of them. Only this was where the chickens were to come in—something that was unnerving both them and me.

I sat cross-legged on the mat, facing the Prophet, who sat on the slightly more comfortable couch. "I'm here to help people, not just do the things that are out of God's way," he told me, in a voice that carried the residue of a thousand souls. He was going to cleanse me and make me *strong*—the word vibrating in his throat in a way that tends to make a person, or a bird, jump—so that I could find the source of any ills in my life. What was he here to do? "Help people," I replied.

Hundreds of years of wisdom were going to heal my life, and I'd be lying if I said that I wasn't ready for it. I had come to Prophet Sithole to witness a miracle, and whether it was God or his ancestors that were going to deliver, I was thrilled by the prospect that a miracle could happen to me.

* * *

Before the white man's God arrived in this part of the world, a man like Sithole would have been a *sangoma*, the Zulu word for the healers and diviners who played an important role in the fabric of Southern African communities. They still do, in everything from directing community rituals to finding lost cattle to advising warriors and kings. There are 69,000 registered sangomas in South Africa today. But many more have gone the syncretic route, combining elements of their native belief systems within an established theological framework. Like Prophet Sithole, they are, effectively, 'shamans for Jesus'.

Many of these churches would dispute that they are a syncretic form of pre-Christian and Pentecostal beliefs. Rather, they say that they are the African expression of the global Pentecostal movement, which isn't owned by the West.[2] However you define it, Sithole and other 'independent' Prophets operating under their own steam are certainly healers bridging the two belief systems. That's Pentecostalism for you: the great strength of this form of Christianity is its ability to shapeshift, to quickly adapt to the cultures opening their doors to it, and then to absorb those cultures into a faith that offers the comforts of being homegrown. Before Azusa Street, other European missionaries who had brought the Christian God to this part of the world had been 'children of the Enlightenment', who had no time for the supernatural. But the Pentecostals did.

By 1908, Pentecostal missionaries from the United States had reached more than twenty-five countries across the world.[3] In

Southern Africa, they reached both Black and white populations, with local leaders marrying traditional cultures and customs with the Gospel. As in Pyongyang, some started to call Johannesburg the 'Jerusalem of Africa'. And yet the region's most influential Pentecostal figure never even made it to South Africa's shores.[4]

John Alexander Dowie was a Scottish-Australian evangelist and faith healer who moved to the United States in 1888 and founded the utopian city of Zion, Illinois. This began the movement of Zionist Churches whose faith healing strongly influenced the firebrand forefather of Pentecostalism, Charles Fox Parham. Dowie also oversaw a culture of tremendous grift that led one biographer to call Zion City "a carefully-devised large-scale platform for 'securities fraud'".[5]

One of his disciples, John G. Lake, had been personally converted to Pentecostalism by Parham in 1907. Parham had travelled to Zion City to mop up the faithful after Dowie was disgraced for his extravagant lifestyle and dodgy business dealings. As it happened, Dowie had recently been deposed by his second-in-command, Wilbur G. Voliva—the same man who, shortly after Parham's revival in Zion City, went on to publicly prosecute the sodomy charges against the Kansas preacher.

After the second of Parham's scandals finished him once and for all—that series of brutal and highly publicised exorcisms that took place in a panic about demons—John G. Lake was among the Parhamites who fled Zion City. He arrived in Indianapolis, where he and Azusa Street veteran Thomas Hezmalhalch conducted a fundraising drive for a mission to South Africa in 1908. Their Zionist brand of Pentecostalism was probably the first to make it to Southern Africa.

Not long after they arrived, they set up the Apostolic Faith Mission (named for Seymour's Azusa Street church, and better known as AFM), whose legacy still permeates the region today— over half of Southern African Christians are adherents of AFM or another Pentecostal church.[6] Many movements call themselves 'Zionist Christian', and they're not referring to the Jewish movement, but to the movement that came out of Dowie's city in Illinois. Key elements of the AFM and Zionist Christianity that took hold in the region were speaking in tongues, speaking to ancestors, and wearing ceremonial robes.

The missionaries might have quickly blended this new American take on faith into the Southern African spiritual landscape, but they had no desire to shake off everything they'd learned from the old country. Lake, denounced by one South African historian as a "congenital and extravagant liar",[7] continued Dowie's legacy to a tee, with faith healing and financial improprieties the cornerstones of his time in Southern Africa. However, his own legacy would be otherwise: inspired by Lake's teachings rather than his deeds, indigenous-founded African Independent Churches, whose Christianity focuses on healing rooted in place and ancestry, became a way for people to deal with the new Union of South Africa—the colonial, white-minority-rule state formed by the British in 1910, after the Boer War.

In the Apartheid era (1948–90s), William J. Seymour, the African-American founding father of Pentecostalism, was a hero and an inspiration to anti-regime activists, having been called by God despite being a Black man in a segregated society.[8] These churches continued to provide spiritual nourishment through the darkest days of Apartheid, and their popularity has only continued to grow since. White rule kept a firm lid on the number of African churches allowed to operate;[9] so, after 1994, they began to spring up everywhere, and gave the opportunity to reassert the 'African' way of doing things. This desire has only increased as democratic South Africa has become tainted by neoliberal economics and resource extraction encouraged by the West. While the jackboot might have been taken off the neck of sub-Saharan Africa, the

Western ideas that were supposed to help countries into an era of prosperity and equal opportunity have failed to deliver.

African-led churches are a homegrown alternative to foreign development NGOs, and increasingly a competitor to governments that have failed to deliver on the promises of post-Apartheid rule. In this context, tithes are effectively a form of taxation, with churches providing the basic healthcare, education and economic development that many people still can't get outside of God's house.[10]

* * *

Lately, the long and storied tradition of African churches has come under threat. The purveyors of God's grace have been overrun by a carnival of miracle men—slick young guys with big claims and bigger personalities, never far from the headlines they love and loathe in equal measure. No one encapsulates Southern Africa's miracle men quite like Prophet Shepherd 'Major 1' Bushiri. On a gloriously sunny Sunday morning in Pretoria, the administrative capital just north of Johannesburg, I attended Bushiri's Enlightened Christian Gathering, a vast outdoor megachurch.

The 30-something preacher is known for his smooth suits and lavish lifestyle, including a fleet of luxury cars, and at least three private jets.[11] Since I first attended an ECG service, 'Major 1' has become a staple of front-page news for allegedly taking the cloth in vain. He returned to his native Malawi in late 2020 while on bail for money laundering, theft and fraud charges,[12] in what he called "a tactical withdrawal meant to preserve lives".[13]

But I was more interested in the Prophet's rise than in his troubles. Among Bushiri's claims are that he has cured people of HIV and made the blind see, and can make money appear in the pockets and handbags of his flock. An infamous, somewhat surreal online video shows him descending a grand staircase, then walking on air, before being lowered to the floor.[14]

The giant, real-life showground is his natural turf, however. Hawkers sell food, drinks, umbrellas and Bibles at the entrances, and posters of Bushiri hang on buildings and poles throughout, with slogans such as "Enough is enough" and "God's open hands". This particular event was called the "Sunday of instant miracles part four", and it was sponsored by the energy drink company Rayon, a subsidiary of Shepherd Bushiri Investments. Tents around the perimeter of the giant hangars sold anointing oils, holy water, and endless books authored by the great man himself.

I was surrounded by Bushiri's followers, who could probably have filled a sports stadium. Trying to glean from them the source of his appeal wasn't an easy task. He was "enlightened", a "true man of God", "the best", and so on—this general, unwavering support felt like the answer you'd get if you asked someone why they love their football team.

I settled for the more accessible option. Bushiri's scores of books would be well at home on any alt-right website: fasting, Forex trading and, in the one I purchased, prophetic codes. Bushiri opens with the fact that he was raised in a Muslim family, but was always captivated by the Christian community: "I remember how my mind was boggled when I heard about the ministry of Smith Wigglesworth; how he brought his wife back to life after she had died."[15]

So many revivals took place around the world in the year or so after Azusa Street that it can be difficult to keep track of them— and, naturally, the faithful saw them as a sign from above. The British Wigglesworth led the Sunderland Revival in 1907, and for many believers he remains a folk hero to this day. He described cancer as a "living evil spirit", something he was known for punching out of people who presented with stomach pains. "What made me laugh," Bushiri writes, "was the fact that there were times when he would even hit the people with so much force that it propelled them across the room. When asked the reason for such a controversial approach to healing, he would respond by saying 'I do not hit them, I hit the devil.'"

Wigglesworth may have inspired him, but Bushiri's mentor is Prophet Uebert Angel, a Zimbabwean preacher who now lives in the UK. He runs Spirit Embassy, also known as the Good News Church, which has branches across Europe and Africa. Angel taught the young Malawian that prophecy comes to him from newspapers; but after that, God showed Bushiri "one hundred and twenty ways in which people can prophesy." Among them are prophetic codes, usually letters and numbers, which reveal a person's story to him "like an encryption." The book promised that, in order to live a better life, I would be "enlightened and edified on how the prophetic ministry operates."

Code 8, The Code Of Facing The Perpendicular Direction, states that you need to face east whenever prophesying "using the perpendicular prophetic line". The code number eight means 90 degrees, illustrated by a diagram showing God's voice as the vertical axis, the Church as the horizontal axis, and man as a square in the corner of the two.

It reminded me of how Sithole had been very specific about the way I had to sit and to conduct all of the rituals. Throwing bones and divining signs from nature are important parts of sangoma practice, although Bushiri's embrace of numerology appears to be more of a contemporary Pentecostal idea, now being used in global congregations as a way of connecting to ancient biblical texts.

As the ECG service went on into the early evening, through interminable hype men, testimonies and singers, the subtext soon became apparent. This was a raucous, ecstatic exaltation of tradition: an open space, opposed to the city's high walls and barbed wire, and a proud celebration of Black culture, in the zipped-up capital once synonymous with the white man's rule. Aside from being conducted in English, this service was distinctly *un*colonial—and this in itself is part of South African Pentecostal tradition.

When the Dutch arrived in South Africa in the seventeenth century, they used the local population as slaves. The abolition of slavery didn't do much for Africans' plight, however, especially after huge diamond and gold reserves were found. Black workers continued to be exploited, have their land stolen, and see every facet of life severely restricted, from their movement to their employment. Apartheid separated South Africa's white minority from the majority (which included a substantial population from the Indian subcontinent), but it also sought to divide Black South Africans along tribal lines in order to reduce their political power. Churches, by contrast, were places where races and tribes could mix; and, with non-white political activity banned—figures like Mandela were sent into exile, others simply murdered by the state—African churches were often the only legal place to hold mass gatherings, proving pivotal hubs for resistance and organisation.

The struggle to end Apartheid may have been won, but democratic South Africa is the most unequal country in the world—an inequality still firmly weighted in favour of the white minority.[16] The enormous hope and sense of possibility as Mandela came to power and founded the 'rainbow nation' have faded, the state seemingly unable to resolve the crises of poverty and inequity, leaving many young people in particular feeling disappointed and unfulfilled.[17] With rampant unemployment, and nowhere near enough conventional opportunities for young Black men to advance their lot, it's understandable that some, blessed with immense charm and confidence, see promoting themselves and their brand as the most effective way to get ahead. Bushiri, in his brash, uncompromising way, is a new man for a new era. While he was raised in Malawi, he's part of the first generation of young Black people in South Africa who have the opportunity not only to make it, but to make it big.

Whether he's raising people up along with him is another question. For many, Bushiri has become a beacon of inspiration: someone to look up to, and someone who can help. But his help comes at a steep fee. Prior to his legal troubles, a 'private consultation' with Bushiri would cost upwards of £400, if you could grease the right palms to get an appointment in the first place. Desperate and upwardly mobile people seeking the Prophet's divine blessing no doubt form a significant source of his wealth. The sacred shakedown has been around since the first days of snake oil—but on this score, Bushiri is far from South Africa's most controversial Prophet.

In my quest to see a miracle in South Africa, I was invited to an online group healing session with Prophet Penuel Mnguni. At only 30, the leader of End Time Disciples Ministries doesn't quite have Bushiri's reputation, but it's not for lack of trying. He is well known for having fed his congregation live snakes and rats.[18] In what the Prophet Penuel himself calls the "church of horror", people have stripped naked as he jumped on them, or hissed like snakes.[19] The Prophet has also encouraged male and female members of his church to strip naked and masturbate to climax, as "the holy fluid of masturbation would produce a sacrosanct fluid which would make the church floor as sacred as heaven."[20]

Penuel's kind of godliness isn't exactly unique. His mentor, only a few years his senior, is 'Professor' Lesego Daniel, famed for having his congregation drink fuel, turning "petrol into pineapple" as a kind of communion.[21] Another of the Professor's protégés, Pastor Lethebo Rabalago, is now known as the Prophet of Doom for spraying his congregants with insecticide: "The Prophet commands demon [sic] to enter into people bodies [sic] so that they can manifest, for demons need flesh in order for them to operate."[22] He then offers the cure—the highly toxic Doom—to drive the demons back out, leading to a conviction for assault in 2018.[23] It's often young women who are in thrall to these pastors, though they compete for the devotion of a range of congregants and families who visit them. In 2019, this prophetic arms race culminated in a spectacular display of the miraculous that gained headlines around the world.

It all started when Pastor Alph Lukau arrived at a Johannesburg funeral home where mourners were weeping over Elliot Moyo, who had reportedly been killed in a car accident two days earlier. Lukau laid hands on this man, and returned him to life. Moyo's family wept and pronounced a miracle, and a video of the event was swiftly uploaded to social media. Soon enough, the cartoonish fake was roundly mocked, and the unenlightened funeral home went on to sue the pastor, as they were never in on this caper.[24] Needless to say, I was interested in what Pastor Alph could offer, but he was unable to meet with me in Johannesburg to talk about the greatest miracle of all—his newfound fame had taken him to Europe, where he was filming a television show.

Penuel Mnguni, though, was still in good standing, and still working. By the time he finally logged on to the Zoom healing session, around thirty of us were waiting—older couples from Mozambique, young Prophets with small Instagram followings, and various others seeking health and hope.

Prophet Penuel opened by explaining that he was simply there to manifest what God has been speaking. We might not be crippled, we might not be sick from a physical illness, but maybe we were depressed or stressed. "These are the last days. These are the End Times," he said, with a softness in his voice. "God has given you such a Spirit to be blessed from above. We have been carrying power already."

He flicked through the faces, asking what they wanted and needed. I had expected craziness, but found something far more familiar: people asked for prayers for promotions at work or for good fertility, and Penuel offered solemn and heartfelt hope and encouragement. "Do what you're good at," he said to one young Prophet, stealing the internet connection from a nearby business. "God loves you so, so much."

Prophet Penuel hadn't brought me any closer to God, but I left the session with a little more faith in humanity. I was open to encountering divine intervention, but in this 'healing' session I had found something far more comforting: the intangible warmth of someone telling you that they care.

* * *

The big business of miracles might be growing apace at a local level, but it's two outsiders who have put evidence of Africa's supernatural traditions back on the global map.

On 30 November 2001, Nigerian pastor Daniel Ekechukwu slammed into a concrete pillar after the brakes failed in his car. He told his wife to take care of the children, and died while being transferred to a second hospital. A doctor took his vitals and "looked at the eyes—the pupils were fixed and dilated." Ekechukwu was pronounced dead. He was taken to a morgue, and the mortician saw that "everything was stiff" and "put him on the last slab."[25] But the dead man's wife had heard of a German-American Pentecostal evangelist, Reinhard Bonnke, who was conducting miracles. With a group of pastors, he set about a prayer vigil.

"Suddenly we saw the eyes started to move and life started coming in," one of them later said. They began massaging Ekechukwu to alleviate rigor mortis, and his "heart started to become hot." The man jumped to his feet and demanded water. An angel had taken him to visit both Heaven and Hell. Down below, he had met a pastor who had stolen church money. Notably, he "never saw any flames in hell, but the torment there looks as if the people are inside fire." The angel was going to send him to Hell too, but gave him "an opportunity to go back for the last warning to this generation."

Ekechukwu eventually moved to South Africa to preach, but it was Bonnke who became the more famous. A crusader known for his week-long revivals on the continent, some called him the Billy Graham of Africa. His Christ For All Nations mission, best known for its dramatic work throughout Africa, claims that Bonnke has overseen more than 79 million conversions to Christianity. In Nigeria, he's known not just for his effect on one man's resurrection, but equally for his association in public memory with many men's death in 1991, having stirred tensions with a widely publicised revival in a northern, majority-Muslim state. The tensions turned to a deadly riot, with street battles between Christians and Muslims killing up to 200.[26]

Not long after Ekechukwu visited the angel, American tel-evangelist Heidi Baker, known to many in Africa as Mama Heidi, witnessed the miracle of revival at her own church. The Tennessee preacher, now in her early 60s, runs a religious fief-dom known as Iris Global, which claims to have 'planted' 1,800 churches. Mozambique, the former Portuguese colony to the east of South Africa, is her primary mission ground. Mama Heidi received a revelation when she was 16, at a Choctaw reser-vation site in Mississippi. She was called to be "a minister and a missionary" and told to go to "Africa, Asia and England". She moved to Mozambique in 1995, where she focused on caring for abandoned and orphaned children.

Iris pastor Lino Andrade is one of more than a thousand in Mama Heidi's network throughout the country. In 2002, Heidi and her husband Rolland wrote an account of how Andrade was "brought from death back to life by the Author of life", one of about ten cases reported in Iris churches.[27] Lino had been des-perately sick for a month, until "his body began to smell of decay". A person called Pastor Joni had arrived with four other church leaders, and they'd begun to pray. "For three hours Lino's eyes were rolled back into his head", but Pastor Joni had done this before. Like Ekechukwu, Lino "was released from his body and given a vision of what might be." He watched his own funeral, and angels showed him things. "But in the vision Lino refused to accept his own death." After a few hours, "he returned to his body and awoke in bed, but was very weak and nauseous from his own smell. Satan did not get his way, and Lino was not buried."

Lino's story was one of many from Mozambique that I had heard about. If Johannesburg is the faith-healing capital of the world, then its eastern neighbour is the resurrectional equivalent. Before I sat down with Prophet Sithole's chickens, I journeyed to Mozambique to try to find out why the country has its reputation for bringing people back from the dead—and to see if there was anyone willing to show me how.

Here, the Spirit has long gone into battle against Satan. Mozambique was a Portuguese colony until 1975. Catholicism was the dominant religion in the south of Mozambique, with much of the northern half of the country Islamic. There were, however, a small number of evangelical missionaries in the country, who had a habit of educating bright young boys both at home and abroad—many of them would go on to leadership positions after independence, in the wake of the Carnation Revolution in Lisbon.

The Portuguese never had the white population to run a full Apartheid regime like the settler colony of South Africa; but life was no more pleasant for native Mozambicans under centuries of colonial rule than it was for their South African neighbours. For a time, the capital Maputo—today a beautiful, crumbling colonial city that doubles as a film set—was a place where Indigenous people could receive a lifetime of hard labour if they were caught inside city limits after dark. Colonial abuses extended to all facets of life—forced labour, high taxes, low wages, and confiscation of worthwhile land among them.

The 10-year Mozambican War of Independence might have achieved its aim, but it took more than the withdrawal of Portuguese power to effect independence. An even bloodier and more devastating civil war took place from 1977 to 1992, largely between Soviet-backed FRELIMO guerrillas and anti-communist forces backed by the white-minority South African and Rhodesian governments. The end of the Cold War forced an uneasy peace, and Mozambique was left one of the poorest countries in the world.

It's not hard to understand why Pentecostalism's resurrections and miracle-based healthcare are such compelling offers here. First of all, we can't underestimate the role of belief in its own right. This is a deeply pious part of the world, and while many turn to faith healing out of necessity, they also take the Bible seriously. In some interpretations, sin is related to sickness. If we can try to eradicate sin from our lives, even if not completely, then it follows that sickness can be 'absolved' too. The emphasis on healing through prayer is a byproduct of the emphasis on sanctification that has always been central to Pentecostalism.[28] But another key characteristic of the movement has always been its positive interventions into the lives of those who are struggling.

In Mozambique, faith healers are taking the place of barely functioning state health systems. Life expectancy in sub-Saharan Africa is 61 years—a full 20 years, or a quarter of a life, shorter than someone in the United Kingdom. But while we in the West tend to die of our excesses, or at the very least are able to exhaust our options in holding off our fate, it's a very different story in Southern Africa. Mother and child mortality, diarrhoeal diseases, HIV, tuberculosis and malaria are the common, horrific forms of death faced by people in the region.

And so, a couple of years after the civil war ended, a blonde American stepped into the gap left by an almost non-existent state. Mama Heidi might be as American as apple pie, but to many in Mozambique, she's a saint. I met with one of her disciples, the extremely charismatic Pastor Joshua. Blessed with an eternal spring in his step and a desire to transform the country both spiritually and politically, Joshua wears an armour of colourful collared floral shirts, jeans, and sporadic bursts of "Amen!" when he's thinking or speaking. An orphan plucked from the streets by Mama herself when he was 9 years old, he has now struck out to preach on his own—but he always returns to see Baker when she flies in on her private jet.

The self-described "bitter, violent kid" hadn't adjusted well to Mama Heidi's orphanage. How could he trust anyone looking to introduce him to a loving Father after he'd been abandoned by his own? But at age 12, something came over him. He asked God to heal him, and not only did he learn to accept this new Father, but he became healed. He had been given the gift of life, and not just for himself: I was told that he has *the* gift. But Joshua finds the celebrity that comes with it irritating.

"The healing is just anointing," he explained, when I asked what it feels like to cure or be cured. "That's why if you were to ask me how many people I've laid my hand on—it's none. Healing is just an electricity that flows, all the glory goes out" from one Spirit-filled person and into another. 'Anointing' is a common word amongst the faithful, a supercharged blessing that personally saturates someone with divine power. Joshua wouldn't deny that he has the power of resurrection—but first, he wanted to show me God *truly* at work.

The next morning, I got a tuk-tuk to the Iris orphanage on the northern edge of Maputo and waited for Joshua and his new wife to pick me up. Since spreading his wings, he's tried a few established churches, but none of them felt quite right. Along with a friend, Pastor Moyane, he'd started a new church, out in a place where the city limits slide into the country and the roads ask something of everyone. Moyane puts the charisma in

Charismatic. Educated in theology in South Africa, this pride of his village had come home and established an adoring congregation. As we greeted people in the carpark, he danced between English, Portuguese, and a couple of regional dialects, priding himself on his ability to speak to anyone who needs him.

A week earlier, a heavy storm had more or less blown away the church; it was now all hastily improvised tarps and breeze blocks. Perhaps twenty of us, led by youngish women with husbands in tow, danced and sang like it was mandated from Heaven above. The men were looking sharp, the women elegant. They tied traditional cloth over their best church outfits, a nod to the two worlds they lived in. Not that appearances really mattered—for an hour, we simply poured out joy through singing and dancing, interspersed with someone taking the microphone to read Bible verse in Portuguese, or the odd moment when the Spirit took a person's tongue.

"Don't worry, we'll teach you how to dance like an African," Pastor Moyane whispered alarmingly, my robotic sways clearly not cutting it. His wife took my hands to help me fall in line with the ecstatic congregation. The joy was transmissible. I no longer wanted to suspend my disbelief about the possibility of miracles—I really wanted to believe.

Once the outpouring was over, we all settled into our plastic garden chairs. Pastor Moyane gave a stirring sermon about how we get too caught up on Facebook, fretting about the failure of our lives after seeing the photos others are posting online. It was, of course, a take on the commandment not to lust after your neighbour's possessions—but without all the thys and thous and the coveting your neighbour's asses. Social media is inescapable in our lives, the pastor pointed out, but our online lives only represent a certain picture. Coveting is a waste of time—why not go out and do something good, for ourselves and for each other?

After the almost-four-hour service, we headed back along the muddy rollercoaster of roads to Maputo. Stopping by the city's garbage dump, home to its most impoverished, we saw that what little they owned had been wiped away in the storm the week before. Joshua gave them loaves of bread; but first, they had to sing a song about how the Lord lifts them up, *lifts them up*.

* * *

Prophet Sithole was furious when I told him that I'd been to see other men of God. "I am a man of principles," he said. "I tell the truth to shame the devil." He had no truck with the young miracle men in their extremely fitted suits. What they do "is welcoming a snake to bring you money, and I am not that person." The new breed of holy men, he added, were "the devil working." If he's right, then Satan must be clocking some overtime, with miracles of the heart and the womb in high demand within the marketplace of razzle-dazzle prophecy. But Sithole is right to say that he is a world apart from the likes of Bushiri and even Moyane. Merging ancient custom with modern Christian religion, he is not only people's first, and sometimes only, point of call for their ailments. He is also a custodian of their traditions—and he wouldn't even know how to livestream Christ's return.

After unlocking the secret codes of my age and marital status, Sithole's first intuition was the false prophecy that I had suffered many miscarriages. He wasn't deterred, though, and you have to give him points for trying—a precondition for prophecy is mastery of the art of vagary. As Prophet Sithole was out in the bush gathering his herbs for my revelation, he continued his flurry of texts between meeting and miracle, emphasising that *he* helped people. He continued to make clear to me that he wasn't happy that I had been seeing other healers, even over Zoom, because they could give me bad spirits and blow up the whole operation.

If he was upset that I'd visited another Prophet, then he was especially displeased that I had been meeting with a man of books.

Before my healing session with Sithole, I spoke with ordained Pentecostal minister and academic Solomon 'Solly' Kgatle, a professor of missiology at the University of South Africa.

"The bigger the prophecy, the bigger the pocket," he said, with a crushing smile. Solly believes that, when it comes to the new breed of pastors, "the gifted person is glorified more than the Giver of that gift." Without saying so directly, they are making false idols of themselves. You might go to church on Sunday to worship the Almighty, but you wind up worshipping at the altar of Bushiri, Penuel—or perhaps, in the local neighbourhood, even Sithole. This side of Pentecostalism is far from unique to Southern African preachers—ever since the days of Aimee Semple McPherson, the power of the messenger has frequently overtaken the message itself.

These young Prophets diagnose the sickness and offer up the remedy—but their popularity also speaks to a very real, and neglected, aspiration in post-Apartheid South Africa. "Penuel and Bushiri wouldn't read Luther," Solly said, referring to the father of Protestantism who first took Western Christianity away from the Catholic Church. "They need to be African; they want to practise power as well as heal. Colonial theology doesn't matter to them or their followers. Some of the pastors know that they are being outrageous—they are populist, and anti-theological on purpose."

The phenomenon of God's millennial showmen goes far beyond them just being good at Instagram. Pentecostalism, through the power of African Independent Churches, helped to bring down Apartheid and colonial rule, and now it's being called on again to help deal with the broken promises, the stomped-on expectations, the failure of what their generation had been told would be their time. Having been let down by hope, they have little choice but to turn to hustling. And what better business to go into than the only thing left that people actually believe in?

Whether it's Sithole and associates taping together a community from the scraps of the inner city, or the local heirs to the Zion City missionaries' empire of deception, an alternative economy in Southern Africa is taking shape. Government remains ineffective at tackling the most basic things for Black South Africans, like poverty and healthcare. And because it can't mediate these challenges, there's a significant gap in the market that people of various intentions can exploit. Approaching the Instaprophets from a distance, you'd be forgiven for thinking that these modern-day P.T. Barnums were full of it. Yet one woman who is not on the payroll says that there's more at work here than meets the eye.

In 2010, the Indiana University religious studies professor Candy Gunther Brown led a group of academics and medical professionals out to rural Mozambique, to test Heidi Baker's bold healing claims. Some medical folks take issue with this study, as it has a small sample size and no control test. Brown is willing to concede that there could have been plants in the audience, but notes that the experiment, which took place in northern Mozambique near Iris Global's headquarters, was also certainly full of genuine people in a tiny community who all know each other.

What Brown and her colleagues witnessed was something life-changing.

They placed headphones on a hearing-impaired young man who, to the best of Brown's knowledge, could not hear the sound coming through them, although it was "as loud as standing next to a motorcycle". A believer would place their hands on his head, or hug him. In soft tones, they invited the Holy Spirit's anointing to heal his hearing, and "commanded ... the departure of evil spirits in Jesus' name."[29] "We heard him able to repeat, in this halting way, words that were being whispered behind his head," Brown recalled to me. "That's dramatic. When you see that, when you're right there, and there are changes in people's experience [of] that scale? I can read about it, I can hear stories, but to actually be present when these things are happening—it gets your attention."

The researchers used a handheld audiometer to measure eighteen ears of eleven subjects, before and after the prayer. In addition to what they had witnessed, they found "highly significant improvement in hearing" in all subjects.[30]

Following up in the long term, the results haven't been easy to measure. Brown said that the subjects in Mozambique didn't have phones or addresses. There's also been the small matter of an Islamist insurgency that has made the area unsafe to visit again. But there is ongoing testing to replicate the studies in places like Brazil, hoping to repeat the results on a larger scale. Most of the time, these tests have found that the healings are lasting and life-changing. "It'd be shocking if there weren't people who thought they had been healed when they hadn't," Brown said. "But I have medical records from before and after. I just spoke to one last week, who felt a tickling in his ear in the process of healing, and he said that his hearing has been perfect ever since."

Another thing she discovered is that the miracle is often bigger than the individual: "The person has this experience, and then they go off and they pray for other people and *they* have a healing experience; and that starts this ripple effect, where one experience then starts off lots of other experiences." Critically, Brown and her colleagues also found that this 'chain reaction' of intercessory prayer only works in person. That is, there was absolutely no healing effect found from distant prayer, such as healing sessions held over Zoom.

In essence, there's something incredibly powerful about the whole village gathering to pray your pain away—a common feature in Brown's study. And, for people who will probably never see beyond the limits of their own small town, it might be especially important. While believers might be looking to the skies as they pray, it's the human element that is the key.

When miracles are the only game in town, it seems that, sometimes, they can happen.

* * *

Armed with all of this knowledge, I had become something of a believer. Not necessarily in God, but in the miraculous, and the power of people coming together.

I returned to Prophet Sithole's clinic to find the chickens awaiting me. "If there's a bad spirit following you, we're going to chase it out," he explained, lighting the candles wedged into the used lemonade bottles. "We can put it on the chicken; it can die in your hands."

"In order to take it out," he continued, as I sat uncomfortably on the floor, holding one of the two unfortunate birds, "you will be wanting it, then I will be praying for you. Then that chicken must die in your hands."

"What?"

"Without cutting it. If there's that spirit to come out from you, it will go in that chicken. So it will be that chicken. Then after that I will take that chicken to the river like the Bible said"—"*errrgghhh*", he belched again—"then the demons will be removed from the people and thrown in the river."

Sithole placed his gold bangle around my wrist, and asked me to snort a little stuff that looked and smelled a lot like black pepper. "Out, out!" he rejoiced, as I sneezed from the herb with a force similar to the belches he kept emitting from all of that energy drink. With the Prophet commanding the bad spirits out of me in a mix of his mother tongue and spiritual tongues, the chicken between my legs started screaming as though its ancestors were speaking to it. Sithole grabbed my hands and had me clutch its wings. I needed to hold the chicken so strongly that it wouldn't move, but I was terrified of hurting it. The Prophet said I needed to be strong, keep my eyes open, and talk inside my heart. Spirits were following me, and it was time to scare them off.

The chicken was very much alive, but seemed paralysed by our hands on it. Sithole pressed down on its spine, and I noticed smears of blood on the bookmakers' flyers that lined the floor of his 'clinic'. I wasn't sure if it was the mysterious pepper or the bad spirits leaving my body, but I was beginning to feel not entirely in myself. I let the chicken half-run, half-fly away under the couch.

It would be fine, he assured me with a wave of the hand, and borrowed 10 Rand to buy us both a Coke. By this time, I think the Prophet was searching for a miracle of his own. My unwillingness to sacrifice the bird was destroying the practice that he had been trained in; but he knew that there was unhappiness in my life, and wanted to help me.

"The things you're going to see," he exclaimed on his return, pointing to the little plastic green mirror with the price tag still on the back, before giving me a list of instructions for completing the procedure at home—mirror under the bed, bathe in the herbs, rub a red balm on my shoulders and the soles of my feet "to stamp down on evil", and begin sipping the bitter medicine he had put in my Coke bottle.

After smoking another bush herb, I went out onto the streets dazed, feeling like I was walking horizontally. Somehow I made it back to my hotel before falling into a deep sleep. I woke up to the sound of my phone: it was the Prophet, calling me to complete my date with destiny. "Tell me what you see," he said, with that growling intensity he had used when he was making me grip the chicken. I unwrapped the mirror from the betting shop flyers, and looked at it without looking in it, seeing a reflection that seemed more like a funhouse mirror than a reckoning.

"Take the mirror, look at the mirror," he urged, his words bending in my mind in line with the distant shapes that were wavering and blinking back at me. "Tell me what you see. What do you see?" I looked again, unable to focus. I squinted one eye and placed a foot on the floor in order to stomp on the evil spirits, or at least find some relief from the spinning. I couldn't make a sound, and Sithole's growls grew louder.

As a paying customer, I'd demanded a miracle, and not just from the Prophet—the thing is, by now, I really wanted one too. A year of chasing the impossible was staring me in the face, and I was straining to see it. I contorted my eyes, and my mind, to try to agree with the blur in front of me. There was an off-centre cross, smeared across the mirror in what looked like rusty blood mixed with the waxen, woody substance I'd bathed in.

"Drink another glass of Coke," the Prophet sniffed. "Drink it fast like I'm doing now," he belched, before slipping into a soft hum of tongues and prayers, and then—"*eeeerrggghhh*".

The poisonous taste of everything I'd snorted, sipped and smoked in his room was ruining a reality I was not yet back to. *Another, another, another* glass of Coke, he kept urging, the fizzy bitterness of bush medicine suddenly calling forth my forebears. "No! Be strong! Another!" he growled. "Tell me what you can see." And with that last sip, I opened my mouth, and all of my ancestors came forth like an army. Generations of warm black liquid shot across the room, and the Prophet went silent.

My head felt like an opened prison, thoughts running rampant that were equally as dangerous locked up. I felt as though I was atoning for the only truly strong belief I think I'd ever held, which was that there's nothing there.

The culmination of months of running around Southern Africa to try to understand why people believe. And it turned out, in spite of my scepticism, that not only did I want super-natural things to exist in the world, but I wanted in. Of course resurrection from the dead was never going to happen—but surely there's a space for miracles to happen to me?

Sithole still didn't feel I was there yet, and wanted me to drink another glass of spiked Coke, but I was ready for revelation. I closed my eyes and searched with a warm, sticky hand for the plastic mirror that was somewhere beside me.

I picked it up for the last time, and suddenly everything came into focus.

6

DO YOU KNOW THE ONE ABOUT
THE GOOD SAMARITAN?

Uncle John wanted my soul, and he's the kind of bloke that you would hand it over to immediately. "It's like a fish 'ook in the mouth, love," he said of his mission to see me reborn. "Might seem cruel, but it's the only way we can get you in."

The former crook knows how to get his way, but these days, he's armed only with a gaffer-taped Bible and a stare that could part the Jordan River. We were angling for converts outside a shopping centre in Bexleyheath, Kent, just beyond the south-eastern edge of Greater London. England was about to enter another Covid lockdown, but Uncle John and the boys from the Light and Life Gypsy Church knew that they had the key.

He's not my uncle, of course, but after a few weekends of evangelising with the lads from the Church's Dartford branch, I was part of the family. Uncle John it was. And he won't stop until every soul is saved, staying out on the streets for hours at a time, wearing Ugg boots against the cold. The Dartford church has five pastors, and they show deference to their evan-geliser-in-chief—well, most of the time. As we stood in the chill, one of the five, Mark Friend, whispered that he knew how to wind the old boy up, and pointed out a group of characters walking down the pavement towards us on stilts, dressed in full Christmas regalia.

Uncle John's lip curled on cue. "What's all this Santa Claus business?" he said indignantly, to sniggers from disciples who had heard it all before. "Not a fan of all this red and green carry-on," he muttered, appalled by the commercialisation of something as important as the birth of his Saviour. But there weren't many souls around for us to convert, and Mark was on a tear. "Dare you to trip 'em over," he urged me. "If the cops come, tell 'em the Pikeys made ya do it!"

I still flinched when they talked like that, but the question of identity is theirs alone. The Dartford boys usually refer to themselves as Gypsies, a word that has been reclaimed with pride, similar to how gay communities have taken back the word queer. British Gypsies are descendants of the nomadic Indian people known as the Romani Gypsies, who migrated towards Europe some 1,500 years ago and arrived in Britain in the sixteenth century. Roma, or Romani, is the name usually used on the continent for this ethnic group. Travellers—a word we well-meaning *gorja*, or non-Gypsies, tend to use as a catch-all—specifically hail from Ireland, either nomadic since the Middle Ages, or itinerant labourers who came over after the famine.

For the Light and Life boys, their born-again Christian identity is as important as their Gypsy heritage. And if their calculations are right, they are evangelising at an untold speed. The Church says that it now has thirty-three congregations and about 20,000 followers in the United Kingdom, which amounts to one tenth of the estimated Gypsy population.[1] Exact figures are hard to come by, but it's thought that the UK is home to around 3 million people who are part of the broad Pentecostal movement.[2]

Beyond Blighty, some estimates state that, across Europe, up to a third of some 12 million Gypsies, Travellers and Roma are born-again Pentecostal, or at least curious enough to have visited a Pentecostal church.[3] Take Spain, for example: according to one missionary organisation, less than 1 per cent of the overall Spanish population is evangelised; but of the approximately 660,000 Gypsies living in the country today, 20 per cent are Pentecostal.[4] Swiss pastor Jacob Zopfi, former leader of the Pentecostal European Fellowship, calls the Gypsy Revival "one of the most powerful that Europe has known to this day."[5] A 2017 report by the French branch of Light and Life estimates that there are between 20 and 30 million Gypsies in the world, with around half of that number living in India. Around 800–900,000 of them "know Jesus-Christ", according to these figures, which count more than 5,000 Gypsy preachers and pastors globally.[6]

The Dartford lads will save anyone they can get their hands on, but feel a special duty to their people. Uncle John's motto is "the only thing better than going to a party is taking someone with you", and when it comes to salvation, it's only a few minutes to midnight. "None of us Gypsies are rocket scientists or brain surgeons," he said, earnest as always. "And it usually takes a Gypsy person to reach a Gypsy person."

Previously a ten-out-of-ten sinner—ten commandments, that is—Uncle John was born again on 16 January 1994. "I plotted a couple of murders, love," he confided in me, after many days out on the streets together. "Never went through with them, but I had murder in my heart, so in God's eyes, I broke it."

Uncle John wasn't the first person of faith who had wanted to save me on the spot, but my usual get-out clause—"I was raised Catholic and am still trying to figure it all out"—wasn't going to cut it here. My old firm was the nominal faith of most Gypsy people before they were saved, and John thinks that they're part of the problem: "Satan got to the Catholics with how they are about Mary." He was referring to the Immaculate Conception: the idea that the Virgin herself was conceived without the stain of original sin, as demonstrated through the virgin birth of Jesus Christ. As a result, she never personally sinned throughout her life—and nor did her son, of course.

"She's blessed among women, that can't be argued," he yelled in my ear as the wind tore through us. To Uncle John's mind, even though she bore the Baby Jesus, she still needed to be saved by Him. "But the Catholics say she's a co-mediatrix with Christ, which is absolutely crazy. There's only one mediator with God, and that's Jesus Christ."

In a few years of running with the world's Pentecostals, this was the most theological bunch I'd encountered—keen biblical students of a religion that appeals to many because it goes *light* on the heavy stuff, and puts everything into the experience of faith. Uncle John's beef with the Catholics' Mary isn't critical to his belief system, nor that of the Light and Life Church. But, as always with Uncle John, he had his Bible at the ready to prove his point. "Sadly, that's what the Catholics believe," he sighed, "and it contradicts the word of God."

We had arrived at Bexleyheath's shopping centre in a big church truck: a lumbering van that looks as though it was made for transporting prisoners. I stopped myself halfway through making that gag, because a brother called Steve was next to me, and he'd only just gotten out. His attention was elsewhere, though. As we directed Mark to manoeuvre the beast in between the parking lines, Steve noticed a flaw in the logo on the front of the truck. "How come it says Life and Light here?" he asked, pointing to the paintwork on the bonnet. Bill Boswell, one of the Dartford pastors who had first invited me along to evangelise with the boys, started laughing. "Let's put it down to racism and say the shop done it wrong," he said with a wink. "See, in French it's *Vie et Lumière*, but the French say everything backwards, so we call it Light and Life. But some of the trucks got done as Light and Life, others as Life and Light. I suppose they're both right."

Boswell, Billy-Boy, is another of the five pastors at the Dartford church. The stocky landscaper might only be 36, but he's the group's natural leader. Blessed with an angelic singing voice and the gift of the gab—including a fondness for telling people that if they didn't take a flyer, he would get in trouble with his boss—he's Uncle John's blood nephew, and witnessed first-hand the transformation that would change all of their lives. "My uncle used to prize-fight, for money. He was a man's man," Bill told me, with the slight stutter of someone delivering an urgent message. "We thought he was punched in the head too many times when he said that he'd got saved."

Uncle John was the first practising Christian in the family, and Bill still feels anxious about the time he wasted before being saved himself, on 15 May 2005 at 7:45pm. "I was brought up to lie and con to get money, and if I couldn't, I was a thief," he said. "If it were up to us Gypsies, we wouldn't have done it. But God is calling His people *now*. It's the most vague and most precise answer I can give."

Bill likens this modern calling to the Parable of the Great Banquet, told in the Gospel of Luke: no one turns up to a feast, so a servant is sent out to invite "the poor, the crippled, the blind and the lame." It is a metaphor to explain how the Jews rejected Christ, which then opened the door for the salvation of the Gentiles: the blessings of the Kingdom of God are available to all who will come and believe. For Bill, the Gypsies have gone hungry for too long, and it's time for them to pull up a chair at the table. Getting in before Christ's return is important, but recent history plays a part, too. An unwanted, stateless people no matter where they landed, the Gypsies know all too well that, when events take over, they need someone in their corner.

One estimate has the Gypsy and Roma death toll in the Holocaust at 1.5 million, out of an estimated 2 million people.[7] Nazi Germany declared the Gypsies "enemies of the race-based state", and they were issued with black or brown triangles to identify them, just as Jews were forced to wear a yellow Star of David.[8] Of this shared history, Bill says that the Jews have not forgotten, especially the ones who lived through it. "I'm friends with a load of Hasidics up in London," he said. "The Jews got a bit of an affiliation with Gypsies because of what happened in the Holocaust—they killed our people as well. It seems like whenever they get persecuted, we go through it at the same time."

A few years ago, a group from the Dartford church went on a pilgrimage to Israel. Bill's daughter couldn't join them, so he tried to collect some keepsakes for her—and the former crook couldn't help himself when the opportunity arose to nick a bit of the Wailing Wall.

"We were doing the *Shema—Adonai Eloheinu, Adonai Echad*—the Lord our God is One. And everyone kept noticing all these crumbs from touching the Wall," he said. "I mean, it's not like I had a hammer and chisel—I just put me hand up and heard *crack*. A shovelful came down, so I grabbed a bit. The bloke with me, he says, we're gonna die 'cos of this, you're gonna cause our *death*,'" Bill remembered, tears of laughter flowing down his cheeks. "I am a bit worried the Israelis might knock on my door one day though."

The undesirables of Europe for centuries, some see serendipity in the creation of a Jewish homeland around the same time as the first Gypsies found salvation in the Holy Spirit. As is often the case with ethnic minorities, there is even a school of thought among some Gypsy evangelicals that they are descended from one of the lost tribes of Israel. Culturally, they argue, both have similar traditions in marriage customs and purity rituals; and, understandably, the shared history of persecution is too great to ignore.

THE ONE ABOUT THE GOOD SAMARITAN

For Bill, the affinity between Gypsies and Jews is a point of pride. A few years ago, he took his family for a holiday to the Greek island of Rhodes. They came across a synagogue and Holocaust memorial. The man looking after the memorial wasn't terribly interested in them, until Bill mentioned that they were Gypsies there to pay their respects. He dropped everything and took them to see an 80-something Jewish elder.

"The bloke was 13 when they took him to Auschwitz, he showed me the tattoo on his arm," Bill said. "He didn't speak a word of English, but he wouldn't let go, wouldn't stop looking me in the eyes. We cried together." The old man's mum and dad had been taken away, and he had been sent to the camp. "The Gypsies was in the compound next to [the Jews]," Bill said. "He was allowed to go out in the fields and work, but my people wasn't. And he said that each evening, when he came back, the Gypsies were playing their instruments. 'Then one night the music stopped, and we knew they was dead.'"

* * *

In the hellscape of postwar Europe, a miracle occurred. According to René Zanellato, a pastor and missionary at Vie et Lumière in France, a poor Gypsy woman called Madame Duvil-Reinhart arrived at a church in the Normandy region one Sunday in 1950, and begged a pastor to help her son Zino.[9]

Zino had become ill with tuberculous peritonitis and perforated intestines, and a doctor had told her that he was "lost", that she should be consoled with her other children. Medics had then told the devastated mother and her relatives to leave the hospital because their tears were causing a commotion. But months earlier, she had met an Assemblies of God preacher in the market square, who'd given her a pamphlet and told her to go to the church, which had a way of getting Jesus to heal the sick. Shortly after the hospital's death sentence, Mme Duvil-Reinhart found the pamphlet, and asked a woman on the street to read what it said for her. The church it mentioned was nearby, and Duvil-Reinhart felt she had nothing to lose.

"The pastor came towards the Gypsy woman and said, 'Why are you crying like that?'," René told me. "'Sir, my son is going to die.' 'Do not cry,' he answered, 'the Lord can do anything. Your son will be healed. God is going to give him back to you.'" The congregation was uneasy with the arrival of a weeping Gypsy, "but the pastor went to the hospital to lay hands on the young man. The next day she went to see her son and found him sitting up in bed, healed. Right then and there, she gave glory to God because she understood He who healed and restored her son."

Duvil-Reinhart's family surrendered to Christ after seeing God's hand, and word quickly spread from family to family, clan to clan. "After this first miracle, the Gypsies began to come to the churches," René explained. "Brother Clément Le Cossec, who was at that time pastor of the French Assemblies of God, received about fifteen Gypsies that night in his church." There, they prayed to receive their baptism in the Spirit, and the gift of tongues came to them.

Mandz, another of Mme Duvil-Reinhart's sons, would go on to become what Light and Life considers to be the first Gypsy preacher.[10] Le Cossec, who was a *gorja*, said that he had received a prophecy about reviving the Gypsy people. He founded Vie et Lumière, and began working among the Gypsies, helping them learn to read at a time when many were illiterate.[11] Since the day Zino was healed, French Gypsies have been active evangelists, using the Gypsy musical tradition to marry their culture with Pentecostal practice and help spread the word to their people across Europe.[12] René believes that there are over 140,000 baptised adult Gypsies in France today, up to 40 per cent of that population.

Saved or not, Gypsies still have a tough time of it in Europe. A 2019 survey found that over half of people in ten European countries have unfavourable views of these communities.[13] René says that many of his people from Eastern Europe continue to "find shelter" in Western Europe, "but their arrival brings fear and dismissal; they are rejected [regardless of] their country of origin." That's usually Romania or neighbouring Bulgaria, where millions of Roma continue to face persecution and poverty.

For René, Romania holds "the record [for] intolerance", one that he traces back to the thirteenth century. From that time, Gypsies in the region were sold into slavery, until the practice was outlawed in 1864. After the Holocaust, he says, Nicolae Ceauşescu's violent regime saw a Gypsy mortality rate in orphanages of up to 50 per cent.[14] After Ceauşescu's fall in 1989, football hooligans and neo-Nazi groups conducted anti-Gypsy pogroms for thrills. René described his people as "marked by poverty, living often in the ghettos, doing hard, dirty, unpaid work, and left to their own resources."

This was the story of Toflea in eastern Romania, a Romani village of around 17,000 held in such contempt by the rest of the country that, until recently, it literally wasn't even on the map. But that all changed in the late 1990s, when the Holy Spirit came to Toflea, in the shape of Marius Banceanu's great-uncle, who had been converted during his travels for work. In a part of the world where Orthodox Christianity is the dominant faith, Pentecostal missionaries have viewed the rubble left behind by the communist Iron Curtain as fertile ground for new believers.

"We started trying to convert people in our village, all the time," Marius told me when we met up on the greyest of London days. This wasn't easy when they started their mission. Most Gypsies in Toflea subscribed to the traditional Orthodox faith. One day, an angry group of village men came to confront his great-uncle on his doorstep about this new rendition of God, "holding their weapons [to] the sky." But the family held firm, receiving visions that "one day they will come to God." The power of their conviction started winning villagers over—helped, as so often with the Pentecostal movement, by dramatic changes to Toflea's way of life.

For as long as they had known, Tofleans, who were almost exclusively Roma, were known as *ursari*, the ones who keep dancing bears. For understandable reasons, that custom has fallen out of favour, and at the end of the twentieth century there was a greater blow to the community's way of life. The town was also famed throughout the region for its metalwork—until the 1990s saw cheap, mass-produced metal products arriving from China. Romani artisanship couldn't compete for price. Help—the only help—arrived in the form of Pentecostal missionaries, who brought education and training, which in turn gave Tofleans new and desperately needed jobs. Within five years, Marius said, "all of Toflea had been born again."

Marius was part of the first generation in the town to receive a decent education, and by the time Romania joined the European Union in 2007, this opportunity combined with the new freedom of movement allowed Tofleans to imagine a life beyond the village limits. Since moving to England in 2014, Marius has become a poster boy for the "perfect" immigrant. Learning English while working in unpleasant conditions at a chicken factory, he is now a father and university student, also dividing his time between volunteering both at his church and with a community group for Roma in the UK.

"At first, they didn't like us, they were very suspicious of us," Marius said of his British neighbours in Ipswich, where a sizeable Romani community from Toflea and surrounding areas has settled. "But after a while they saw that we were hardworking, religious people. We don't like to evangelise in the street or something—we think it is better for people to see *this*: our character, what we're doing."

Blessed with a humility that would make you blush, Marius isn't interested in dwelling on a life story his forebears couldn't have dreamed of. What makes him most proud is the odd British neighbour who pops into the Gypsies' church to pray with them, or at least check out their music. One Romanian *gorja* even drives down from his home in Oxford to attend. An outsider wanting to worship with the Roma remains something that would be unthinkable back home.

My stories of a rapidly evangelising Light and Life Gypsy Church surprised Marius—he wasn't aware that the British Gypsies had been saved too. After experiencing generations of discrimination and violence for being who they are, his people just want to put their heads down, and make the most of a better life that they believe has been mandated from above.

* * *

They're not alone. For many immigrant and minority groups in the UK, the Pentecostal faith is critical to helping them navigate life. It's a phenomenon as common to domestic cleaners as to Premier League footballers. People arriving in the country for its economic opportunities, particularly from Eastern Europe, Latin America and Africa, are being born again; or renewing their faith as a way of coping with the transition and of making connections in a big, cosmopolitan city. What is left unsaid is the sense that being a practising Christian makes an outsider more accepted in post-Brexit Britain—just as we've seen with North Korean defectors trying to settle in Seoul.

There are an estimated 17,000 Pentecostal churches in the UK—about one congregation for every two pubs in England.[15] Step out of any large Tube station in London and you'll probably walk past the red-heart logo of the 'help centres' run by the Universal Church of the Kingdom of God—the Brazilian Church started by Edir Macedo with an ever-expanding global focus. Hillsong's largest chapter worldwide is also a London fixture, with around 5,000 of its members gathering each week in one of

London's largest theatres, the Dominion. Tellingly, some 70 per cent of its members are under 25.[16]

West African communities are served by branches of major Nigerian churches such as the Redeemed Christian Church of God, which has over 800 congregations across the United Kingdom. Black-majority churches are also booming among the third- and fourth-generation descendants of Windrush migrants from the Caribbean, seeking a connection to their heritage. Some Pentecostals in the UK might be looking to their faith as a bridge to the past; others are very much focused on the present. Uebert Angel, mentor of South African preacher Shepherd 'Major 1' Bushiri, has grown his Spirit Embassy supporter base by moving its headquarters to London. Taking a very different approach from Marius and the Tofleans, Angel is highly engaged in politics, leaving no doubt as to the role he sees for his modern-day army of God. An enthusiastic social media user, he is best known for his full-throated support of Nigel Farage, applauding the Brexit leader for taking on "leftist demonic narratives".[17]

A relatively recent phenomenon has emerged in the West that sees people from Global South countries such as Nigeria, South Korea and Brazil engaging in "reverse missions"—trying to bring the gospel back to the UK and US, societies they believe have lost their way and grown distant from the Lord by embracing liberal ideas such as gay marriage. But beyond reviving what we might think of as old ideas, Pentecostal churches in the UK are also giving new life to old facades. The dwindling numbers at many Church of England or Methodist congregations have seen them shutting up shop and renting out their buildings to the new kids on the block. That's how Bill Boswell and the brothers got set up down in Dartford: a philanthropist bought up a number of unused churches and offered the Light and Life Gypsies peppercorn rents to start this modern-day revival.

The mission spirit runs thick through Bill's veins, and along with many in Light and Life, he travels frequently to the former Soviet Union, trying to help the large Romani minority be saved. Light and Life recently built a church in Soroca, 'the Romani capital of Moldova', around 300 kilometres north-east of Marius' village, Toflea. An eternal student, Bill has learned the Romani language, which is still widely used in the region. Before he started going on missions, he only knew slang and swear words in his people's historic tongue.

During those freezing afternoons spreading the word south-east of London, the Dartford lads liked to muck around and play up to stereotypes of how *gorja* see them. "When we're evangelising, 99.9 per cent of people we're talking to are non-Gypsies, though the Gypsy ratio changes when we're in prisons—there it's more like 95 per cent," Bill joked. But trying to live the travelling life in modern Britain is no laughing matter. While recent decades have seen advances in the human rights of Gypsies, Roma and Travellers across Europe, institutional discrimination has become more cunning. Many look at their persecution in Eastern European countries, but the west of the continent, where René Zanellato says so many seek shelter, is often no kinder. France and Italy have undertaken expulsions of Romani communities, usually back to Romania and Bulgaria.[18]

In the United Kingdom, the traditionally nomadic Gypsy existence is under threat.

Britain has around 200,000 Gypsies and Travellers, most of whom settle for periods before moving again. This means that around 10,000 will be on the road in England at any given time. The number of caravans has risen by 13 per cent in recent years, and with it, levels of persecution.[19] In 2005, the *Sun* newspaper launched an anti-Gypsy campaign called "Stamp on the camps".[20] Three years later, it was found that Gypsies experience a higher degree of discrimination than any other minority group in the

UK, including asylum seekers[21]—but the rot goes deeper than a tabloid-led crusade.

Gypsies have the lowest level of education and highest rate of disability of any ethnic group in the UK. Child mortality is twenty times higher than for the rest of the population, while life expectancy is 10 years lower.[22] A 2015 lawsuit over denying Gypsies entry to pubs confirmed what they all already knew: a third of Britons admitted to being prejudiced against Gypsies, according to one 2011 survey.[23] The travelling existence appears to be a particular issue to some in political office. Ahead of 2019's general election, the Johnson government campaigned on a promise to make intentional trespass involving vehicles a criminal, rather than a civil, offence, if the camp contained two or more vehicles on public or private land.[24] In January 2020, Cabinet minister Jacob Rees-Mogg reaffirmed the government's commitment to the crackdown in parliament, referring to alleged "defecation in public places" by such trespassers as "absolutely revolting".[25]

A 2021 High Court case ruled unlawful a series of blanket bans preventing Gypsies and Travellers from stopping on parcels of land, but the hostility goes on.[26] Shortly after the ruling, columnist and former Tory MP Matthew Parris wrote a piece denouncing the ruling in *The Times*, under the headline "It's time we stopped pandering to Travellers—Indulging those who claim to be nomads by giving them designated sites and ethnic minority status has gone too far".[27]

Laws have been tightened to make it harder to obtain official status as a Gypsy or Traveller, with confirmation of this identity needing to be "granted" by local councils or the national planning inspectorate. The criteria used by the authorities to make the designation have set up a cruel paradox that effectively makes the nomadic way of life illegal. Those who settle lose their status as a Gypsy or Traveller—which in turn makes them ineligible for a mobile home or caravan site.[28] If they want to put down roots, they must prove that they live on the road.

In a compromise with the impossible, some Gypsies now settle, but maintain caravans as an homage to their culture. Bill Boswell ships his over to France each year for the annual gathering of the Light and Life faithful, a pilgrimage to the place where the Ghost first appeared in 1950 to save Mme Duvil-Reinhart's son, and save them all.

* * *

It wasn't until decades after that fateful day that the French Gypsies made it over the Channel to save their British brothers. Jackie Boyd, Light and Life's unofficial 'Archbishop of Canterbury', was one of the first to be converted by the French when they arrived with the good news. If Uncle John is the tireless fisherman of Gypsy evangelism, reeling in unsaved souls across south-east England, then Jackie Boyd is the grizzled sea captain steering the Light and Life ship. "The French mission came over evangelisin'," Jackie told me over the phone in his typically gruff manner. "The first Gypsies to start gettin' saved was in '81, and we formed the mission in '83."

The Dartford lads had taken their church onto Facebook for the pandemic, but Jackie, not the most tech-savvy of men, invited me to the service that Light and Life was maintaining in the Surrey town of Leatherhead, about 30 kilometres south-west of London. Down there, the path to Salvation is simply not on the map—Salvation being shorthand for the church's home at 9 Salvation Place, that is. Jackie sent me a dropped pin on WhatsApp to show its location off the busy bypass.

A small sign identified the church, bearing the Romani flag: blue and green with a red wheel in the middle. Around a dozen houses were clustered as if in secret along the small, muddy lane leading to the church. As I stepped onto the bitumen at the end of the dirt road, a 6-year-old boy in a three-piece suit escorted me to the church door by dribbling a full water bottle down the street. He kicked a goal through the makeshift tarpaulin door into the church's overflow segment.

Inside, Jackie was looking on as a junior preacher with a heavy Irish accent delivered a stirring sermon about the state of the world. We need to stick together, he said, and stick to the word that binds us. The Spirit-filled people can still leak out their godliness, "because of the cares and problems in the world." We drip and we drip, and we need to be filled daily.

Before Jackie stood up to deliver some final thoughts, we took communion. A few strapping young lads—and only lads—came around with two trays of tiny plastic thimbles, one filled with broken wafers, the other with apple and raspberry cordial. Jackie called on suggestions for prayer, and the congregation began calling out names: members of the community at home sick with Covid; neighbours struggling with the drink; family members who still, in spite of everything, won't believe.

When it came time for personal prayer, it wasn't a quiet moment. It was an outpouring; a cacophony of tongues and invocations. The young woman next to me laughed as I looked around: it was clear from the looks I was getting back that I was not one of them. "You know us Gypsies, we're all loudmouths who won't shut up," she whispered, her supermodel legs wrapped in tight leather pants and shakily high stilettos. Not that she paused for this punchline. Like all the other women, except for me, she put a shawl over her head—a direct instruction from 1 Corinthians—and launched into private but loud prayer, in her own words and the tongues gifted to her by the Spirit.

Jackie, on the other hand, did not conform to the gabby Gypsy stereotype. I joined him after the service to try to coax some words out of the man. On the question of the doctrine his church subscribes to, he had even less to say than usual. "We used to have contact with other evangelical groups, but that's faded out," he explained, between handshakes with the men in his congregation. "Most of them went liberal, so we parted ways." When pressed about what might have caused the split, he replied, "Just general liberalism." As Light and Life sees it, "through our small eyes," as Jackie said, "they were not sticking to the Word of God—not being true to their original convictions."

Jackie has been around too long, and spoken to too many journalists, to be pressed further on the meaning of "liberal"— but I knew what he meant. As with other British Pentecostals, many Gypsy evangelicals have pushed back against certain secular ideas filtering into modern churches, such as anointing female clergy and welcoming LGBTQ people. Jackie wasn't about to discuss it, but this became apparent when I asked about joining a group that he had mentioned would be going evangelising next week. "Women aren't allowed," he said curtly. "No way, sorry."

Like their global Pentecostal fellows, Light and Life are biblical literalists and religious fundamentalists. Many see their faith as the last way to stay 'pure' in secular, libertine modern Britain, helping them hold on to their traditional culture, which might seem dated in today's world. Gypsies already have a hard enough time—their faith might just be the last acceptable way to maintain strict ideas about gender roles and sexuality. But the exclusion of women from evangelising isn't an entirely hard-and-fast rule—the Dartford branch of the church was not only happy to have me along, but pleased by my interest. And it should be said that no member of Light and Life was ever hostile to my presence as an outsider, let alone a woman—quite the opposite.

After church, I began sliding along the muddy path that led back to the motorway. Just as the dirt road was beginning to look impassable on foot, a small red car as worn as a hotel-drawer Bible pulled up alongside me. "I know it's not the normal thing to offer a lady a lift these days," a white-haired man called out of a jammed window, "but I saw you in church."

His name was John, and I wedged myself next to a baby carrier in the back seat for a ride to the station. John "wasn't one for big words," and fretted about the "protocols, I guess you'd call them," of offering a strange woman a lift. "Once upon a time you would offer a lady walking on the side of the road a ride," he said, "but the modern woman might find it weird." I didn't—it had been highly Christian of him to save me from certain disaster in the mud—but his terribly embarrassed teenage grandson Levi, who was sitting in the front, seemed to feel otherwise.

"I was born nomadic," John told me, flashing his technicolour smile in the rearview mirror. "We used to take a horse and cart out along here. The horses would eat the grass on the side of the road. But we had to move, and it's almost another country now." Trying to distract from a voice that had tipped into sadness, he pointed to the Box Hill lookout where, in summer, you can see all the way to London. Since John became settled, he feels more born-again Christian than Gypsy. That I was raised Catholic and am still trying to figure it all out was quite okay with him—after all, it had taken him long enough to see the light.

We arrived at the station, and Levi and I got out, the kid going in whatever direction I wasn't. John fired up the hatchback and began to drive off, before stopping suddenly as he was about to lurch into second gear. "Elle," he called out excitedly. "Do you know the one about the Good Samaritan?"

I had vague recollections from the Sunday school of my childhood, but John helped me fill in the gaps. It's a story Jesus told about a Jewish traveller who is robbed and left for dead on the side of the road. A priest and then another man both cross the road to avoid him, but a Samaritan—the enemies of the Jews—bandages him up and gives him shelter.

To Gypsy evangelicals, the story of the Good Samaritan has been turned on its head.[29]

Like the Jews, they've been beaten up and ignored as people cross the road to avoid them, but Jesus has stepped in. In their evangelising work, Gypsies want to be the Good Samaritans lifting up their fellow travelling people, having first been beneficiaries themselves; as far as Gypsies go, the Pentecostals among them have come the closest to fitting in with the rest of British society.

"We were the last ones they bothered saving," John said, that unmistakeable sadness back in his voice. "We were the last ones they told."

* * *

The snap Christmas lockdown came into effect, and that ended up being the last time I was able to visit Britain's Pentecostal Gypsies. But I was considered part of the Dartford congregation now, and over that miserable time, I continued to hear from the lads on WhatsApp, concerned for my wellbeing and by the fact that they hadn't yet managed to save me.

Like Uncle John, Bill had decided that my soul was his number-one target while I was in the country; but I couldn't lie to him. He conceded defeat after making sure I knew that I could call him anytime, from anywhere, with any of my problems. After all, there was a broken country to repair, and far more important souls than mine that the boys needed to get to work on. In his messages, Bill would cheekily use the Black skin colour option in his emojis, a reminder that his lot are different. Yet since he has been reborn, he just wants everyone to be the same. "I want to see a Christian prime minister. Someone that has my values," he said. "It's like when my daughter's boyfriend asked me if I would okay him marrying her. My only concern was who he *was*—and that's a Christian."

It's just that, in the UK today, who *Bill* is remains an issue of contention.

"There's no smoke without fire, and mostly, I don't blame the *gorjas*," Bill said, referring to the continued discrimination that Gypsy and Traveller people face, while acknowledging his and his uncle's criminal past. But rather than standing up to the people who would cast them out and cross the street to avoid them, Bill would rather bring the unfaithful in for that great banquet. "It's only right that we try to make a witness of 'em," he declared, with his usual optimism.

For both the Light and Life Gypsies and the Roma of Toflea, God isn't moving in mysterious ways. He's set them on a clear path. But it's one that comes at a cost—conversion is not only life-changing, but changing the Romani way of life. Being saved makes Gypsies more acceptable in modern Britain, and for Bill, standing under the Lord's banner is proof that they have assimilated.

"It's only really that God has made us more civilised than we were," he told me. "Gypsy culture used to be travelling, running to and fro. Now, once most of our people become saved, they stay put."

PART TWO

SPIRITUAL WARFARE
THE BATTLE TO BUILD HEAVEN ON EARTH

7

A COMPANY TOWN

It might have been Laura's morning off, but if Jesus never stops working, then why should she? The 26-year-old sat in her car, saving lives with a soft Taylor Swift track as backing. "Are you here to pray?" I asked, and she slid her hand back out of a large Doritos packet on the passenger seat, sustaining her vigil. "Y-yes," she replied, postmarked with caution. "They said we're allowed to be out here if we stay in our cars."

A steady stream of patients on gurneys were being wheeled into the emergency room at the Shasta Regional Medical Center in the northern city of Redding, as California struggled to deal with its Covid surge. Restrictions on hospital visitors meant that Laura couldn't enter the waiting room to lay hands on the sick, so she waited in the carpark alone, a thin silver bracelet indented on her forearm from an hour of prayer on her steering wheel, her palms raised to the windshield to transmit her healing energy.

Laura is a member of Bethel Redding, one of the biggest and best-known Pentecostal megachurches in the United States, if not the world. Led by charismatic pastor Bill Johnson, its army of foot soldiers wants to conquer the globe, to prepare it for the

3

Lord's return—but first, they have to complete their takeover of Redding, population 92,000.

Inspiration comes in many forms, and it was something a lot smaller, in the cosmic scheme of things, that had sent Laura into battle for the sick that day. Earlier in the week, she had lost her phone while she was juggling bags outside of a supermarket, where "all kinds of homeless" were hanging around. She only discovered it was missing when she arrived home, and it was gone by the time she made it back to the carpark.

She took a breath and made "prayers for whoever took it", trying not to think about how a new phone would blow her meagre savings. And when she woke up the next morning, a friend was at her door to tell her that someone had found it and gotten in touch. For Laura, this wasn't simply a relief: it was a reminder from God that He performs miracles great and small. It was also, she realised, a clear warning that "we have to manifest the Kingdom."

Much like Hillsong, Bethel has ditched the Pentecostal label in favour of its own branding, led by an eponymous recording group. Bill Johnson operates with a far heavier theological touch than his Australian friend Brian Houston, but the two are among the most important figures of the new generation. With massive churches that are monuments to the faith—you could even say themselves—they've been at the forefront of giving religious consumers what they want: direct access to the supernatural, and putting on one hell of a show.[1]

Bethel counts 11,000, or one in eight, of Redding's residents as members. Laura "didn't grow up with much" and never attended the church's large college campus, the Bethel School of Supernatural Ministry, but she was now a member of an unofficial Facebook prayer group of the Bethel faithful, encouraging members to continue socially distanced carpark vigils during the pandemic. "Invite as many friends as you can!" one callout said enthusiastically. "We'll be declaring healing, joy, peace, resurrection and an end to the coronavirus."[2]

Even prior to Covid, Laura regularly joined missions to local hospitals to heal the sick. Hospital staff would sometimes "come out and tell us that it's working already," she told me. Her past experiences made her feel all the more guilty that she'd drifted from healing missions since Covid began reshaping daily life. Losing her phone had been a sign to refocus her faith—and also, her lack of it.

They—you know, doctors, politicians, experts—cannot be trusted. "There's so many voices around trying to change our stance and opinion on things," she said, "and they completely changed the narrative." Refusing to be drawn on what "the narrative" is, she added, "I pray so hard for the doctors and nurses, but only God can heal people. We have to declare healing and an end to the virus in *Jesus'* name."

The pandemic had been a reckoning for Laura in more ways than one. Now, she got her information from "a few doctors on Instagram". It's all out there, she said, but she couldn't stick around any longer to educate me—she had to go to her job as a medical administrator at another facility across town.

* * *

When it comes to direct experience with faith, someone who knows all about the megachurch's healing programme is Ronda Snyder. A tireless citizen reporter and Facebook warrior, she's an admin for the group Investigating Bethel, which documents the church's growing influence in Redding.

She joined after her mother, who had developed an illness that confined her to a wheelchair, was approached by a group of Bethel students, who asked if they could lay hands on her. "She came home and was really upset," said Ronda. "She said, 'No, I don't subscribe to that.' Instead of taking no for an answer, they

145

blocked her wheelchair with their feet underneath one of her wheels so that she couldn't move, and they subjected her to it. She was humiliated to the point of tears."

Snyder believes that students and churchgoers are inspired by Bethel Redding and the Johnsons to demonstrate public expressions of faith and feats of loyalty because of the competitive element at the School of Supernatural Ministry. "There's intense pressure to prove Apostle or Prophet status among the ranks and out-do each other," she explained. But this unofficial army of healers operating in the town goes well beyond hospital carparks and enthusiastic student groups.

One medical professional in Redding told me that the church has issued a call to arms: *Redding will be a red line for cancer.* They added that a number of doctors and specialists who attended Bethel conferences have been recruited to work in the town—they believe that at least four of Redding's twenty ER doctors are involved with the church. And two nurses confirmed to me that, before Covid restricted hospital visits, it was common to encounter Bethel-inspired healers in emergency wards and waiting rooms.

"We've had problems with them here in town at both hospitals," one told me. "They push their ways into there and go beyond medical staff to do the healing and prayers. I've seen patients who made a special request [that] no one from Bethel is allowed to come into the room, because they'd become that disruptive."

In 2007, after years of the church trying to build Redding's reputation as a "cancer-free zone", Johnson's wife Beni was diagnosed with breast cancer.[3] Bethel's first lady turned to a more conventional route to be "healed of cancer", undergoing surgery to remove her tumours. On discovering that she had the genetic mutation that makes her susceptible to breast and ovarian cancers, Beni then travelled to Spain for "holistic treatments" under the watchful eye of a personal "health coach".[4]

If only Bethel workers received these kinds of benefits. Some have complained to local reporters about unsalaried, hourly pay at low rates—sometimes minimum wage or barely above.[5] The church offers only partial healthcare coverage for full-time employees. According to the website, perks of working for Bethel include two free lunches per month, an email address, and discounts on church events.[6] 'Supernatural Ministry' students at BSSM don't even receive that. In addition to conducting their healing work pro bono, they're paying up to $5,250 per year to attend the college.[7]

For some of these students, learning ways of the miraculous not only has a financial price, but takes a deep emotional toll. Zach, who was a BSSM student in the 2010s, and whose family still attends the church, told me that he began to grow disillusioned with Bethel when he realised that, despite being taught that he and his fellow students had been invested with supernatural powers, they were using them incredibly selectively. "We're supposed to be powerful and messengers for God, we have anointment," he told me. "But then I started wondering, 'Why aren't we clearing out children's hospitals and healing homeless people of addiction and mental illness?'"

The school's way of accounting for miracles that don't occur instantly is that "acts of faith" are the true key to healing through God, something that requires ongoing belief and prayer to work over time. Born and raised in this theology, Zach wanted desperately to heal people. After a lifetime of faith, he also wanted to see people be healed. He joined Bethel healing groups, which see people fly into Redding from all over the country seeking to be cured.

"A guy with bad vision wanted to get healed, and I was so certain that I could heal him," Zach said. "We prayed for each other for two hours and then stood outside looking at posters, taking off our glasses to read them. And there was just—just nothing. I remember how crushing that was. I saw him later that day at the conference, and he was wearing his glasses again."

* * *

A guide to Redding left in my cheap motel room cheerfully warned not to engage in political conversations with locals, especially if you have liberal or moderate views. Ringed by snow-capped mountains but subject to vicious summer wildfires, Redding signals the beginning point of the Pacific Northwest. A traditionally red meat kind of place, not very diverse and now politically dominated by liberals, there is an awareness that the region's demographics are now against a Christian, conservative, white American future. But that constituency isn't ready to give up yet: the Northwest has become the chief battleground in their rearguard action.

Militiamen regularly flood regional cities to brawl with "Antifa" real and imagined, turning the Northwest into a laboratory for the country's post-democracy future. Different parts of the region are tackling the project in different ways: rural Oregon was home to a 2016 standoff between the Mormon Bundy clan and federal officials; Portland sees almost weekly militia parades; people in Forks, Washington ran a mixed-race family out of town, believing they were part of a Black Lives Matter takeover. They had come on a camping trip.[8]

Bethel, and by extension Redding, has its own way of transforming the world: a Christian 'Dominionist' project called the Seven Mountain Mandate. A plan by a shadowy group of 'Prophets' and 'Apostles' to take over the world sounds like the stuff of a bad airport novel, but it is one of the most important ideas in the Pentecostal movement today. The premise of 7M, as it's often called, is that the seven pillars of society have been taken over by demonic powers. Believers have to reclaim control of these 'mountains' so that Christ can return to rule over the earth.

Before setting out to change the United States, Bill Johnson first had to change Bethel. A fifth-generation preacher and son of the megachurch's former lead pastor Earl, Bill took over in 1996. Since then, few churches have been more closely associated with the third wave of the Holy Spirit than Bethel—in spite of the church firmly rejecting the Pentecostal label. They are simply Bethel. A year before Johnson Jr took over, he'd been at the Toronto Blessing,[9] the revival that brought together North America's major Pentecostal leaders at the end of the twentieth century (see Chapter 2). At the time, Toronto was undone by press reports of animal noises and hysterical "holy laughter"; but, in the long run, it also marked the rise of thinkers like Peter Wagner, more focused on the 'work' to be done for God than on individual believers' experience of the Spirit.

Returning to Redding, Bill Johnson made a personal pact with God that "the outpouring of the Holy Spirit" would be the sole purpose of his existence.[10] He declared that Bethel must be a revival church with an emphasis on the supernatural, causing 1,000 members of the congregation to walk out on the church. The remaining faithful of the new Bethel would vote to leave the Assemblies of God in 2005.

In becoming independent, they were also becoming part of something bigger. Umbrella organisations like AOG are starting to feel old-fashioned. Today's Pentecostal leaders are transnational figures in charge of their own brands: Johnson's Bethel, Houston's Hillsong, Heidi Baker's Iris Global, Edir Macedo's Universal Church of the Kingdom of God, David Yonggi Cho's Yoido Full Gospel Church, and a few other key international organisations we'll come to meet in later chapters. They operate a lot like the kings of Silicon Valley a few hundred kilometres south of Redding: united by a 'disruptive' ethos and clear common interests, but each with their own distinct identity. But while figures like Jeff Bezos and Elon Musk have their sights set on dominating space, Bill Johnson and his fellow Toronto alumni have the more pragmatic ambition to take over Earth.

A church with the look and feel of an app (and yes, Bethel has one of those) is difficult to square with one that wants to rule over us under direct instruction from God—but amid all of the stadium spectaculars and Instagram inspiration, a distinct theological shift has taken place.

The apocalypticism that marked the early Pentecostals has taken a back seat. After all, predicting doom runs counter to the Pentecostal optimism that has been growing since the postwar Latter Rain movement (see Chapter 2), and isn't much use to anyone wanting to effect change in the here and now. So, what drives global Pentecostalism today is still an inevitable Judgment Day, only now it's imbued with the idea that believers can work *towards* it, and in anticipation of it—they can bring it about through their actions here on Earth.

Eschatology, the theology of the End Times, is deeply important to Pentecostals, and evangelicals in general. The Book of Revelation, the violent, evocative final book of the Bible which prophesises Christ's return to Earth, shapes a lot of their thinking. There are infinite schisms surrounding interpretations of Revelation, but they fall broadly into camps divided by views on exactly what will happen, and in what order, before, during and after the End Times.

Most adherents to 'dispensational' doctrine say that there will be seven of these 'dispensations', which are distinct ages—up to and including the thousand-year rule of God over His Kingdom. Pentecostals used to be largely 'dispensational premillennialists'—that is, they believed in a brief period of intense tribulation before Christ returns to Earth to rule. This is why events such as the San Francisco earthquake in 1906 were seen as a sign by many inside and outside of Azusa Street. After this Second Coming follows the Rapture, when believers alive and dead will meet the Lord in the clouds, before Christ's thousand-year reign over Earth.

This idea was in stark contrast to 'postmillennialists', who believed that they had to create the conditions of Heaven on Earth before Christ could return. Though we can say that today's Pentecostals have switched sides to join this camp, they have also put their own spin on it: a new line of thinking has emerged called '*victorious* eschatology', an optimistic view of the End Times that says Satan won't take over, because the time of tribulation has already been and gone—thus accommodating both schools of thought, with the idea that "we are now living in the days of God's advancing Kingdom."[11]

Rich Schmidt, pastor and lead Bible instructor at BSSM, says that Bethel has "moved away from negative prophetic words" in its work. "We're not emphasising destruction and darkness, but focusing on the positive things God is doing." After all, he told me, "Look at Europe. These great cathedrals took the Church hundreds of years to build. You don't invest 500 years to build a cathedral in the city square if you think that the end is going to happen next year." In other words: Pentecostals—once the trembling disciples of William Seymour who feared the End Times were coming at any moment—have now given that destiny a modern, upbeat, political sheen.

This is where the Seven Mountain Mandate comes in. It's part of a shift towards "Kingdom now" theology—another of John Wimber and Peter Wagner's ideas, meaning that believers have to start doing everything they can to create the world for Christ to rule over. Instead of fretting over interpretations of the Book of Revelation and what will happen when those events come to pass, Pentecostals are increasingly concerned with the here and now. Particularly, with the overarching idea that secular society is taking over the world, and that they need to fight back.

The Seven Mountain Mandate first came into being in 1974, when God delivered a concurrent vision to three evangelical figures to take over what they called the "seven spheres" of influence—that is, education, religion, family, business, government, arts and entertainment, and media (the number seven also represents completeness in the Book of Revelation.)[12] This idea then remained dormant for 25 years, until the late-century tide of globalised capitalism came to meet Pentecostalism. One of the three 1974 'visionaries', a missionary leader called Loren Cunningham, met with Dallas business consultant and self-proclaimed Prophet Lance Wallnau. Wallnau recognised 7M's potential and began selling seminars and training courses on this "template for warfare" for the new century. In 2013, he co-authored the movement's call to arms, *Invading Babylon: The 7 Mountain Mandate*, with Bethel Redding's own Bill Johnson.

Authority to take over the world's seven spheres comes from Isaiah 2:2, which says, "Now it shall come to pass in the latter days that the mountain of the Lord's house shall be established on the top of the mountains." Believers must overcome Satan and create God's Kingdom ahead of the Second Coming (fulfilling the line in the Lord's Prayer: "Your kingdom come, Your will be done, on Earth as it is in Heaven.")

Invoking the presence of evil forces all around us also serves a purpose, in this culture of signs, wonders and thick metaphors. If satanic forces have descended on society like fog, the peak of the mountain is the one thing that rises up above them. Those on top of the peaks, like Wallnau and Johnson, are able to look down through the demonic haze, and call upon everything—from social media presence to bank accounts and, increasingly, boots on the ground—to act.

Taking over the world requires action from the bottom up as much as the top down, and the mission is clear. There is "no such thing as secular employment for the believer"; the role of government is to "create a realm of safety and a realm of prosperity", because "poverty is demonic".[13] In other words, reshaping

America and the world so that Christ can return just so happens to look a lot like gaining power in the here and now. Either way, the 7M movement is providing supernatural justification for the politics of a Christian right coming to terms with the diminishment of white Christians as a proportion of the US and world population, a trend set to continue in the coming decades.

As Kris Vallotton, Bill Johnson's second-in-command, has put it, "If we are going to be a force of hope in our communities then we must ditch the passivity that is present in the philosophy of so many Christians." Vallotton finds himself taken aback by those who "make [Jesus] sound like a Buddhist monk instead of a radical world changer!"[14]

Ultimately, the Seven Mountains Mandate shifts the Pentecostal narrative from one of restoration and liberation to one of conquest[15]—a 'victorious' reading of biblical prophecy that puts aside theological differences to get everyone acting in concert *now*. An old-school evangelical preacher might have been hellbent on stopping a woman getting her abortion, but the preachers of 7M are looking at the far bigger picture. They want nothing short of a complete transformation of society.

* * *

Before Peter Wagner's disciples were hatching a plan for total world domination, he had come up with another idea critical to modern Pentecostal thought. His concept of 'spiritual warfare' came out of his time as a missionary in Latin America in the 1950s and '60s, after which he returned to the United States and met up with John "doin' the stuff" Wimber.

According to Wagner, spiritual warfare comes in three forms. There's ground level, where people are fighting possession by demons; occult level, which sees them work towards domination of other religions and spiritual practices; and strategic level, where the battleground is territorial spirits possessing either geographical places—anywhere from a gay nightclub to the nation of Iran—or institutions, such as a progressive political party or the mainstream media. For Wagner, who died in 2016, strategic-level spiritual warfare was the most important battle.

Biblical justification for this comes from Ephesians 6:12, which speaks of a struggle that is "not against flesh and blood, but against the rulers, against the authorities, against the powers of this dark world and against the spiritual forces of evil in the heavenly realms." Believers engage in 'battle' in their everyday lives. 'Warfare' takes the form of waging 'violent prayer' (persistently and aggressively channelling emotions of hatred and anger against Satan), 'spiritual mapping' (identifying areas where evil is at work, such as the darkness ruling over an abortion clinic, or the 'spirit of greed' ruling over Las Vegas), and 'prayerwalking' (groups roaming the streets, "praying on-site with insight ... in the very places that we expect God to bring forth his answers").[16]

Though Wimber would eventually fall out with Wagner over this emphasis on the demonic, Wagner was proved right in the end: the idea of spiritual warfare has only accelerated through the Christian world since his death, and the Seven Mountains Mandate has been working in tandem with it, offering believers the justification that anyone or anything that gets in the way of their quest for institutional power is demonic, or at the very least evidence of hidden forces at work.

Equally as importantly, the doctrine has made its way into elements of the Republican Party, even among those who might not believe that God speaks to and through them directly.

Project Blitz, also known as Freedom for All, is a Christian-Dominionist 'shadow network' that claims a network of 950 legislators in thirty-eight states.[17] It provides model legislation for state governments to copy and paste, for instance allowing adoption agencies to discriminate against LGBTQ people. The steering committee for this opaque organisation includes the influential

David Barton—a former senior Texas Republican and close ally of Lance Wallnau—who believes that "If you're going to establish God's kingdom, you've got to have these seven mountains".[18]

With some seriously powerful people being directly influenced by the ideas in Wallnau and Johnson's *Invading Babylon*, you would think that Bethel would be trumpeting it from the hilltops. Instead, the Redding church has effectively disavowed the manifesto co-authored by its leader. Bethel's director of communications, Aaron Tesauro, told me, "We do not believe Christians should 'conquer' or 'take over' any sector of society." A graduate of BSSM, Tesauro said that Johnson and Bethel's vision is simply a refreshing change from when he was growing up, a time when "the eschatology" of Pentecostalism "was that the whole world is going bad, and that Christians need to separate themselves from the world government structures" in order to save themselves.

Pentecostals were not supposed to be part of worldly affairs—they were to stay in their church and survive until the end of the world. "And," Tesauro noted, "the end was coming very soon." In far more upbeat language than the grim total-war outlook of 7M, he told me that Bethel takes a "fresh look and approach", that it wants to "release Christians to be more intentional". According to Tesauro, the church teaches that Christians should bring the values of their faith into their daily lives. Unlike in the past, when some Christian movements taught that working in the Church made people more holy, Bethel believes that "everyone's call is equally valuable and important—whether you're called to be a pastor, a nurse, an inventor, a business owner, or any other profession." Put this way, those Seven Mountains sound less doomsday-like, and more aspirational.

Unfortunately, however, Bethel's network does teach that some people are more equal than others. "Once-gay" Bethel pastors Elizabeth Woning and Ken Williams run the Equipped to Love ministry and its CHANGED movement, for people who "experience same sex attraction or gender identity issues."[19] That's a polite way of saying organisations for conversion therapy, the traumatic practice aimed at 'reprogramming' congregation members, often teenagers, to abandon their gay or trans identity.

Woning is also a teacher at BSSM, which has been a huge part of transforming the church from its Redding roots to global influence. Vallotton started the school in 1998, and has grown it into the largest vocational college (that is, it doesn't issue degrees) for international students in the United States. It's undoubtedly a cash cow for Bethel, income from the multiple school tuitions providing $13.7 million, or 22.5 per cent of the megachurch's total earnings.[20]

Redding residents who aren't members of Bethel quibble with the church's insistence that it isn't sending its people out to the mountaintops. At a bar downtown—one of the few places in town where you won't find Bethelites—Bob, a keen fly fisherman, said the only thing he catches these days is "damn students trying to fix me". He called BSSM a "bearpit" where young people are taught to "go out and dominate" in order to win favour with the Johnsons. His mate Alan, a retired real estate agent, said, "In business, you'd call what they're doing to Redding a hostile takeover."

Criticising Bethel isn't something most people like to do loudly, for the organisation's influence extends well beyond the church doors. Some of the town's most prominent businesspeople are members and operate commerce networks "to partner with God at work."[21] Tesauro himself mentioned to me that, reportedly, over 50 per cent of new startups in Redding were founded by entrepreneurs who attend the church. Bethel donated $500,000 to the city's police in 2017 to allow a neighbourhood watch scheme to continue, and later led a campaign to raise $740,000 to fund the salary of four police officers.[22] Not long after, they donated a further $25,000 for a drone programme.[23]

Julie Winter, a longtime member of Bethel's council of elders, has been on the city council since 2016; in 2019, she served as mayor of Redding.[24]

* * *

The few downtown bars are the only places to avoid the throngs of excruciatingly enthusiastic young people with passions for music, God and social media, and an even greater passion for talking about these things really, really loudly.

Relentless positivity is a hallmark of the Bethel brand. Local reporter Annelise Pierce, who attended the Bethel School of Supernatural Ministry in 2010, said the church encourages students to "get activated" in the community. "They have connections with schools, they have connections with businesses, they have connections with local government, connections in the arts—they're very strategically going after each of those mountains," she told me.

Annelise and her husband, who are still active Christians, began to doubt the teachings of the church, as they "felt there was a colonial mindset" in the way that Bethel was doing Christianity. "There was a lot of going out to conquer other people and other ways of thinking."

Most people who are at the school didn't grow up in the area, but the strong networks mean that many who arrive will stay on. "They think that if we can transform Redding, then the whole world will look at it and see what Jesus does when He comes in and transforms a community," she said. "The goal is to make Redding the prototype for the Heaven that all of us could become if people get on board with the Kingdom."

In order to understand what Heaven on Earth looks like, I walked 90 minutes from the heart of downtown Redding to Annelise's old stomping ground, the Bethel campus, which sits in a wooded, private estate area, off a junction of interstates.

Apart from another coffee shop bursting with enthusiastic conversations, most people come this way to visit the Alabaster
Prayer House. These 24/7 prayer rooms are another feature of
megachurches, with some—such as IHOP Kansas City—featuring never-ending live music and the ability to stream the room
from anywhere in the world.

Alabaster's wooden interiors form a hexagonal shape. The
windows look out over landscaped gardens and tree-lined val-
leys, a peaceful space with a centrepiece fountain offering the
sound of running water and a distinctly Eastern, meditative feel.
A few months before I came to look around, BSSM had also
been the site of a 247-person superspreader event[25]—but the
exceptionally good-looking young people lying on the floors or
quietly praying were still maintaining the general town-wide
disdain for face masks.

Similar to the Temple of Solomon in São Paulo, Alabaster had
a collection of 'Hebrewics' paraphernalia that must be mass-
produced to appeal to Christians. One wall had a banner reading
"Seek first the kingdom and his righteousness"; another had a
large Star of David flag and a wooden replica menorah. Pulling
up a window seat, I noticed that I was sat next to a small stand
of little plastic flags, representing scores of nations whose members I imagine frequent the campus. My eyes suddenly settled on
the Saudi Arabian flag, the unmistakable green with Arabic
script above a sword. This was probably a political statement, but
no one was around to ask—only beautiful 20-somethings prone
in prayer, scattered like playing cards on the floor.

Alabaster is only an entry-level experience to the world of
Bethel. For those who really want it, there's so much more. The
megachurch's sermons have become famous, or infamous, for
'glory clouds' of gold glitter and feathers that fall out of nowhere
in the middle of someone preaching. In one YouTube video of
this 'phenomenon' that has had almost 500,000 views, the

church says that it doesn't "claim to understand it," but knows that "there is a biblical precedent."[26]

And then there's the practice of 'grave-soaking', an ancient idea that a person can roll around on the graves of deceased revivalists to 'suck up' their 'anointing'. There are photos in circulation of Beni Johnson engaging in grave-soaking and grave-hugging.[27] According to people I spoke to in the town, Bethel's best-known alumnus, anti-lockdown musician and politician Sean Feucht, is also known to indulge. A YouTube video from Ben Fitzgerald, the Australian ex-Bethel pastor turned European stadium spectacular promoter, explains how students lay over the grave of Smith Wigglesworth, deceased hero of South Africa's 'Major 1' Bushiri (Fitzgerald denies he participated in this act).[28]

Kris Vallotton and other church elders have publicly disavowed the practice of grave-soaking,[29] but a 2006 post on Bethel's website explains how BSSM students were taken on a mission trip. Titled "The Power of Soaking", the post declared: "Since Jesus has commissioned us to raise the dead, it is the heart's cry of many staff and students to be used in this way." Multiple students "received the opportunity to pray over the deceased body", but sadly the teenage girl in question "was not raised". A few weeks later, Beni returned to the same venue for a youth conference, where she "began teaching on soaking (intimacy and encounters with God's presence)".[30]

In 2019, Bethel captured global attention when congregants tried to raise a 2-year-old girl, Olive Alayne, after her mother, a Bethel Music singer-songwriter, asked them to "pray for a miracle of resurrection".[31] Another BSSM graduate, Tyler Johnson, has formed an organisation called the Dead Raising Team, "which has brought about 15 resurrections amidst the 60 teams worldwide that are committed to fulfilling the commissioning of Matthew 10:8."[32]

But that call to action from Matthew is not only about healing the sick and raising the dead. More broadly, it's about casting out demons—and this brings us back to the 7M Mandate. For the ultimate anointing, Sean Feucht was part of a group of worship leaders invited to the White House in late 2019 to pray for President Trump as he went through his first impeachment trial. Among the fifty or so leaders gathered around Trump in the Oval Office, including Hillsong's Brian Houston, only one hand reaches out to rest on the president's arm—that of Feucht.[33]

* * *

Using the threat of the next life to gain power in this one isn't exactly new. The excesses of many a megachurch mean that the word for such an institution has become code for fraud, flock-fleecing and falling from grace. But that's all old hat, like whiskers on a preacher. Bethel is leading an altogether different proposition.

Right at the end of the twentieth century, that boom period for unfettered global capitalism, the Christian right was largely defined by fire-and-brimstone Southern Baptists—Jerry Falwell Sr's Moral Majority, and campaigns against contraception, abortion, euthanasia and sex education. But today's no-label Pentecostals are coming to define that same political force at a time of *bust*, ushered in by the Great Recession and through the pandemic. And their approach makes that of their spiritual forebears look positively antiquated.

Led by American figures such as Johnson and Wallnau, Pentecostalism's religious entrepreneurs have become political entrepreneurs—they're not really pastors anymore, but executives who oversee a morally charged business operation. In fact, the new breed of (mega)church leader has become so commercially focused, and so dependent on visionary figureheads, that former preacher William Vanderbloemen has opened a recruitment firm specialised in "executive search" for Christian organisations.

"The Neo-Charismatic Pentecostal movement creates an experience in a worship service, and not just a data transfer," he told me from his office in Houston. In other words, you're meant to *feel* God when you're in church, not just have biblical information thrown at you by a pastor. "There is a hunger in people for experience, especially through music, and the theology of worship in the Neo-Charismatic world is to transport people from one place to the next."

Vanderbloemen says that the movement's leaders worked out how to keep people coming through the gates, even before the pandemic started giving believers the opportunity to stream the preaching they desire on demand. They've also perfected storytelling, and understand the power of pulling for the rebel, or the underdog. "They have done a wonderful job of accepting those rejected by others and picking up people whose lives have fallen apart—they're particularly good at it," he added. "They're also the one branch of the Church in the States that is racially diverse, and that, along with the music, is incredibly appealing to millennials and Gen-Zs."

For all that third-wave Pentecostals have continued the tradition of empowering the marginalised, Bethelites have been accused of ignoring rampant poverty and homelessness in the area, and an environmental crisis quite literally on their doorstep. Seven Mountain Mandate theology might be about a total revolution via seven pillars of society, but the way word on it is spread is all about positive reinforcement, equipping true believers with the spirit of conquering things in their everyday lives, rather than the less sexy ideas of remediating broad social ills, or pursuing incremental change. The church is simultaneously focused on the immediate priorities of its members, and on the far larger prize of preparing the Kingdom—on anything, you could say, except what's going on around them.

Bill Johnson and Bethel might be going hard on the positive aspects of creating Heaven on Earth, but studying the works of Lance Wallnau, the entrepreneur who cowrote the 7M manifesto *Invading Babylon*, is revealing. He has remarked that the "business of shifting culture or transforming nations does not require a majority of conversions." Instead of winning a consensus, "we need more disciples in the right places, the high places. Minorities of people can shape the agenda, if properly aligned and deployed."[34]

Wallnau believes that Christians have been divinely appointed to take this on, in the United States and around the world. The rhetoric is aggressive, focusing on battle, violence, war, satanic forces, urgency and victory. Heresy is no longer a religious idea—it's a political one. True believers in the Seven Mountain Mandate are not simply dangerous because of what they want to overtake; because they believe that everything outside of their control is demonic, their threat lies equally in what they can destroy. Wallnau's regular Facebook sermons show how this theology of conquest can quickly turn into a lust for confrontation and disruption, with titles like "Destroy the 'Public Education' System before it destroys America".[35]

It will come as little surprise, then, that the 6 January 2021 "Stop The Steal" storming of the Capitol in Washington DC involved some 7M soldiers. An army with a broad range of grievances and beliefs, they helped provide supernatural justification for what was to come. Pastor Ken Peters, of the highly amped-up Patriot Church Network, spoke in the nation's capital the day before the riot, saying: "we are not just in a culture war, we are in a Kingdom war."[36] Meanwhile, prominent Pentecostal magazine *Charisma* published an article and posted it on Facebook with the caption: "'There are but two parties right now, traitors and patriots.' #StopTheSteal."[37] It has emerged that one charismatic pastor from Florida has been charged in connection with the storming of the Capitol: according to *The Washington Post*, which viewed the court records, the FBI has footage of the man of God roaming the halls.[38] His church's motto is "Restoring Hope to a Hopeless Generation".[39]

For what it's worth, a week after the storming, on 14 January, Bethel Redding posted a condemnation of the protest on

Facebook, stating: "As a leadership team, we condemn the acts of violence and destruction that occurred during the protest at the capitol building".[40] The church stayed silent, however, on Beni Johnson's highly charged Instagram posts before and after the attack,[41] and on allegations that she may have attended a 'patriot rally' of militia groups at California's state capitol on 6 January itself.[42]

The idea of a force of 'overcomers' emerging to wage spiritual warfare—known variously as Joel's Army or the Manifest Sons of Destiny—has been floating around 'hyper-charismatic' circles since the postwar Latter Rain movement. A 2008 report about controversial Canadian Prophet Todd Bentley said that he had military dog tags reading "Joel's Army" tattooed on his sternum, advancing an agenda that "prophesied to become an Armageddon-ready military force of young people with a divine mandate to physically impose Christian 'dominion' on non-believers."[43]

Joel's Army has since been picked up by patriotic and conspiracy groups in the US, the three ideas of religion, conspiracy and patriotism forming a deadly trinity for the people marching that day. Such 'believers', in more senses than one, embrace this prophecy as confirmation that their mission is preordained.[44] Christian leaders preaching a God-given 'mandate' help to suppress doubt, and to inspire violence and fanaticism. This mission has now gone well beyond the traditional evangelical idea of converting individual souls, or "a majority of conversions", as Wallnau put it. The Dominionist movement is seeking to turn whole groups into disciples—or soldiers—and to transform society through them.

This is called the Great Commission, and is based on the Bible, Matthew 28:18–20:

> And Jesus came and said to them, "All authority in heaven and on earth has been given to me. Go therefore and make disciples of all nations, baptising them in the name of the Father and of the Son

and of the Holy Spirit, and teaching them to obey everything that I have commanded you."

At least one participant in the 6 January insurrection has direct links to the 7M movement, having studied under the major figures and become a pastor himself (although he was fired within weeks of the attack).[45] Pastor Tyler Ethridge posted multiple Parler videos of himself "in the Capitol", sometimes with chants of "STOP THE STEAL!" audible in the background.[46] Just a few years prior, Ethridge had graduated Colorado's Charis Bible College, a school founded by Lance Wallnau associate Andrew Wommack, with a degree in 'Practical Government' founded by that 7M-promoting Texas Republican, David Barton. The course curriculum states that "students will learn to identify the various arenas of society, and how they interact and overlap. Particular focus will be given to the importance and influence of Government."[47]

Barton promotes the idea that the Founding Fathers of the United States were all born-again Christians, meaning the constitution needs to be interpreted in a Christian Dominionist manner. In a 2011 radio interview, he explained that "Jesus said 'you occupy 'til I come.' We don't care when he comes, that's up to him. What we're supposed to do is take the culture in the meantime, and you got to get involved in these seven areas."[48] David Barton blamed the attack on the Capitol on Antifa and Black Lives Matter activists in cahoots with the police, who were "actually opening doors, pulling down barricades and then letting people come in."[49]

Following the insurrection, the Charis Bible College put out a statement that it "adamantly" opposed the "violence or other violations of the law that occurred." The 7M-promoting school added that it doesn't "condone or teach insurrectionist practices in our School of Practical Government". The college founder Wommack's Truth & Liberty Coalition—a political advocacy group he started with Wallnau—was reported in February to be promoting a documentary called *Absolute Proof: Exposing Election Fraud and the Theft of America by Enemies Foreign and Domestic.*[50]

This isn't to say that America is about to become a seven-mountained theocracy, but it's not only people radicalised enough to storm Congress who are buying in. Republican politician Michael Watson is the son of an Assemblies of God preacher, and Mississippi's top election official. He told a National Day of Prayer event in May 2021 that "we need Christian men and women in office today more than ever before." Highlighting the stamp of Pentecostal ideas on American Christianity as a whole, the event invited speakers from all of the "seven centers of power", describing its purpose as the offering of prayers "for the seven spheres of influence in our culture."[51]

What happened on 6 January wasn't only important for its symbolic value, but also in highlighting the value of the whole show—Trump prophecies, deep-state conspiracies, political adversaries possessed by demons—as entertainment. While it would be difficult to call these beliefs anything other than genuine, in the crushing modernity of the third Pentecostal wave, faith is being gamified. The Seven Mountain Mandate is now part of a cinematic, right-wing Facebook universe, where people can post themselves into a frenzy about good and evil, grand plots to take over the world, and a group of believers banding together to fight back. We only need to look at some of the people who went out to perform it in real life, dressed in crazy costumes, nicking souvenirs and live-streaming themselves taking part in a wild carnival.

It was at that point in the coverage on 6 January when I reached for the remote, and decided to go for a walk in Redding's crisp winter air. Wandering around the local cemetery, a maintenance worker came to ask me if I was lost, and I sheepishly explained that I was hoping to catch some grave-soakers. "Yeah,

I've seen them, but not much lately," he said, a grin slowly spreading across his face. "But it's not in here where I'd be worried about them."

8

FULLY CURSED AND ABUNDANTLY BLESSED

Overnight rain in Lagos washed away the last of the bloodstains from the anti-government protests. The mood was celebratory: the rolling 24-hour curfew imposed in response to the protests, which had seen security forces open fire on peaceful demonstrators, had finally been lifted. It felt as though all 20 million of Lagos' residents had burst onto the streets at once—and into its notorious traffic.

"It's church day," my taxi driver Wale said matter-of-factly, as we inched along the smoggy highway, noticing that I was admiring the parade of believers walking into churches: evening gown–clad women, and men buttoned up in traditional or Western suits. "If you have a family of ten, all ten of them will be going today." He laughed when I asked if the Sunday dress code was a cultural or a religious thing. "Nigerians are religious without being righteous."

By the time I arrived at my destination, I was running, and running late for the morning service, pulling and preening my cobbled-together, comparatively dowdy outfit. Thankfully, there were only a few glances as I burst through the door to a service deep in prayer, but I was more immediately embarrassed by the elegant style of the women around me. 'Pious chic', I suppose you'd call it: the art of covering all the right places while leaving little to the imagination.

After a brief preamble of the typical stuff—up, down, chapter, verse—we sat down on the tiled floor, on our long dresses or prayer mats, to listen to a roiling sermon that encouraged ecstasy and prosperity. Then we jumped back to our feet to project our way to the skies, hands behind our headscarves in a manner that felt only a few degrees of sexiness short of a nightclub.

"Allah! Allah! Allah!" the imam cried. "Praise Allah!" he continued, holding his microphone like a beatboxer and strutting through the male section of the mosque. "Take it back to Allah," he urged, pointing, working up theatrics as his assistant sang spurts of praise. "Take it back to the Messenger!"

It might have the feel of one of Lagos' sprawling mega-churches, but I was at the mosque of the Nasrul-lahi-li Fathi Society of Nigeria, better known by its acronym NASFAT. This all-signs, all-wonders Islamic prayer group is the face of Born-Again or Charismatic Islam; and its leaders hope that this growing movement will staunch the flow of Muslim believers converting to the Pentecostal faith.

This kind of Muslim/Christian syncretism first emerged during the 1970s, a critical time in Nigerian history. The newly independent country was coming out of a particularly nasty civil war and into the oil boom. For most Nigerians, ethnic affiliation has long been more important than religious orientation. Lagos is the port and the major city of Yorubaland, which spans south-west Nigeria and the neighbouring countries of Benin and Togo; in this region, Christians and Muslims have long lived cheek by jowl. Around two thirds are Christian, about one third Muslim.[1] Many Yoruba will have one parent from each religion and will have experienced both growing up; commerce and neighbourhoods are equally mixed. So, in many ways, Charismatic Islam reflects the 'Yorubaness' of its origins.

Not that NASFAT will call their faith anything other than Islam, or admit to doing things the Pentecostal way. After prayers, I met chief missioner Imam Abdul-Azeez Onike, the group's spiritual leader, who isn't thrilled with the charismatic label. "We're making Islam attractive to elites and young people, to make them proud of Islam," he told me, noting that the Society has more than a million members in Nigeria, and branches across West Africa, the UK, the US and Canada. NASFAT began in 1995, he explained, with "ten elite families" meeting in the living room of one of the founders. Within three years, they had outgrown this first home and moved their "enlightened Muslim society" to the Alausa Secretariat Mosque in Ikeja, an administrative city within the megacity of Lagos. This was where I had been invited to prayers.

The imam might be the only person left in the world using the word 'elite' in a positive sense, and it's not by accident. When most people think of Nigerian Islam, they think of Boko Haram: the "*bastardious* ones" up north, as a source put it, who terrorise small towns with their hatred of schools, books and modernity. Among other things, NASFAT is trying to change that. "We are going against the ones who give Islam a bad name," Imam Onike declared, arguing that the Society offers a better alternative for Nigerian Muslims than any hardline, sectarian view of Islam. "We organise summits against radicalisation, against religious conflicts, to educate our people."

But Islamist fundamentalism isn't the only competition for NASFAT. The Sunday prayer service lasted from 8:30am to midday, fitting between the Islamic day's first two *salahs*. But it's deliberately timed to coincide with something else, too: Pentecostal church services.

Many Lagosians, often with mixed religious backgrounds, have been hedging their spiritual bets. In recent decades, the city has seen a phenomenon of young people in particular attending Friday prayers at mosque, *as well as* Sunday Pentecostal church services. Over time, they tend to stop turning up on a Friday. NASFAT's Sunday service is a "gathering to promote brotherhood, and members supplicate to pray together—it's not an act of worship," Imam Onike clarified. As for losing followers to churches, "The Quran says it is not allowed to attend both church and mosque," he replied tersely, "but we live peacefully with our Christian neighbours." What he didn't mention is that the mosque's Sunday service now tends to attract more people than the traditional Friday prayers.

While policing my headscarf—which was refusing to stay in place during the service—one of the female attendants handed me the NASFAT prayer book. The back cover bore an ad for *zakat*: one of the five pillars of Islam, the act of almsgiving. This charity can go straight to the needy, and doesn't have to be directed to a religious institution, but NASFAT clearly sees *zakat* as equivalent to Christian tithing, due to the church—or mosque, in the case of NASFAT's foundation. The ad offered the slogan "One donation, many rewards", and an invocation to "secure your wealth with *zakat/Sadaqat*".

This encouragement-slash-warning refers to the Islamic idea that not giving away some of your money dirties it, and leaves you open to being cursed by Allah. It's also more than a little reminiscent of Pentecostalism's prosperity gospel, where if you give to the church, your wealth will grow; the Society's version seems to suggest that if you *don't* give, you'll lose the wealth you already have. Listed inside the back cover was a range of merchandise for sale, including headscarves, backpacks, analogue clocks and table water. "Quality Brand Management," read a small line at the bottom, "our BUSINESS." Sunday services aren't the only thing NASFAT has learned from the Pentecostals—such vigorous requests for donations and branded products set the Society apart from more traditional mosques.

FULLY CURSED AND ABUNDANTLY BLESSED

Next to me on the floor, a young woman called Lola had a blue NASFAT handbag next to her prayer mat. The book I'd been handed had each prayer in Arabic, Yoruba and English, and Lola was determined that I wouldn't lose my place. She can't read a word of Arabic; but, when not sending texts on her phone, fluidly recites prayers in the language from memory.

"I started coming here because of my brothers," she told me after the solemn prayers finished. We were watching on televisions as the Imam returned to his exultant worship, moving through worshippers in the men's section. "They show us the beauty here. It makes me a better Muslim, and we can show a better Muslim *way*." Better than what? Lola, like Imam Onike, was referring to Boko Haram, a phenomenon that—along with online scams—is a source of deep embarrassment to Nigerians of all stripes.

Unlike the imam, she didn't seem bothered that some young people will go to both mosque and church, sometimes on the same day. "It's not so unusual here," she smiled, and reminded me that Mariam, Jesus' mother, is the only woman mentioned by name in the Quran. Christians celebrate one prophet, Muslims another—it's no big deal, really.

But not everyone has such a conciliatory outlook. As we packed up our mats, I asked whether Lola had any fears about religious conflict spreading in the country. "Excuse me," she said quietly, and picked up her things and left.

* * *

Peaceful coexistence is understandably prized by Nigerians, and for most of the country's modern history, relations between Christianity and Islam have been relatively harmonious. But some with power and influence have been tempted by the incentives to put this peace at risk. Pentecostalism, with around 200 million African followers, now accounts for over a third of the continent's Christians, and 17 per cent of the total population.[2] At the same time, fundamentalist Islam has also been increasing in influence across Africa, and there are growing tensions wherever the two religions collide.

One of the world's largest cities, Lagos is the commercial centre of both Nigeria and West Africa. The Sunday after my visit to the mosque, I went north of Ikeja to the Lagos–Ibadan Expressway, Nigeria's most travelled road, and a place where it feels as though the entire country has been unfurled in front of you. People say it's the road that leads to everywhere, and for a long time it had fallen into disrepair, a symbol of a faltering nation.

Or rather, that was all the highway represented until the early 1980s, when enterprising Pentecostal pastor Enoch Adeboye realised that the hundreds of thousands of people who travel and work on this route every day have spiritual needs—around the same time, and in the same manner, as Edir Macedo was discovering how to make worship fit into the lives of Brazil's working class.

As with Macedo, Adeboye's instinct was right. His Redeemed Christian Church of God opened its campground almost 40 years ago, and today scores of megachurches line the Expressway. By the time I arrived, though, the pandemic meant that the kinds of mass gatherings you're normally likely to see out here—we're talking 100,000 worshippers per service—were on hold. The Expressway is a place that, if the rest of the world bothered looking at Africa, would be proclaimed as a charismatic Vatican, such is its significance to the Holy Spirit's revival. And if the capital of Catholicism is a treasure trove of Renaissance art and architecture, this centre of Pentecostalism—improvised, austere, and bubbling with the miraculous—is proudly the opposite.

You could fit two Vatican Cities inside Redeemed's *small* camp—which measures 1 kilometre by 1 kilometre—and more than six Vaticans in its big brother, which is 3 kilometres by 3; it would take more than a couple of hours if you chose to walk the perimeter. These camps, with their high roofs, look like airport hangars. They can hold the dreams of millions at a time. Redemption City, as it's known, doesn't have the status of a city-state, but it functions like one. In addition to the notably paved roads, it has its own housing estates, private schools, university, hospitals on site—and more functioning ATMs than you'll find in the ritziest part of Lagos. After all, as Pastor Adeboye has explained, "Anyone who is not paying his tithe is not going to heaven, full stop."[3]

Adeboye is suspected to be eight- or nine-figures wealthy,[4] so it's little surprise that his success, and the success of his church, has been replicated by other Pentecostal megachurches up and down the Expressway. This is not to say that he's simply a charlatan on the make—as well as anyone, he understands the Pentecostal allure. "Pentecostals have such an impact because they talk of the here and now, not just the by and by," he has said, in defence of preaching the prosperity gospel. "While we [do] have to worry about Heaven, there are some things God could do for us in the here and now."[5]

A regular church service can clog the road for hours—and when there are Pentecostals around, NASFAT is never far behind. The Society is in the process of reconstructing its giant mosque 5 kilometres from Redemption City, on the Lagos–Ibadan Expressway. For NASFAT, this campground represents something even bigger than its square footage: the idea that they have *arrived*, as a force equal to Redeemed or any other major Pentecostal church.

A year after moving out to the Expressway in 2000, NASFAT caused a day of even more chaos than usual on the choked road, when the cars of thousands of worshippers leaving Sunday prayers caused gridlock. A senior member of the Society later admitted that NASFAT orchestrated the paralysis so that the Pentecostals would "know that they are not the only ones who can block the highway." At a place that symbolises the route to power in Nigeria like no other, this was an important sign that the Society is not subordinate to Christians.[6]

At first glance—which is a couple of hours' crawl on a good day—it's difficult to understand why a benevolent God would make the Expressway His gathering place. A few hours of exhaust fumes will leave most lungs with a hacking cough; with the exception of the most well-heeled church camps, there's little out here in the way of infrastructure. Hawkers wander through traffic standstills to sell everything from cold water to biographies of Silicon Valley entrepreneurs to distract from the tedium.

Over time, many in Lagos have come to view the Expressway as a moral space, removed from the money and corruption of the city proper—even if the megachurches and their leaders tend to do quite well for themselves, and certainly far better than most Nigerians. The campgrounds may boast some of the best schools around, but a number of sceptical Lagosians pointed out to me that the preachers don't tend to send their own kids to them, preferring overseas education.

Even if the wealth of religious leaders does raise eyebrows, the all-encompassing role of Pentecostal Churches in the lives of Nigeria's believers is difficult to overstate. It can be hard for a worker stuck commuting for hours each day to find love, so megachurches take on the role of Cupid, hosting speed-dating nights and Facebook singles groups. As we've seen in Southern Africa, when the state healthcare system is barely functioning, church is often the only place where a person can attend to their mental and physical wellbeing, even if it is generally by way of miracle. An aspirational outlet for young men in a nation of severely underemployed youth, one of Redeemed's major competitors, Mountain of Fire and Miracles, even has its own football team in the national league, MFM FC.

It's probably no surprise, then, that megachurches so ingrained in the daily lives of their congregations are also deeply and increasingly invested in the affairs of the nation. Fifty years after the civil war that shattered newly independent Nigeria, some of the most influential Pentecostal leaders are using their authority to muscle in on the established order of peace.

The line between the majority-Christian south and the overwhelmingly Islamic north is like a ligature mark across the centre of the country. The Sahel, where the Sahara transitions into the savannah, is a febrile region across the continent. Traditionally, the Sahel has divided what is today Nigeria along more ethnic than religious lines. Though Nigerians belong to around 250 different ethnic groups, the country is for all intents and purposes divided into three blocs: the rural Hausa-Fulani herders and farmers of the north, mainly Muslim; the mixed Yoruba in the south-west; and the largely Catholic Igbo in the south-east, where most of Nigeria's oil is found (and, yes, there is movement underway to convert the Igbo to Pentecostalism).[7]

With these communities bolted together into 'Nigeria' by the British, whose colonial project was so nakedly to divide and conquer, some would argue that conflict has been the nation's unavoidable destiny. Historian Olufemi Vaughan explained to me that Nigeria is "three fundamentally different countries wrapped in one", with conflicts that are regional and civilisational, not simply religious. "The fault lines are real and very deep," he added. "It doesn't look good now, and it doesn't look good in the future."[8]

The many tribes and kingdoms of these historic civilisations had their own distinct faiths. After centuries of the British engaging in the slave trade along the West African coast, in the 1850s, the Empire began to assert its political power in Lagos. Catholicism had been introduced to the area by Europeans centuries earlier, but British rule meant that a wave of Protestant missionaries arrived.

Thanks to their reputation for being good with books and money, the Igbo have long been likened to another dispossessed people. In a 1969 memo to President Richard Nixon, national security advisor Henry Kissinger called the Igbo the "wandering Jews of West Africa", describing them as "gifted, aggressive, Westernized; at best envied and resented, but mostly despised by their neighbors in the Federation."[9] For some Igbo, the association is literal—they believe that they descend from at least one of Israel's lost tribes. The Igbo have a longstanding political culture that is highly individualised, often described as looking like Athenian democracy. The north was almost the opposite, with a political tradition of hierarchical sultanates.

By the time European traders set up shop on the West African coast, Islam had been firmly ingrained above the Sahel for hundreds of years, thanks to the Muslim conquest of the Maghreb in the seventh and eighth centuries, and the powerful Mali Empire founded in the 1200s. Religious leaders wielded incredible power, and Christianity became a civilisational threat before the white man's rule did. At the same time, Yoruba trading with the Hausa in the north led to Islam filtering down towards the coast.

A midpoint between the cultures of expressive democracy and absolute monarchy, Yorubaland was divided up into small kingdoms, and over time the leader would come to decide which religion each polity would take up. This is why you see a mixed religious makeup among the Yoruba today, and it's one of a number of reasons why Nigerians have traditionally felt more affinity to their local community, as opposed to their faith.

These three 'civilisations' might have lived side by side, but it's difficult to believe that they would have come together in such an obviously fraught way if it hadn't been for the British. By 1914, the Empire had cobbled together these disparate societies into a country. In true colonial fashion, harmony wasn't exactly the aim. The Igbo's 'Athenian democracy' was certainly not the kind of thing a colonising force would appreciate; the British preferred dealing with the northerners, whose authoritarian sultanates were easier to buy off or at least rule by proxy. To hold up their end of the bargain, the British made sure that Christian missionaries knew not to bring their work into the Muslim areas, insulating the Hausa-Fulani from Western culture and education that could have changed their way of life.

In the wave of postwar acknowledgement that the colonial jig was up, the British agreed to depart in 1960—but not before putting their thumb on the scale to ensure that power in independent Nigeria would still be weighted in favour of their northern allies. It was still a time of optimism, and some ambitious Igbo and Yoruba went north looking for opportunities in the new nation; but the spirit of hope was short-lived.

After only seven years, everything came to a head—the northern grip on power, military figures asserting control through coups and counter-coups, disputes over the division of regions into states, and the great stain of oil money. It started with a series of pogroms that killed up to 30,000 Igbo plying their famed business acumen in the north.[10] The promise of independence was nowhere in sight, and Igbo military men had had enough. They wanted to go their own way, and in 1967 declared that the south-east region would become the independent nation of Biafra.

A romantic idea in theory, but in reality, when the people seceding held most of the assets—oil—and the people they were divorcing held most of the power—the northerners—it was only ever going to end one way. The ensuing civil war was short, but as gruesome as they come. With the British and the USSR supporting the Nigerian Army, the Biafrans never stood a chance. A blockade saw 2 million Igbo starve to death, and by the beginning of 1970, Biafra was no more.

The Biafran War was one of the great humanitarian tragedies of the twentieth century, but outside of Igboland, it's been largely forgotten. This historical amnesia is a disgrace and a problem, given that Nigeria is Africa's largest economy, and the world's seventh most populous country. On current trajectories, by 2050 Nigeria will rank behind only India and China for citizens.[11] But no amount of demographic growth can bury the legacy of inter-faith tensions.

NASFAT places a great amount of store in living harmoniously with Christians, and the group's clergy repeatedly emphasised to me that they do not encounter any problems with Pentecostals, whether believers or church leaders. Then one high-ranking NASFAT official quietly introduced me to Disu Kamor, suggesting that he might have more to say on the matter.

Kamor is executive chairman of the Muslim Public Affairs Centre, better known as MPAC, a body that represents Islamic organisations across Nigeria. He hails from Igboland, where Muslims are a small minority. He grew up alongside, and works with, many Catholics and Anglicans, and never encountered problems—until about 20 years ago, when he first noticed a distinct change.

"I was registering the birth of my child," he explained. "And I called the evangelical lady who was working at the office 'sister'." Clearly offended, the woman replied that she wasn't his sister because she was not Muslim. "I was taken aback by her antagonism. It might not be true of every Christian, but I've become familiar with this attitude." Kamor told me that since the Pentecostals became a dominant force, problems that Nigerians and Igbo thought were confined to the Biafran War have returned. Since the 2010s in particular, the Pentecostals have become especially fervent, he says—entirely different from the Christians he grew up alongside.

"There is a notion amongst many Pentecostals that if they are good to the Muslims, it shows a lack of commitment to their faith," Kamor went on. "This is something that is being *taught*. You only need to go online to see their hostility, their religious arrogance. They feel that Muslims are lesser to them."

While NASFAT is preaching that everything is good and well, Kamor says that a lot of other Muslims don't feel the same. "Islam is haemorrhaging," he told me, in an almost pleading voice, grateful for an audience. There's no reliable national figure, but MPAC believes that the number of Muslims has reduced by about a million in recent years—even though Nigeria's demographics mean that the number of Muslims should be growing. Added to this, there's one significant fact that Kamor thinks has gone unnoticed. "A lot of the leading Pentecostal pastors in Nigeria were once Muslims," he said. "I think that the hostility from Pentecostal groups is related to this." Kamor puts this figure at about 30 per cent, but there's no way of telling. All he knows is that "there's a special antagonism, from this crop of Christians, for Islam. Most of these preachers behave like they have a score to settle with the Islam they left. It's something well known within the Muslim community that the ex-Muslim Pentecostal Christians are the most difficult to deal with."

Trying to verify any statistic about Nigeria is close to impossible, but I spoke to scholars who agreed that Kamor's conversion narrative is certainly plausible.[12] It may also speak to some of his wider fears about where Pentecostalism is leading the country. Either way, the biographies of some of the country's most prominent Pentecostal leaders also lend it weight.

Johnson Suleman, also known as "God's oracle", is a televangelist and the leader of Omega Fire Ministries, an empire stretching to Ghana, Turkey, South Africa, and the United States. He was born to Muslim parents, though there is a version of his story which explains that his mother is Christian—but these are minor details. According to Suleman, he was anointed from day dot. A few days after he was born in Benin—the small, largely Yoruba country next to Nigeria—prophets arrived with a message from God that he was to become one of them. Suleman's parents were curious, but ultimately dismissive due to their religious beliefs. But this kid "had a soft spot for the things of God", and was doubting his parents' faith from the first time he went to a mosque.[13]

These days, Suleman is known for his colourful suits and electric stage presence. His ministry markets itself with the line "no more tears"—and the more incendiary claim that "the devil and his cohorts has [sic] no scriptural right to control and manipulate the destinies of the children of God."[14]

Standard Pentecostal stuff, right? That is, until you give the enemy a name. In a video that went viral in 2017, Suleman claimed that he had received a call from someone who told him that Fulani herdsmen had been sent to assassinate him. "I told my people, I said, any Fulani herdsman you see around you, kill him," he said. "And I have told them in the church here, around these premises, that any Fulani herdsman that just entered by mistake and want to pretend, *kill him. Kill him. CUT HIS HEAD.*"[15] Suleman later said he had been speaking in self-defence, referencing his claim that there was a Fulani plot against his life;[16] but his sermon also justified this incitement to violence on the general grounds that such people were "busy killing Christians" without consequence.[17] In 2018, he also accused homosexuals of being "paid", or being possessed by demons "from hellfire, a demon with capital letters."[18] In 2019, Suleman expressed strong opposition to reforms that have increased the maximum fine for hate speech, calling them "a deliberate attempt to silence Nigerians".[19]

Another prominent preacher with a Muslim or mixed background is Bishop David Oyedepo of the Living Faith Church, better known as Winners Chapel International. Headquartered at a big campus not far from Lagos, which he calls 'Canaanland', Oyedepo's network of churches spans 300 cities in 65 countries—and he has a history of stirring up resentment, blaming the unattributed murder of his pastor on "Fulani demons", cursing them in his capacity "as a Prophet" and declaring that "in the name of Jesus, their end has come."[20] Meanwhile, the then president of the Christian Association of Nigeria, Musa Asake, claimed in 2018 that there was a grand plan to wipe out Christians in the country, and that "Any Christian that does not prepare to defend himself is stupid, unless you are in government and being protected by the government."[21]

With such Apostles turning up the volume on decades of Pentecostal rhetoric that has painted fundamentalists in the north as backward fanatics, there is a very real concern that this caricature is now being made of Muslims in general. Incensed by what he believes Pentecostal leaders are knowingly stirring up, on the streets, on television and online, Disu Kamor isn't interested in peace gestures. "We will never resolve our doctrinal differences," he feels. He told me that he cannot foresee the Muslim community having any good relations with Pentecostals.

"It's all about perceptions—and in Nigeria, perceptions are facts."

* * *

There's a palpable embarrassment among many Muslims that Boko Haram is perceived as Nigerian Islam. Founded in 2002 as an Islamic purity movement in the north of the country, the sect's popularity was an expression of frustration at perpetual problems of corruption and unemployment; but the group grew increasingly militant, and within seven years had become a terrorist insurgency.

With its terror largely confined to the north, it wasn't until Boko Haram abducted 276 schoolgirls in 2014 that the organisation, and the plight of people subjected to its tyranny, became an international concern. But that spotlight has been no comfort to the tens of thousands murdered by the group, nor the millions it has displaced.[22] At the time of writing, its influence is growing in the troubled Sahel, causing regional famines and helping spread terror to neighbouring countries.[23]

Boko Haram's primary grievance is the 'Western' style of education in Nigeria, a system that members feel has been imposed on the north since independence, and one that is culturally incompatible with their way of life. *Boko haram* is broadly translated as 'Western education is forbidden', though the group claims that it means "Western *Civilisation* is forbidden", and that they are not "opposed to formal education coming from the West" but "believe in the supremacy of Islamic *culture*".[24] But whatever the precise meaning of the movement's name, its terrorists are railing against what they see as southern imperialism, something they'd not been subjected to when the British first pushed entirely different cultures into the forced marriage of colonisation.

Boko Haram blames the south, along with the return to democratic rule in 1999, for the lack of job opportunities in the north. Even for those who receive education, prospects are grim. The group's founder, Mohammed Yusuf—executed by police in 2009 after being captured—openly argued that, since university graduates had no opportunities even with their piece of paper, they might as well join his insurgency to earn a better time in the *next* life. With destruction as its guiding ethos, in 2015–18 Boko Haram actually attacked more mosques than churches.[25]

The leaders of NASFAT and MPAC are working overtime to distance themselves from Boko Haram's activities and doctrines. Imam Onike attempted to mediate in the group's kidnapping of 344 schoolboys in late 2020, warning that "Islam abhors aggression in whatever form".[26] But for many Christians, the threat of Boko Haram fits into a historical narrative. It isn't just the unlikely idea that they may one day come and kidnap your daughter from school and marry her off—it's the suspicion that these thugs could be next in the long line of northerners holding power over the south.

FULLY CURSED AND ABUNDANTLY BLESSED

After the Biafran War, debate arose over whether Nigeria should become a secular state or adopt sharia (Islamic) law; either way, the military regime was supposed to hand power to civil politicians (it didn't do so permanently until 1999). During the three decades of military rule, oil revenues at least helped the country to rapidly urbanise and allowed more young people to reach higher education. New ideas were reshaping old faiths, and universities in the 1970s were great places to foment those ideas. The growth of Pentecostal churches down south, in Yorubaland, was paralleled by the establishment of an Islamic reform movement in the north, financed by Persian Gulf nations.[27] Within a decade, these new ways of religion had moved off campus and into the cities.

The rise of both movements has undeniably contributed to increasing tensions between Christians and Muslims. Too often, they are viewed as and reduced to their most extreme edge or caricature: some Muslim leaders in the north see only the outrageous prosperity of many 'health and wealth' preachers, while Christian preachers in the south see only the nihilistic violence of Boko Haram. Yet the two religious movements are closer together than some of their more strident leaders might like to think. Olufemi Vaughan describes a theological arms race, in which the two "outspoken" and "weaponised" versions of faith currently dominating Nigeria—'renewal' Islam and Pentecostalism—are in fact two sides of the same coin, their fates entangled.

They obviously differ in methodology—we certainly can't compare Boko Haram's terror to a Pentecostal Prophet's gold watch—but Vaughan says that, broadly, the respective rises of Pentecostalism and Islamic reform have been reactions to the same poverty and corruption that haunts all peoples and all parts of Nigeria. "Fully cursed and abundantly blessed" by oil, as sociologist Ebenezer Obadare puts it,[28] the military state atrophied in the '80s and '90s; the corruption that tends to go hand in hand with reserves of 'black gold' took over. Zealous forms of Pentecostalism and Islam began to grow rapidly, and provide structure and meaning not on offer from the government.[29] The military always had the final say, but there was a rise in "violent language" and the Pentecostal "obsession with enemies", alongside a belief in occult powers and evil spirits as an explanation for how things were going wrong.[30]

In his examination of global religious extremism, sociologist Mark Juergensmeyer argued that people are attracted to radical religious ideas when secular nationalism fails to deliver on its promises "of political freedom, economic prosperity, and social justice"—offering only moral corruption in return.[31] We've seen in Part One of this book how deprivation and marginalisation are driving people the world over to Pentecostalism; when you add to these everyday problems a widespread awareness of seemingly insurmountable corruption, as is the case in Nigeria, it's no wonder people are looking for an alternative authority to trust. Whether through the preachers with easy smiles, or the militants with compelling stories, these modern forms of faith were the first stop for Nigerians looking to interpret and cope with what was going on around them in the late twentieth century. A spiritual identity is easy to adopt—and, if necessary, go into battle for. But religious divide is far from Nigeria's only, or primary, problem. People don't actually move to take up arms without context, and the modern Nigerian state provides plenty of that.

The precarity facing Africa's largest national population over the decades has been described as "a permanent, radical sense of 'uncertainty, unpredictability, and insecurity'",[32] or as "comprehensive social deprivation" engendering a sense of "impotence in the face of Leviathan".[33] Nigeria might not meet the textbook definition of a failed state—that is, a country where the government is no longer in control—but it is undoubtedly a state that is being failed.

FULLY CURSED AND ABUNDANTLY BLESSED

The permanent state of economic and physical insecurity isn't a special Nigerian problem: with a few lucky exceptions, countries rich in oil tend to follow a certain pattern, known as 'resource curse'. They are less democratic, more corrupt, more economically unstable, and quicker to go to war. When people can't trust the police or the politicians, and they also have suspicions about two thirds of their countrymen, it's not hard to understand why God has such currency here, nor why men of God, both Christian and Muslim, do well in collecting it.

Those who can leave Nigeria tend to in spades. Nigerians are the United States' most highly educated group, and have above-average incomes in that country; this is a diaspora overwhelmingly made up of doctors, academics and businesspeople.[34] As for their friends and family back home, the sense of positive connection to America has remained strong, even when the other side has tried to weaken it. When President Trump brought in a 2020 visa ban affecting travellers from Nigeria, one of his "shithole countries", many Nigerians loved him all the more. One poll found that 58 per cent of Nigerians had confidence in Trump, behind only Israelis, Filipinos and Kenyans.[35] Another, also from 2020, found that 56 per cent of Nigerians approved of US world leadership, compared to 24 per cent of Europeans.[36]

Arguably, much of this support was down to the job Trump was perceived to be doing for evangelicals.[37] But there was also local resentment for those who have opportunities the vast majority of Nigerians do not. When the country was added to his 'Muslim ban' list, some saw it as a good thing. One Lagosian explained a common view to me: "Nigerians are saying, hang on, you have your medical degree? It's good that the door is being closed—they can stay here and work in our hospitals."

The grievances of the Nigerian people, north and south, east and west, Pentecostal and Islamist, are understandable. My arrival in the country in October 2020 coincided with a fresh and more powerful wave of End SARS protests against the lawless and unaccountable state security apparatus, after the Special Anti-Robbery Squad unit (SARS) opened fire on and killed at least fifty-one civilians. Eleven police officers and seven soldiers also died in the clashes.[38] Beyond the specific brutality and injustice that SARS represented, the unit also represented Nigerian power dynamics in microcosm. A small elite runs the country under a kind of gentleman's power-sharing agreement that crosses eth-noreligious lines—after all, the size of these individuals' bank accounts alone means that they have far more in common with each other than the people in their hometowns. The dividing line that the British exploited, and the inequality that this pro-duced, can still be seen in Nigerian elections today: a Muslim northerner can more or less take their turf for granted; a south-ern Christian can't do the same.

Since the resumption of democratic rule in 1999, known as the Fourth Republic, Pentecostals have had the *cultural* ascen-dency, while northern Muslims tend to hold a disproportionate number of senior *political* positions. The Pentecostal elite, including Redeemed's Adeboye and Winners Chapel's Oyedepo, are content to be kingmakers—or, as they're more politely described, 'spiritual advisors'—seeing to a long line of Christian and Muslim politicians willing to bend the knee in return for a public endorsement, an electoral blessing. What the megachurch leaders get in return is a different kind of power. Ebenezer Obadare identifies the benefit they gain as a tacit agreement to define Nigeria's problems in spiritual terms, with relentless bat-tles of good and evil the order of the day.

The sociologist calls the Fourth Republic the "Pentecostal Republic", for it is ruled by a "Pentecostalist world view of ubiq-uitous and apparently inexhaustible evil", where dark forces are highlighted as the reasons why Nigerians, and by extension Nigeria itself, have not fulfilled their potential. What's more,

Obadare believes that, alongside the movement's muscular form of Christianity, its violent rhetoric of discarding the old self and old ways is an important part of being born again.[39]

And so Nigerians are left with Pentecostal leaders lobbing verbal bombs, and Boko Haram detonating actual ones—Christian fundamentalists are equating all Muslims, northerners, Fulani or Hausa with terrorism, while Islamic fundamentalists are burning and murdering Christians, liberal Muslims, and anyone who gets in their way. The two are not equivalent to one another, but the growing sense of confrontation and irreconcilable difference mirrors the multitude of problems facing the country.

* * *

You won't see many of the big Pentecostal preachers cursing Islam far outside the comfort of their megachurches. They're not wrong, though, that in some parts of the north, practising Christianity can be a death sentence. This hasn't discouraged Oscar Amaechina, who runs the Afri-Mission and Evangelism Network, from taking clothes and basic supplies to poor communities in the north—along with a helping of the good news. He told me that he has been held hostage by a group of Boko-like thugs, who he claims were desperate, angry young men he was able to talk down and, the way smoothed by some aid, convert to Christianity.

A deeply considered guy who believes that the End Times are near, Amaechina rails against preachers whose motives don't go beyond their fingertips; men who, he believes, have lost sight of the mission to save souls in the rush to build empires: "They only talk about prosperity, signs and wonders, and prophecy. The vast majority of Nigerian Christians do not know anything about Christian suffering. All they are looking for is how to live comfortably on Earth. If the Antichrist comes, these churches will invite him for a miracle service." In other words, the self-interest of flashy Pentecostal 'miracle men' is such that they'd even try to collect a tithe from the devil himself.

Most Nigerians need no explanation of suffering—and when personal hardship has been folded into a narrative of visible and invisible enemies, the Antichrist's return can be seen as part of a pattern of social disaster. Amaechina might be a critic of the megachurch preachers, but his outlook still sounded familiar by this point in my travels. "The Gospel is the only antidote to terrorism, division, insurgency, banditry and kidnapping," he told me, with his customary intensity. "If only we can take the Gospel massively to the north. We have northerners who are Christians, and there's no division between us and them."

So, everything will be fine, so long as everyone is like us. This could be the unofficial motto on both sides among those most invested in Nigeria's religious divide. The born-again project boils down to winning, and in the Pentecostal Republic, the battle of good and evil is not an abstract issue, but an everyday one.

Since the mid-2010s, Christian communities have suffered a documented rise in armed abductions and killings, typically involving herders who are Muslim coming south and attacking settled farmers.[40] Nigeria's president since 2015, Muhammadu Buhari, is a former military ruler from the much-accused Fulani tribe. His ambitions for the top political job were given the nod by Redeemed leader Adeboye and other influential Pentecostals;[41] but, in spite of these key leaders' backing for the administration, anti-Christian attacks and the general lawlessness continue; and people of all faiths see a political establishment that is serving fewer and fewer of them.

Even members of that very establishment, without accepting any of the blame, are openly stating that the country could be sleepwalking into further conflict. In 2019, Olusegun Obasanjo—the born-again Pentecostal who ruled Nigeria first as military head of state in 1976–9, then as the Fourth Republic's first democratically elected president in 1999–2007—wrote an open letter to President Buhari about the "problem of insecurity in the land," which he called "the issue of life and death for all of us".[42]

Obasanjo, a staunch nationalist who considers himself as Nigerian first and Yoruba second, warned that "a very onerous cloud is gathering". He fears that "spontaneous or planned reprisal attacks against Fulanis" on the part of Christians may "inadvertently or advertently mushroom into pogrom or Rwanda-type genocide that we did not believe could happen and yet it happened." He echoed the words of Disu Kamor, noting that "Perception may be as potent as reality at times."

Buhari's vice-president Yemi Osinbajo, formerly pastor at a Lagos branch of Redeemed, spoke at a virtual NASFAT youth conference during the pandemic. What was supposed to be a rousing speech about interfaith values instead served to highlight the growing climate of concern. "As resources become scarcer, identity-based claims to a share of the national patrimony become more aggressive and lead increasingly to conflict," he told his young Islamic audience. Rejecting the "bleak view" of history that says Nigeria can never be a multi-ethnic, religiously plural country, he nevertheless added that, in a situation of shortages, Christians and Muslims "are liable to see each other as competitors ... instead of compatriots, and eventually we begin to demonise each other as enemies."[43]

For the time being, it remains in almost everyone's interests for the bloodletting to stay at the margins, with scapegoats made out of ethnic and religious minorities in dusty outposts far from the big cities. As we saw with the anti-establishment End SARS movement, which ultimately saw protesters of all stripes gunned down in Lagos and elsewhere, there's a small elite relying on the status quo, and living in fear of ordinary Nigerians finding common cause. But, as Vaughan put it to me, the insistence of faith leaders from both sides on upping the stakes risks turning the country's historic faultlines from regional to religious.

Nigeria's Pentecostals might not want war, but when you create a climate of daily struggle against "evil" that needs to be combatted, you're going to find a lot of people signing up to be the spiritual warriors C. Peter Wagner dreamed of, fighting for a Pentecostal society however they interpret the third-wave idea of 'violent prayer'. Spiritual tensions are escalated while earthly peace is preached, a dance as freeform as NASFAT's euphoric worship during Sunday prayers at the mosque.

In a state so marred by corruption and injustice, some believe that faith is a way of building a movement that breaks through and overcomes the enormous problems of the country.[44] Perhaps better than anyone, Nigeria's Pentecostal preachers understand and stoke the optimism that still exists in the country, even after the darkest days of the crackdown on End SARS. And nowhere is this hope more apparent than off the Lagos–Ibadan Expressway.

I took a final journey along that road, which had become a second home, a place I'd come to love. Just beyond Enoch Adeboye's Redemption City, we had to stop for petrol, and I jumped out to stretch my legs. This was the unofficial border between sacred and secular, where the paved roads end and potholes that ride like rodeos begin.

Small stalls along the side of the road sell the essentials: SIM cards, cold drinks, or a seat to watch Real Madrid on television. I noticed that some of them were run by women and girls dressed all in black, wearing niqabs covering everything but their eyes. These traders worked side by side with women and children in shorts and t-shirts, hosting advertising signs for the scores of local churches. The clash of faiths was as apparent as the hope that everything is going to be okay— because frankly, it needs to be.

FULLY CURSED AND ABUNDANTLY BLESSED

Not everyone is so optimistic, however. As I packed my bags, my phone pinged with another message from Disu Kamor. "There's an African adage," he wrote, "which says that hate speeches precede wars."

9

NOT YOUR GRANDMOTHER'S CHURCH

Pizza had been ordered for lunch, and greasy police fingers were now all over the officers' weapons. Not their guns—their holsters were slung in a corner of the roadside motel room. For this sting operation, the detectives were armed with iPhones, texting their way into the coming frenzy.

"I know what the eggplant emoji *is*," said Detective Gene, of the oft-used sexting symbol, "but do we know if the prosecutors will take it as an agreement for sex?"

The youngest of this sting team in Brazos County, Texas, Gene's thumbs were called into action for maximum authenticity whenever older detectives had someone on the hook. Police in Texas and many parts of the United States regularly conduct these operations to catch men buying sex, who they call johns. This is, after all, a country in which consenting adults selling and buying sex remains illegal in all but a tiny strip of Las Vegas.

But before we could reel in any johns, we had to put our guesses up on the whiteboard: how many we'd bust today, and of those we would bust, how many would cry, possess drugs, carry unlicensed guns, or have outstanding warrants. I had just finished my tally when the room suddenly came alive.

"He's coming," crackled the police radio, and we moved into position.

Sergeant Paul Mahoney, the officer in charge, grabbed my wrist and led me into the bathroom. There, he and his largest officer strapped on their gun holsters and selected a pair of handcuffs from a neat row lined along the edge of the sink. Gene and another detective waited silently behind the motel-room door, opened by a tiny, bird-like female cop in jeans and ill-suiting makeup, the closest woman in their orbit who looked enough like the blurry photo they had posted, offering her sexual services.

"Come in," she greeted the john with a huge smile, beginning her Ginger Rogers moves backwards into the room. She was dancing to the words of the District Attorney, who had strictly warned Mahoney that a foot has to be inside the door for an arrest to stick. Once the guy had stepped in, the moves were precision: this wasn't their first dance—or rodeo, as they would have it. By the time I made it out of the bathroom, the john was in cuffs and his pockets were turned out.

"Fuck," Mahoney said, his crew still moving swiftly, looking for anything that might get the john on the scoreboard. "He's pissed himself."

The other men arrested that day would fight, or promise that they weren't going to fight, but Fernando stood quietly as the officers went through his pockets, his fear spreading across the front of his work trousers.

Gene, the male cop Fernando had been unwittingly sexting with, asked him why he'd been so stupid. Fernando, his wet pants sticking to his legs, replied softly, "I got to live with what happened." He went on to calmly, politely answer questions that revealed a wife, two jobs, and two toddlers at home.

Pissing himself would only be the first in a series of humiliations for Fernando, and thousands of guys like him caught in john stings around the country. His mugshot, name and engagement in "sex crimes" were splashed on the local evening news as a matter of course, and will live on the internet forever.

Puritanical readings of sex and social relations have long bound faith and politics to one another, but the Pentecostal movement has put a new veneer on American efforts to combat the world's oldest profession, coating advocacy in the language of social justice and sisterhood. Fernando is another casualty in the war on sex—the fallout from a moral panic that is destroying lives in order to save souls.

* * *

A week after Fernando's arrest, I was in a church basement in downtown Waco, Texas, with eleven johns who had been busted while attempting to procure sex. They were avoiding each other's gaze, keeping their heads down under their baseball caps—and even more carefully evading the eyes of the man standing before them.

"This won't be a hug-athon," warned Brett Mills, co-ordinator of an anti-prostitution programme known as a 'john school'. "We're kind, but we're not faint of heart." Mills has been running this john school—a mandatory education programme for men convicted of first-time solicitation offences—since 2016, through Jesus Said Love, a not-for-profit organisation that he runs with his wife Emily.

Class rules were read out: sleepers and phone-checkers get one warning before being asked to leave the room; anyone showing up drunk, high or late will be kicked out of the programme altogether. Mills instructed the johns to "own their story" by sharing how they had been arrested—he wasn't going to tolerate anyone protesting their innocence. Each man attending the class had had to pay $525 for the privilege, as part of a misdemeanour charge for soliciting a prostitute online. Mills might tout reform, but his idea of justice retains a strong sense of punishment.

"There shouldn't be no payment plan," he told me, criticising his competitors in the growing john school marketplace. "And johns should have to take a day off."

If Mills had his way, the class would cost twenty times more than it already does, so that the johns would feel the true weight of their crime. For instance, he says, the average DUI costs in excess of $10,000 when impounding, fines, court and attorney fees are taken into account. Even if the costs were equal, Mills was clear that to him, the crimes are not equivalent: driving drunk is nothing like trying to *buy* a human being. "And don't tell me that legalisation is the way to go. The only one who wins there are the regulators, 'cos they get the money. Go to a bar and meet someone!"

The guys had been arrested in a series of police stings, which are increasingly taking place across Texas. Of the johns in the room, seven were Latino, one was Asian, and all were blue-collar workers. The three white guys were all serving military personnel, low-level.

Mills commanded the room, switching between cool youth group leader and drill sergeant. "There are eight women in our office right now that have been perpetrated on by guys like you!" he yelled, to silence and soft expressions. Jesus Said Love, or JSL, is primarily focused on helping 'janes' leave the commercial sex industry, and its john schools, which teach that women should not be bought and sold, have become a core part of that mission. It does no harm that they have also become a lucrative line of business, and attracted significant political support.

Unable to shrink any further inside himself, Tanner was called on to share his story. A tall, thin, 24-year-old suburban Dallas kid, he clenched his fists around the side of his t-shirt, his eyelids at half-mast. While others fidgeted and downed energy drinks, he talked about the day he was arrested—the day before he was due to go on deployment. "I just wanted to talk to a female face before being stuck in a box," he remembered. "I tried to call and got a text back, I thought it was weird, but I just wanted to see a woman. Then these two guys are comin' at me. I tried to fight back; they didn't ID as cops. There was no video or audio surveillance—it all seems kind of sketchy to me."

Mills asked the other johns who had had their mugshot posted on the news. They all raised their hands. "And on Facebook, everyone saw it on Facebook," Tanner added quietly. Mills yelled, "I don't give a fuck about your face on the news, I care about these women!" He'd tell me later that he calls these interventions "front-end alignment moments." At the same time, he says that his philosophy is that they can't condemn the johns. "Holding up a bloody foetus is shaming, and it's weird," he told me. "We treat people with kindness no matter how awful they are to women, so that we can get in their ear."

Before we broke for lunch, we met Sheronda and Jackie, two of JSL's presenters with stories to shock. Sheronda is a former john-robber. She ran away from home after being sexually abused by her stepfather, and channelled her anger towards men into a scheme of posing as a prostitute, then making off with her would-be clients' money and cars. Jackie, a Department of Health nurse, wheeled out her projector for a stomach-churning slideshow of the worst effects of untreated STDs in men and women, before offering free swabbings to the johns as they filtered outside. Several complained they'd gone off the idea of lunch.

Out in the carpark, a number of the guys shared cigarettes and embarrassed jokes, but one figure stood apart. Tanner, the military kid who'd tried to voice an excuse, was walking in anxious lines up and down the empty parking spaces, painfully alone. He didn't want to talk about what had happened, but the words tumbled out like a waterfall anyway. "I just want it all behind me. I hope that this is the end."

Tanner was arrested with thirty others in a sting at a motel near Fort Hood, one of America's largest military bases. Local media ran his mugshot, plus a report that he had been found in possession of a knife, six strands of rope, duct tape and a body bag. He told deputies he'd brought the rope up to the room because he had a bondage fetish. The other items were later found in a search of his car. "There was no investigation," a broken Tanner said. "The sheriff told the media that I was a serial killer."

Sergeant Mahoney, from the sting that nabbed Fernando, had also been there that day, participating in a cross-county exercise. "We arrested a lot of johns that day, but I remember Tanner," he told me. "I was on surveillance. I saw that he had put on his big bowie knife on his hip. They dunked him pretty hard 'cos they knew about this knife.

"He was a squirrelly dude. I remember after they arrested him that he wouldn't tell them his name, wouldn't say he was buyin'. Maybe he wasn't going to kidnap her, I don't know."

The day after class, and that haunting conversation with Tanner, I arrived at the Waco office of the McLennan County sheriff, Parnell McNamara, to talk to him and his human trafficking team. Sheriff McNamara greeted me with a hug and asked if I wanted anything to drink. Within minutes, he was showing me a DVD highlights reel of his greatest law-enforcement triumphs. After we were done, he asked me to pose for photos with his collection of Tommy submachine guns, and handed me an autographed photo and some merchandise promoting his re-election campaign.

"Some of these guys should have been shot," he declared, when we finally sat down and I managed to steer the conversation back to crime. "The johns are the root of the evil, creating the demand. It's a big effort: the pimps, the johns, the molesters are all in it together." McNamara paused and asked me to write down one quote verbatim: "Child molesters should be tied to a post and horsewhipped every day."

Moving on to a gateway theory as to why a guy might want to see a prostitute, McNamara argued that soliciting is like the marijuana of sex. "I think prostitution leads to child molestation. Johns get bored and escalate to something weirder, kinkier."

The good sheriff describes himself as a lawman who "just inherited the job." His family has been a mainstay of Waco law enforcement since 1902, and his sprawling office is a shrine to three generations of the badge—one cabinet alone holds seventeen framed photographs of historical lawmen, as well as seven guns underneath scales of justice.

McNamara is something of a Waco legend, and that's no accident. It's what happens when you do things like form a posse of old-school lawmen to track down a thief dumb enough to steal a horse belonging to your daughter.[1]

That much-publicised event took place in 1996, but more recently, the 73-year-old sheriff was cited as the inspiration for Jeff Bridges' character Marcus Hamilton in the 2016 Academy Award–nominated film *Hell or High Water*. Bridges plays an ornery US Ranger not ready to face mandatory retirement at age 57—which is exactly what happened to McNamara after 30-plus years as a Texas deputy marshal. "You gotta get the right lookin' hat," was his advice to Bridges, who shadowed the Stetson-loving sheriff to prepare for the role. "If you get a stupid hat, you'll wind up lookin' like Howdy Doody." To seal their friendship, McNamara "put him in the posse", making Bridges an honorary deputy sheriff, before travelling with the actor to the Oscars—an experience he recalls almost as fondly as he recounts tales of his colourful career.

Of the Jesus Said Love john school he has not visited, McNamara said, "The Mills are good, good people, and it's a wonderful programme they have. There's a place for them, at least as an attempt to straighten people out." It's debatable, though, whether john schools, or 'stop demand' programmes as they are sometimes called, have any effect beyond humiliation. The first of its kind was launched in 1981, in Grand Rapids, Michigan, and was then developed into competing models, first by Minneapolis therapist Steve Sawyer, then to greater acclaim in San Francisco by women's rights activist and former sex worker Norma Hotaling.[2]

"Norma was extremely shrewd as an advocate," Michael Shively, an independent researcher who has evaluated john schools extensively for the Justice Department, told me. Hotaling developed a close working relationship with San Francisco's then district attorney Kamala Harris, now Joe Biden's vice-president. "Ideologically, john schools are all over the map," Shively explained. "One of the partners is often a charitable organisation, or something that is really survivor-focused."

In 2011, Texas passed a state law allowing any county or city to create a john school as an alternative to fines or incarceration. As with drunk driving, it is the local prosecutor's decision whether attendance at a john school is required under misdemeanour charges for soliciting. "It's the Wild West, totally unregulated," says Shively. "It is almost impossible to find out whether they work, and there is almost no accountability. The criminal justice system is heavily discretionary—there's a lot of latitude on restitution versus punishment."

Shame is driving so much of this activity. Convicted johns live with the very real possibility of losing their jobs and families, and so they rarely fight their cases in court, unable to bear the cost and desperate to put the event behind them. Of course, many of them stand trial regardless—paraded on the evening's news—and, in the event anyone didn't catch that, their shame lives in perpetuity online.

By Shively's count, in the early 2010s there were roughly fifty john schools in existence nationwide, though many may be no longer in operation, and many more may have started. If Texas law has its way, they'll be popping up like taco trucks. As with many other startups, the "moral entrepreneurs" behind these schools might have to contend with the flow of supply and demand, but such initiatives are undoubtedly money-spinners. The fees paid by johns to attend these classes are seen as a key component of the restorative justice philosophy that underpins the movement. It probably goes without saying, then, that 'stop demand' operators are backed to the hilt by local politicians and law enforcement.

Jesus Said Love is no exception. A charity financed by private donations and revenues from its monthly john school, according to its annual report, JSL averages revenues of around $500,000 a year.[3] Its annual fundraising weekend getaway, Wild Torch, is attended by a who's who of local business leaders, church leaders and political figures, including Sheriff McNamara.

"Marketing is a strength of ours," Brett Mills told me back in JSL's Waco office, a converted warehouse decorated with chic lamps, couches and cowhide rugs in every room. "We're in talks to do a corporate programme. A local company approached us after their foreman was arrested in a sting. It had affected their business."

* * *

If Mills likes to be the balls of the operation, then his wife Emily is the heart. She first felt called to work with women in the sex industry about 15 years ago. She now spends much of her time organising gift-bag runs to Texas strip clubs—often hubs for prostitution—providing women with high-quality toiletries as well as resources if they want to leave the business of sex.

"I believe we're divine beings, not for sale. But it doesn't matter in secular terms, and I get that," she told me. "Sex is a $3.2 billion industry—look at the economics, look at whose backs it's built on. This country fought a war over slavery as economics. Is that why we're not doing anything? Is it just about money and white male power?"

Brett and Emily aren't Pentecostal per se, but the Spirit-led faith has profoundly influenced them, and the entire anti-sex work industry, far more than many realise. Raised typically Southern Baptist, Emily recalled the Britney Spears-era chastity pledges and other strict moral measures that felt outdated, even for a conservative Christian like herself.

Much as Bethel plays an outsized role in Redding, a non-denominational megachurch called Antioch Waco is a pillar of town life here, right up with Sheriff McNamara and the Baylor Bears football team. And the church's anti-human trafficking organisation, Unbound, is an increasingly powerful force. Antioch, which got going as a charismatic church in 1999, has helped to rebrand opposition to sex work as an 'anti-trafficking' and 'anti-modern slavery' stance, bringing to mind Christian abolitionist figures such as John Brown who helped end the enslavement of Black people in the American South.

Today, Unbound is an international operation: as well as its ministries in three US states, it's working on the ground in Asia and South Africa. Back in its home state, Unbound has become one of the largest anti-trafficking groups operating in Texas. It works across multiple cities, assisting police in sting operations, monitoring online prostitution ads, and putting together school programmes. It enjoys the support of other megachurches in the state, and the head of its Houston chapter, Kerri Taylor, is the wife of a Texas senator. Jessica Sykora, head of training at Unbound Waco, told me that they felt the county district attorney, Republican Barry Johnson, was "going to be a good asset", who "has the right attitude, but needs more education to be accurate."

Sykora gave a 45-minute presentation on human trafficking at the Jesus Said Love john school. "I was on the phone last week with a director of the governor's demand-decrease unit," she told the johns. "They are sitting, waiting, to get a strong enough case to make one of these a felony. It hasn't yet happened in our state, but everyone wants to make it happen. Scaring the hell out of buyers is the best way we can end this industry."

When I asked her after class about this claim—that Texas wants to change first-time solicitation charges from a misdemeanour to a felony—Sykora said that she was "just spitballing".

When Michael Shively told me that these anti-trafficking groups are "survivor-focused", he was referring to the fact that they're not just about targeting the johns: their first order is to look after women. So, while Brett likes to give his balls-to-the-wall treatment, this has undoubtedly been a women-led movement. After a few days in each other's company, I came to realise that the Mills, who were usually deeply distrustful of the mainstream media, had let me spend time with their john school because Emily's idol is my compatriot Christine Caine—a Hillsong alumna whose popular talk on "anti-slavery" inspired Emily's calling. Not long after my time in Waco, I went to see Caine on her Propel Women Activate tour. She was speaking at a megachurch outside of Jackson, Mississippi, just off the interstates that are supposedly a hub of women being sold into slavery.

Not that Propel is going to bring anyone down about the way things are in the world. Caine's show is an extravaganza of female empowerment that sells out theatres and megachurches across the United States. The auditorium, in the whitest white-flight suburb of the Blackest state in the union,[4] was heaving with identical-looking women, and they were there to have *fun*.

"It's going to be a day of miracles here in Jackson, Mississippi," Caine whooped exuberantly into the microphone, in her thick Greek-Australian accent. "We came here to do business. This is not your grandmother's church conference—we're gonna kick some arse today!"

Caine knows how to put on a show, having risen through the ranks at Hillsong before branching out on her own. While she reportedly remains close to founders Brian and Bobbie Houston, she has long since swapped the council housing of her upbringing in Western Sydney for a beachside community in Orange County, where she lives with her husband and business partner, fellow Hillsong alumnus Nick, and their two daughters.

"Immaculate conception is a bit cray-cray," she joked. This event might have been a world away from her upbringing, but Caine knew her audience. Through waves of laughter, she led a prayer for Jesus to "bind our bladders" so that we ladies wouldn't need to take a bathroom break—you know how it is. This was a display of feel-good Christianity at its finest; and with women worldwide at the front of the pack among Pentecostal converts,[5] it's also good business.

For the bladders that didn't receive Jesus' blessing, anyone venturing outside the auditorium would find rows of merchandise stands selling Caine's books (*Undaunted, Unstoppable, Unashamed, Unshakeable*, and so on), several branded clothing lines, and invitations to form their own Propel Women chapter—a kind of spiritual Tupperware party for God-fearing gals. But the self-education curriculum isn't free, and if you add in the price of admission to the show, which ranged from $50 to $100, the Christian women's empowerment business is clearly a significant earner. Tax documents in the US show that Propel Women's parent company—Equip and Empower Ministries, led by Caine's husband—brings in millions.[6]

Similarly, the Caines' anti-human trafficking organisation, which has fourteen offices on four continents, brought in $8.9 million in 2018, and $8.05 million the next year.[7] The family of former vice-president Mike Pence are supporters of the charity, called the A21 Campaign, which received a portion of the sales from a series of children's books written by Pence's wife and daughter.[8]

But, while Caine might specialise in helping good millennial and Gen-X women feel that they're doing social good, the anti-modern slavery or 'abolitionist' movement isn't all that it seems.

Back in Waco—part of what's known as the Texas Triangle, formed by the interstates connecting Dallas, San Antonio and Houston—the stretch of I-35 between Austin and Dallas is routinely invoked by anti-trafficking activists as one of the nation's hotspots for modern slavery. Using the carefully formed language of social justice, advocates avoid talk of borders and illegal immigrants, but what they're really talking about still retains a humidity in the post-Trump political climate. Waco's place along this edge of the Triangle, and its status as a major college town, make it a mecca not only for the sex trade, but for the real indentured labourers. The town's economy is fuelled by strip-mall greasy spoons and commercial nail salons, which are all too often staffed by enslaved workers, particularly from Asia.

For some women like Norma Hotaling, the sex-worker-turned-anti-sex-work-campaigner, life in the trade was hell. For others, it's a choice, and a perfectly valid way to make a living. It's invaluable and commendable that organisations like A21 or Jesus Said Love provide shelter for abused women, and opportunities for them to pursue new lives—but you don't tend to hear those groups arguing for the kind of welfare that might spare people from feeling they had no choice but to enter the sex industry in the first place.

After launching in Australia, Christine Caine next set up A21 in Greece, a country the charity says is a hub for exploitation of women from Eastern Europe and, increasingly, of refugees from war-torn places like Syria. One refugee advocate in Athens told me that his organisation had been repeatedly approached by A21 and offered training on how to detect human trafficking. On further inquiry, he understood that A21 works closely with police and immigration authorities, and declined to partner with it, believing that this co-operation with the state would ulti-mately lead to deportations, and a greater risk of violence against vulnerable women.

In other words, evangelical-founded anti-trafficking groups may be offering exactly the kind of 'female empowerment' that I witnessed in Texas, which is more about affirming the saviour than understanding the real needs and lives of those to be 'saved'. And it's hard to get away from the signs that, in the US itself, the movement interests itself only in a certain type of victim. For all of the genuine altruism in the work of JSL and Unbound in Waco, they're only ever waiting in carparks outside of strip joints—not helping the dish-washers and nail salon workers who have been trafficked into other kinds of work. They might mean well, but it is clear that 'anti-trafficking' and 'modern slavery' mean more to the people who call it such than to those they've selectively identified as its victims. These are just buzzwords for a certain kind of sexual ethics that has become the stock in trade of today's Pentecostalism.

The modern Pentecostal woman isn't attending to her uncut hair or home-schooling a brood of children. Much like Christine Caine and Emily Mills, she's an educated, savvy person; not one for feminism, but all in for the sisterhood; speaking in the lan-guage of social justice to promote fundamentalist Christian val-ues; weaponising society's ills and the latest cultural trends as the movement has always done, but with a new goal for the twenty-first century—not converting believers, but changing the world.

* * *

Whether the johns are paying much attention in class isn't important. It is evident that the people listening most intently to 'stop demand' entrepreneurs are those in positions of power.

Legislation in Texas saw a raft of john schools open up in the late 2010s. Governor Greg Abbott (2015–) began an anti-prostitution campaign, saying that "anyone who commits these crimes should be behind bars." The raft of harsh new measures includes cracking down on the promotion of prostitution, and on online sex advertising.[9] With a strong law-and-order focus, Abbott has been a particularly enthusiastic 'anti-human trafficking' crusader (with the added bonus that this cause can be tied in to the perpetual issue of 'illegals' crossing Texas' borders).

Stings are increasingly focused on johns rather than janes, usually via ads posted by police on foreign websites that were set up in the wake of the federal shutdown of Backpage, the major sex ad site. Incidentally, credit card companies almost effectively did the same to PornHub after a sustained campaign by Exodus Cry, an organisation linked to popular Prophet Mike Bickle's International House of Prayer in Kansas City, which runs 'restoration' shelters similar to those of Jesus Said Love and A21.[10]

I witnessed another john school leader in Dallas warn her students, "You know, the governor is trying to get y'all on the sex offender registry," bringing to life a room of guys terrified that they might lose their jobs, or not be able to see their kids again. Men buying sex are being reframed as pimps and paedophiles—well, not all men, exactly. In a high-profile case from late 2020, prosecutors in Florida dropped the solicitation charges against New England Patriots owner Robert Kraft, who was alleged to have bought "rub and tug" services at a day spa.[11]

Billed as laws finally going after the perps, not the victims, these efforts are only hurting those they claim to help. Women in the sex trade often work in pairs or groups for safety reasons, driving each other to jobs and helping to manage calls—this means that they get ensnared in these laws, frequently being arrested for trafficking each other. The three Chinese employees arrested as part of the "human trafficking" sting against Kraft, including the two women alleged to have provided services to him, have been convicted for soliciting one another into prostitution, and ordered to pay thousands of dollars in fines.[12]

After visiting a number of john schools and witnessing the Brazos County sting, it also seemed clear to me that police operations are targeting a certain type of john. In 2012, Rachel Lovell of DePaul University studied mugshots taken by the Chicago Police Department over two years. She found that almost all of its stings had taken place in poor, African-American and Latino neighbourhoods, targeting clients of street-based sex workers.[13] Over 85 per cent of the men arrested were Black or Latino.[14]

Luis, a Dallas john schooler I spoke to after his humiliation, knew the score: "I grew up in south Dallas. I know it's where they do most of their surveillance and stings. Prostitution is more discreet in higher-class neighbourhoods, but it goes on, there's just more palms being greased."

Christa Daring, former executive director of the nationwide Sex Workers Outreach Project, agrees that the 'anti-slavery' movement is targeted at the most poor and vulnerable. They told me, "We've seen a lot of bills introduced in line with the end-demand philosophy which also prop up civil forfeiture"—taking property that may be suspected to be part of a crime—"which is already a really sketchy business, and technically illegal in the United States. Legislation we're seeing being introduced could result in people having their cars seized if they cannot pay their john school fines of only $250."

Not content with labelling men caught buying sex as pimps and perverts, the movement is also classifying sex workers as unwilling victims, ironically against their will. Ayesha, a 30-year-old sex worker who has been working the Triangle for 15 years, says that she made a decision to enter that line of work, and did so with her eyes open. A Texas native, Ayesha ran away from home at 14 because she didn't get on with her grandmother—both of her parents had been incarcerated for low-level drug offences. Recently arrested for the first time in her career by authorities pushing this new line, she worries that the law's sudden obsession could see her wind up in prison too.

"I got caught in a sting in Dallas. They didn't want to let me go," she said. "It was the FBI's human trafficking squad, they were trying to make me say that I was a victim. I'm like, look at me, check my demeanour—I don't look like I'm being forced."

Law enforcement agencies are taking on the rhetoric given to them by faith-based groups such as Unbound and Jesus Said Love. And, in turn, those organisations are sounding an awful lot like policymakers. "The mortality rate for trafficking victims is seven years from entry—usually through suicide, violence, and drugs," Emily Mills told me, using a frequently cited but false statistic.[15] "People don't realise that they are victims. We tell them that they are a walking miracle. The victims have to learn to say that they are victims."

Ayesha couldn't disagree more. For a high school dropout like her, getting into sex work felt like an astute decision: "What else am I going to do, bag groceries in Walmart for $7.25 an hour?" She added that this new police obsession with 'sex crimes' means that, for her, the risk of getting a criminal record is now too high. She's trying to finish a business degree at college. "I'm done. It's not how it used to be—stress free—with the police and all." And the worst part, she says, is that there *is* really serious crime happening within the world of soliciting; but the forces driving this crackdown don't seem interested. "We have more things going on than just the hobby. There's a lot of violence, there's girls getting raped—those are the guys they should go hard on."

Ayesha counts a former sheriff among her clientele, most of whom are older white guys, but says that you only need to glance at the skin colour of her colleagues' and clients' mugshots to see who is actually being arrested. For her, full legalisation of sex work is the only way forward—not least because sex itself is only a small part of her work. "A lot of my guys can't perform," she told me. Many of them just want company—much as Tanner, the army guy at the Waco john school, put it.

But legalisation of sex work is definitely not the direction police are moving in. As Ayesha said, they are ramping up their efforts to stamp out sex work altogether—with Pentecostal groups at their side. The operation that nabbed Tanner wasn't just another sting for the Waco boys in blue. It was a showcase for the way that, beyond not-for-profits pushing 'anti-trafficking' policies nationwide, local law enforcement agencies are reaching out across borders to crack down on commercial sex. I met Tanner at the Waco john school in McLennan County, but his arrest—and subsequent trial by television—had been part of a *Bell* County show-and-tell operation, an on-the-job training exercise for officers visiting from elsewhere in the state.

Parnell McNamara, the McLennan sheriff, had been jubilant after Tanner's bust, telling local papers, "I'm so proud of Bell County for jumping on the bandwagon." The Bell County Sheriff's Department had learned everything they knew from McNamara's team, which began conducting stings as part of the National Johns Suppression Initiative in 2014. Speaking to the cameras at the end of the operation, McNamara described those arrested as "every kind of weird sicko you can think of".[16] His comments were picked up nationally, and a star was born. Today, he invites television crews to his many busts, and he has been working on his catchphrases. During our chat, he appeared to riff on Tolstoy when I asked him why people buy sex. "There are all sorts of excuses, like unhappy homes—but there's no excuse for someone like *that*."

In 2015, buoyed by the effectiveness of cross-county prostitution busts, McNamara started another posse of a kind, called FAST: Fugitive Apprehension and Special Tasks. Access to his "personal SEAL team" only takes a call to the sheriff, and the team spends much of its time chasing down "pimps". The work has taken them all the way to Las Vegas and New York City; when I spoke with McNamara, they had most recently tracked down a Waco brothel owner in Dallas. The FAST team is "run-nin' and gunnin' day and night", powered by Homeland Security clearances that allow it more or less free reign to conduct opera-tions all over the country.

* * *

Republicans such as Governor Abbott and Sheriff McNamara feel there is a moral blight on the Texas landscape, cities where pimps, prostitutes and 'illegals' run the streets and threaten traditional values. In a climate of disinformation and conspir-acy, it hasn't taken long for this idea—that pimps and paedo-philes are roaming our neighbourhoods, ready to take our children—to be picked up by people willing to take matters into their own hands.

Troublingly, during the height of the pandemic in 2020, ideas peddled by the 'anti-slavery' movement saw the birth of an online vigilante movement. #SaveOurChildren is closely linked to the far-right conspiracy theory QAnon—which, at the last count, enjoyed the support of a disturbing 15 per cent of Americans.[17] Conspiracy is often the twin of prophecy, and QAnon has been described by some who track it as a repurposed Christian apoca-lypse cult, which enjoys a lot of crossover with Pentecostalism.[18] The #SaveOurChildren movement has provoked an explosion of protests, and lured well-meaning 'Instagram mums' into its mythology. Like QAnon, it has been called an outgrowth of the New Christian Right. Charismatic Pentecostals have often been found at #SaveOurChildren protests, speaking in tongues and having ecstatic experiences.[19] The movement has also prompted some people to destroy their lives and relationships, becoming obsessive online conspiracy warriors trying to expose global Satanist paedophilia networks.[20]

Law professor Bridgette Carr of the University of Michigan Human Trafficking Clinic told me that these movements are ignoring the way trafficking actually happens: vulnerable people being exploited for profit, usually through an existing relationship. "I've represented hundreds and hundreds of victims and consulted on many more cases, and never, not one time in my case work, has a child been snatched by a stranger. Not one time."

"There is a willingness for a lot of nonprofits to say whatever they need to say to get donations," Carr added. "Many only do awareness and training, and they have no on-the-ground experience." She cautions that many of the "glossy" online groups affiliated with evangelical megachurches "may never have actually served a real trafficking victim".

Brett Mills, of course, would say differently. He's busy searching for a repentant john to round out his curriculum at the Waco john school. That is, someone repentant enough to join his team. There is no one better equipped to counsel the sex-addicted than a former addict, he reasons, and the number of jobs that publicly branded sex addicts are welcome to apply for are few. The only option, then, is for humiliated johns to turn pro—to become part of the system that destroyed them.

Moral panic takes many forms, and sex is its current obsession. The prison industry can no longer rely on weed-smokers to fill the cells, so it is looking to sex offenders—and that is what johns will be classified as—to pick up the slack.

No one's crying over this, of course. Moral weakness is a disease—until the doctor comes down with it, anyway. But the fact is, real people are having their lives turned upside down for sexting cops. John school graduate Tanner is now effectively in hiding, jobless and living with his parents; understandably, he's finding being 'exposed' as a 'serial killer' difficult to deal with.

Under the cover of goodness, the john school movement rolls on. As states are increasingly underfunded, and under attack, these moral entrepreneurs are dictating public policy without ever receiving a single vote. They're completely changing, and sometimes ruining, lives—casualties of the Pentecostal drive to transform society. Or, you could say, it's one part of the Seven Mountains that looks well on its way to being conquered.

10

SIN TODAY, REPENT TOMORROW

Killing Domingo Choc Ché was like burning down the Great Library of Alexandria. The Mayan healer held centuries of traditional medicine in his head, and his final moments proved that he was right to have lived in fear because of it.

On the morning of 6 June 2020, most of the 1,500 inhabitants of Chimay, a village in northern Guatemala not far from the Belizean border, gathered at the football field in the centre of the town. What happened over the next few hours is a matter of who you ask, but the final moments of Tata Domingo's life are not in question. That's because his horrific death—doused in gasoline and set on fire—was captured on video and shared widely on social media.

Though it is referred to locally as "the accident", Tata Domingo's niece, Angelina Valle, who witnessed the murder, said that her uncle "raised his hands three times to the sky and said: 'God knows I did nothing, forgive me gentlemen, I did not do anything, I am not doing anything.'" But it was too late. The call went out: *set him on fire*.[1]

In 28 seconds of shaking footage, Tata Domingo, a screaming ball of fire followed by a dark trail of smoke, tears through the crowd, and no one helps him. The 55-year-old father of twelve ran out onto the only road that runs through the village and collapsed, his charred ruins smoking in front of a small *tienda*. Villagers buried his remains in the nearby cemetery, where the whole sorry chain of events had begun 10 hours earlier.

Within days, police arrested siblings Edin Arnaldo Pop Caal, 21, and Magalí Pop Caal, 27; their cousin Romelia Caal Chub, 49; and one other relative. All four were charged with murder.[2] There have been further arrests since, though reports conflict on the details; in June 2021, however, these three were convicted and sentenced to 20 years each in prison.[3] One man from Chimay, confronted with cameras after the initial arrests, confessed his involvement. "Yes, yes, of course I participated," he said. "*Gasolina, si.*"[4]

Witnesses, evidence, arrests and a confession might make the murder of Domingo Choc Ché seem an open-and-shut case. But the events leading up to his death are also part of a disturbing trend in Guatemala. The long tail of Central America's dirtiest of dirty wars is a crusade against invisible enemies who are invading everyday life.

* * *

A petrol station wasn't what I had in mind when Mayan priest Romulo Pop invited me out to his office in San Luis, Petén, about 10 hours' drive from Guatemala City. The town of 8,000 is the nearest regional centre to Chimay, a further 90 minutes north-east of the village along a solitary, unpaved road.

Out the back of Romulo's petrol station, we sat in a courtyard littered with bottle caps, with a sign promising "genuine beer" printed on the wall. Though he wears serious glasses and a strict side parting, Romulo has the easy charm of a man with a much younger wife. She brought us coffee after a couple of hours of listening to Romulo talk, for we were "still only at colonial times", and he could talk Mayan history for days.

A Q'eqchi' elder like his late colleague Domingo Choc Ché, Romulo is what is known as an *Ah Kin* or *Ajq'ij*—a Mayan spiritual guide, or priest; this role is distinct from Tata Domingo's, as an *Ajilonel*, or traditional healer. Both men came from a long line of practitioners, and both disciplines of priests are being persecuted for their practices, a new front in an old war that began with the European invasion 500 years ago.

"When the Spanish arrived, the Inquisition was already underway," Romulo explained. "They were cruel and wanted to step on our cosmology; they didn't understand how strong our beliefs were." A small tear rolled down his cheek, pooling like candle wax in a fold of his face. "They began killing off our deities, saying that our beliefs were a sin."

Duality is critical to the Mayan belief system: spirits can be used for good or evil. Romulo explained that most *Ajq'ij* are 'good' priests, but there will always be some who use their powers for ill, something he blames on envy. But none of this nuance mattered to the morbidly Catholic Spanish, who forced their faith on the local people, and "tied Mayan priests to trees before burning them."

In time, some learned priests helped to build bridges between the faiths. Many Guatemalans practise a syncretic, uniquely Mayan Catholicism, which evolved over time as a way of physical and cultural survival. The people in Petén generally have good relations with the Catholic Church, but now there's a new competitor on the spiritual landscape, and Romulo cannot say the same for them. Once someone turns *evangelico*, he said, "they reject their native culture."

Romulo suggested we drive out to a sacred ceremonial site not far from his petrol station. We parked on the side of the road and walked down half a kilometre of unmarked track, through thick subtropical forest, before arriving at a natural clearing. A canopy of trees, easily 50 metres high, let only beams of light through, while a large cave signified the passage between the underworld and the material world.

We lit candles from a small flame pit and prayed to each of the four energies as we turned in each direction. Romulo gave Mother Nature an offering from a palm tree, and asked for her blessings. "Burning everything reminds us that nothing belongs to us, everything belongs to nature," he told me. "I am praying for you to find the right words to write about what is happening to the Maya."

After the ceremony, he proposed a healing session, but not one that an *Ajilonel* like Tata Domingo would offer. The medicine he stocks is Gallo, the chicken-logoed beer jokingly referred to as Guatemala's national bird. Finishing the story of what happened to his town required a dose of something that wouldn't have had approval from the people who irreparably changed its history.

In the 1960s, Romulo explained, American missionaries Matthew and Rosemary Ulrich arrived in San Luis, with a new twist on an old story. They translated the Gospels into the language of the Maya who traditionally lived in the area, the Mopan. Despite the centuries-old Catholic presence in the town, the arrival of these Pentecostals altered the way the people of San Luis understood God's will.

Everything started to change, and quickly. Romulo says that before the Ulrichs appeared, the people of San Luis didn't think in terms of sin, but about respecting nature, living in harmony with it. They didn't speak of Hell, and didn't fear death, which they saw as a natural cycle between earth and the underworld; between the material and spiritual life.[5] The modern missionaries "brought new rules" about being reborn through baptism and "burning in our sins". The cycle of sin, penitence and absolution is present in all forms of Christianity; but for the born-again, repentance is a critical step in salvation and rebirth. Many Pentecostals also believe in the idea of progressive sanctification—that is, continually repenting your sins, in the ongoing desire to be more Christlike.

The American God was similar to the Mayan cosmology in that it had a distinct duality of good and evil—but in every other sense, the two religions are worlds apart. "The new denomination changed many things in the mind," Romulo said. "People felt free to sin, because the next day you could repent." The status of absolution applies from moment to moment in Pentecostalism. 'Good' and 'evil' often comes down to a collection of deeds in Christianity, but traditional Mayan ideas about good and evil were more of a way of life, and of relating to other people and the natural world.

The theology may not have been a good fit, but in spreading their faith, the Ulrichs likely encountered what so many other Pentecostals had before them, in places like Brazil, South Africa and Korea: promises of healing were strong draws for local communities. And the religious business model so reliant on these practices requires a monopoly on spiritual power. Since the Ulrichs' arrival in San Luis, Pentecostal conversion in the region has exploded. To put it in perspective, there are five Christian churches in the municipality of Chimay, where Tata Domingo lived and died; four are Pentecostal, and only one is Catholic.[6]

Romulo has attended regional meetings of elders since the murder, and believes that "the accident" was a matter of "revenge and emotions" that got out of control. The healer's three convicted murderers were the relatives of José Pop Caal, a powerful man in the village who had recently died. Villagers believed that Tata Domingo was a witch who could place curses on them.[7] While the facts leading up to that day may be in dispute, their consequences are not, says Romulo: "Since the accident, everyone out in Chimay is doing Christianity."

When they showed up in the '60s, the Ulrichs wouldn't have known exactly what they were presaging—but, as we know, in

Pentecostalism what's critical is not merely being Christian, but *doing Christianity*. Romulo's wording reminded me of John Wimber, who emphasised "doin' the stuff" and started the modern third wave of Pentecostalism with C. Peter Wagner in the '80s. That wave, of course, led to Wagner coining the phrase 'spiritual warfare', giving a new name to the old idea of slaying demons in our midst.

Spiritual warfare rests on the assumption that everything bad in the world is the result of demonic forces—whether due to 'satanic' beliefs, such as those held by Indigenous Mayans; or to what spiritual warriors see as the bastardisation of Christianity, whether syncretic practices like Charismatic Islam, or even established religions that pre-date Pentecostalism, such as mainstream Islam or Catholicism. A student of faith in the Global South, Wagner's time as a missionary in South America gave him the idea that the world is in an apocalyptic struggle between good and evil—the kind of cosmic duality that Romulo says his people have practised for millennia. Only, in Wagner's version, the 'good' is radical Christianity, and the 'evil' is traditional Mayan belief.

Unsurprisingly, encouraging people to constantly meditate on demons ruling over them is a recipe for paranoia and fear, where slippery denunciations of evildoing carry undue weight. Not only that, but we've seen in Nigeria that, when belief systems collide, spiritual warfare becomes not only a cosmic struggle, but a political one. In Central and South America, spiritual warfare has come to mean the violent rejection of non-Pentecostal beliefs, and the annihilation of Indigenous peoples and cultures.

Another way of looking at it is that dehumanising your opponent is the oldest trick in the book of conflict. For almost 40 years, Guatemala has been a testing ground for spiritual warfare, and it appears to be succeeding. A series of political leaders have put on their biblical armour, and shown how to take strategic-level spiritual warfare from the page into practice. Fully realised, spiritual warfare is a dictatorship of the faithful, going into battle against anyone who doesn't believe their claims.

* * *

It took the CIA three attempts before it successfully deposed democratically elected President Jacobo Árbenz, in 1954. The coup was launched in the name of anti-communism, the 'communism' in reality being nothing more than land and labour reforms. The CIA had stepped in on behalf of the US-owned United Fruit Company—the largest landowner in Guatemala, with annual profits twice the revenue of the entire country.[8]

Árbenz was no communist. He had simply been trying to liberate large swathes of the population out of effective agricultural slavery, and in fact to transform Guatemala into a "modern capitalist state". United Fruit, however, had engaged in an influential lobbying campaign, persuading the Eisenhower administration to show the newfound American way to a country in the neighbourhood. After the coup, the Americans installed a military dictatorship; but by 1960, leftist rebels were actively opposing the regime—and they had broad support from the Indigenous Maya, who made up around 60 per cent of the population.

The Roman Catholic hierarchy supported the military government—that is, until the Second Vatican Council (known as Vatican II), a 1962–5 conference on modernising the Catholic Church which brought about a profound examination of the faith, opening the door for some to take a more liberal view of religion. The idea of 'liberation theology' (a renewed Christian emphasis on liberating the poor and oppressed) swept Latin America, first powered by Vatican II, then boosted by the local Acción Católica movement, which focused on serving the needy and the marginalised. Many Guatemalan clergy embraced this shift.

This coalition of left-wing guerrillas, Indigenous Mayans and liberation theology Catholics began to coalesce against the dictatorship imposed on them, becoming enemies of the regime, and therefore enemies of the state. The result was perpetual turmoil for Guatemala after Árbenz's overthrow: insurrection, massacres and revolving coups continued until 1976, when an even more devastating force intervened. A terrible earthquake shocked the country, killing 23,000 and rendering an estimated 1.5 million homeless—about one in four people.[9]

Into this crisis and despair stepped Gospel Outreach, a Californian Pentecostal outfit that had been a part of the Jesus People movement led by Lonnie Frisbee and John Wimber in the '60s and '70s. American evangelical missionaries such as the Ulriches had been arriving in Guatemala at a slow trickle for a decade already, but following the 1976 earthquake, Gospel Outreach—known locally as *El Verbo*, The Word—quickly earned a significant following thanks to its charity work. Besides this practical aid, intense spirituality is a part of Guatemalan culture: many, if not most, people saw the natural disaster either as a sign of God's displeasure, or as a divine call for redemption ahead of the Second Coming—much like their predecessors in California 70 years earlier, who saw a clear line between the Azusa Street Revival and the great San Francisco quake.

The best-known of the new converts was General Efraín Ríos Montt. The young military man had played a minor role in the 1954 coup. More importantly, he was a graduate of what would become known as the School of the Americas: the notorious CIA finishing school for dictators and genocidal maniacs who would go on to overthrow left-wing governments across Latin America.[10]

Ríos Montt probably won the country's 1974 election, but the Guatemalan Congress decided the outcome in favour of the more right-wing candidate, Kjell Eugenio Laugerud García. In this injustice, Ríos Montt saw a conspiracy by the Catholic Church and the Mayan people, and vowed to "one day even the score". First stop on the road to revenge was studying a different kind of muscular American theory. Four years after his defeat, he converted to El Verbo, and became a preacher and leading member of its Guatemalan operations.[11]

This religious turn didn't mark a retreat from public life, however. In 1982, alongside two former military colleagues, he seized power in a fresh coup that appeared to catch even the Americans off-guard.[12] The new junta leader had remained popular in the country after his defeat eight years earlier. In Nicaragua, the left-wing Sandinistas had taken over in 1979; now, Guatemalan guerrillas were reportedly on the verge of taking over much of the country's highlands. Amid the mounting anxiety about left-wing insurgencies, it was widely believed that Ríos Montt would be a force for stability—clean and honest, and "committed to ... rooting out the corruption and political killings" increasingly associated with the regime he overthrew.[13]

"We feel a great door has been opened," said an El Verbo elder, on the afternoon that Ríos Montt assumed office. "We don't understand what is going to happen, but he will be operating with a power that is not like men's corrupting power. He is going to have an anointing from God."[14]

You might say that he had been anointed by something even more powerful: the political-evangelical elite of the United States. Two thirds of Ríos Montt's cabinet had been trained at the future School of the Americas, and once in power they applied their American education wholeheartedly. The general's ascent marked the culmination of decades of US soft and hard power in the region. After he came to power, a meeting was held in Washington DC about how to support him, involving senior political and diplomatic figures like the ambassador to Guatemala (and practising evangelical) Fred Chapin, along with religious leaders such as Pat Robertson, Jerry Falwell and Loren Cunningham, one of the men who originally came up with the idea of the Seven Mountain Mandate.[15]

But Ríos Montt's faith was no stunt to win favour with the Americans. Deeply pious, he earned the pejorative nickname Dios Montt. As with all good Pentecostals, his project was far bigger than saving souls: he wanted to redeem an entire nation. Dios Montt's project, La Nueva Guatemala, would give the country unity and direction, through morality and order.

The 'new Guatemala' might have been steeped in morality, but violence was its true ideology. At least sixty-nine massacres took place in Ríos Montt's first 100 days in office.[16] During the same period, he appeared on television each week to deliver "Sunday sermons". Marrying his two American educations, the general believed that "A Christian should carry his bible and his machine-gun."[17] Within two weeks of coming to power, Ríos Montt had initiated a scorched-earth policy, prosecuting a brutal counterinsurgency against real and suspected guerrillas and their sympathisers. Historian Virginia Garrard-Burnett has called his 17-month rule in 1982–3 "the violent and bloody nadir" of Guatemala's 36-year civil war.[18]

For Ríos Montt, the victory he craved meant more than defeating the enemy—because after that, he could save the soul, and souls, of a nation. He had his own personal desire for revenge on the Catholic Church, but the eyes (and guns) of the entire regime were firmly trained on the many clergy who had adopted liberation theology, and on their allegiance to a left-wing, socialist view of the world. The enemy wasn't simply the guerrilla/Catholic/Maya coalition—the enemy was evil personified, and the terms of the battle were widely understood.

Nine months into Ríos Montt's reign, a pastor at El Verbo told a group of Americans that "we hold brother Efraín Ríos Montt like King David", the biblical figure who defeated Goliath and went on to become the first king of Israel. "The army doesn't massacre the Indians," the pastor continued. "It massacres demons, and the Indians are demon-possessed; they are communists."[19]

In the context of the Cold War, this Pentecostal justification was the soft-power sheen over decades of monetary and military might. It offered a moral impetus, beyond protecting America's interests, that people in the region could actually believe in. It was, quite possibly, the first time that spiritual warfare had been put into practice.

The civil war long outlived Ríos Montt's rule, raging from 1960 to 1996, but the orgy of anti-Mayan state violence, often called 'the Silent Holocaust', peaked in the early '80s, then slowed after the general left office. A truth commission has found that some 200,000 people died due to political violence during the 36 years of the conflict—and that 86,000 of them, 43 per cent, were slaughtered during Ríos Montt's year-and-a-half in office. The overwhelming majority of deaths, up to 90 per cent, were committed by government-led forces.[20]

Under Ríos Montt, the military launched what can only be described as a final solution, attacking 4,000 villages, wiping 626 of them off the map, and driving 1.2 million people into internal or external exile. Foetuses were ripped from mothers' bodies, children had their heads caved in and were thrown into wells, women were gang-raped, men castrated. It's estimated that 80 per cent of the victims were Mayan—in contrast to earlier years of the war, when the victims were largely Ladino, or mixed-race, and generally political targets such as students and trade union leaders.[21]

The UN's Commission for Historical Clarification on the war's atrocities concluded in 1999 that "the massacres, scorched earth operations, forced disappearances and executions of Mayan authorities, leaders and spiritual guides, were not only an attempt to destroy the social base of the guerrillas, but above all, to destroy the cultural values that ensured cohesion and collective action in Mayan communities."[22]

A CIA intelligence memo written during this reign of terror noted that the commanding officers had been "instructed to destroy all towns and villages which are cooperating with the Guerrilla Army of the Poor (EGP) and eliminate all sources of resistance."[23] Ríos Montt spoke to Ronald Reagan in a language the US president could understand. "We have no scorched-earth policy," the general insisted. "We have a policy of scorched Communists."[24] Bishop Mario Ríos Montt—his brother, who ministered in an area severely affected by the violence—called the general's campaign a "holy war", and condemned it publicly.[25] The bishop would later head the Catholic Church's inquiry into the human rights abuses of the Guatemalan state.

Sister Bernice Kita of the Maryknoll nuns arrived in Guatemala in 1970, and remembers the way the new religion flooded into the countryside with the American missionaries. They were given an easy ride, while the Catholics were under constant suspicion and threat of violence. "Pastors were knocking on doors and convincing people that Catholics were all going to Hell," she told me. "Soon enough, I remember hearing people say things like, 'We don't want any statues in our chapel.' These are things that were part of their culture and heritage."

If the Pentecostal pastors couldn't convince you, the army would. "They were saying that Acción Católica is evil, they're all guerrillas and communists and against the government," she added. "They said, 'We're killing Catholics—but if you become an evangelical, you'll be safe.'" The consequences for the nuns of continuing to practise their faith amidst this Pentecostal wave were plain: next door in El Salvador, four American church-women were raped and murdered by the National Guard in 1980, including two sisters in Bernice's order.[26]

Sure, you could be caught in the wrong village during the wrong massacre, but converting to Pentecostalism was at least a shield, if not a sword. Indeed, the Catholic Church in Latin America was learning the same lesson as the people: giving over to the Holy Spirit to stay alive. Catholic churches in the region are now largely Charismatic Renewal (Renovación Carismática Católica)—Pentecostal in all but name, a way for the Vatican to cling on to its waning influence in the part of the world where it has the most followers.[27] Sister Bernice thinks that the Acción Católica movement she is a part of will be "dead in ten years."

Wishing to turn the page on so many decades of corruption and violence, people were behind what they saw as Ríos Montt's moral vision. As in many communities across the world that have turned to Pentecostalism, after so much despair and hatred, the movement seemed to offer Guatemalans the first sense of positivity to reach them in a long time. To this end, many Indigenous people actively participated in the counterinsurgency. During his short reign, Ríos Montt's network of 'civil patrols' grew from 25,000 to 700,000, meaning around 10 per cent of the population eventually took part. During this time, El Verbo members were the preferred patrol leaders, liaising between the military and local communities, and flushing out guerrilla sympathisers.[28]

Even during the worst of the bloodshed, the general was considered a stabilising force. In the words of one rural villager years later, at least under Ríos Montt, "you knew what you needed to do to stay alive." In August 1983, he was deposed by his own defence minister, over the "fanatical and aggressive" religious leanings of his regime, now threatening the military's power—what this really meant was that Ríos Montt had launched a crackdown on corruption, threatening the generals' personal prosperity. Even after his fall, though, he remained popular across broad swathes of the country, including the areas worst affected by the genocide, and continued to enjoy electoral success and important positions right into the early 2000s.

The tide turned during his final presidential campaign of 2003; by this time, two truth commissions had revealed the extent of his violent reign decades after it ended.[29] But it had taken a long

time for Ríos Montt's appeal to wane—maybe too long for the
ideas he upheld ever to have been truly set aside in Guatemala.

Shortly after the general's overthrow, a prominent Pentecostal
leader and businessman preached to a crowd of the faithful. The
evangelicals, he said, "began to understand that Satan was rob-
bing, killing, and destroying Guatemala and began to resist in
the name of Jesus." God showed them spiritual warfare, and "He
wanted his church to dominate in this environment." The pastor
claimed that, under Ríos Montt's reign, the guerrillas had
retreated, the economy had improved, and corruption had been
brought under control—but it was bigger than that. "God began
a great harvest of souls ... Satan, in the name of Jesus, we grab
you and we order you to leave Guatemala, from border to border
and from ocean to sea, in the name of Jesus: LEAVE!"[30]

Guatemala's truth commission into the civil war concluded
that Ríos Montt's Silent Holocaust to rid the nation of its
demons "came close to destroying one of the world's great native
cultures."[31] The peace treaties that ended the civil war in 1996
were supposed to stop the slaughter of the Indigenous Mayan
people—but it seems that only one side laid down their arms.

* * *

A month before Tata Domingo was murdered, Mayan rapper
Tz'utu Kan was woken in the middle of the night by two young
men, who told him that the house he was building was on fire.

"At first, I thought it was a kidnap attempt. But they convinced me to jump in their tuk-tuk to check it out, and when I
got there, the fire was 30 metres high," he told me. "I went to
my knees to give my offering of energies to the *nawals* [spirits],
to the grandfathers and grandmothers, praying and praying as I
watched the house collapsing down."

Situated some 500 kilometres from San Luis, near the famous
Lake Atitlán in the Guatemalan highlands, the house was going

to be dedicated to the Mayan calendar. Tz'utu had spent six years carving sculptures devoted to the snake *narwal*, which represents inner fire. The house fire had begun late at night, not long after the town had turned off the water, "so there was no water in the pipes to douse the flames." Along with neighbours, he threw dirt on the fire for four hours until it smouldered; the house was made mostly of wood, so only a few central pillars remained.

"The next day, I started investigating," he said. The local council informed him that a CCTV camera near his house had been turned off a few days before the fire. "Neighbours told me there had been people drinking at the swimming pool nearby that night," he added. "I have reason to believe that people from the town council were involved. This town is very, very, very conservative evangelical."

By promoting Indigenous culture, changing his name to a traditional Mayan one, and trying to encourage people in the village to speak the Tz'utujil language, the musician has upset people. "Pastors are talking a lot of bad things about Mayan culture. There's this guy, he gets so mad that you see white saliva foaming in his mouth, just talking about my culture. He's screaming in the church and scaring people," he said. "The brainwashing is coming from the church. The snakes, they see them as the devil."

Tz'utu had thought that he would be too big a target to kill, because of his profile in the country and his performances in the United States; but seeing Tata Domingo's death on the news, just weeks after the fire, freaked him out—the healer was, after all, working with international universities, and they'd still got to him. Then, on 3 January 2021, another Indigenous spiritual leader he knows went missing: Jesús Choc Yat, 57, from Uspantán in the department of Quiché.[32] "They disappeared him, just like in the war," Tz'utu said. "Violence is in the plan of the evangelicals—some of the Catholics too, but mostly evangelicals. They want to erase Mayan culture to get more people into their church."

Tz'utu said that his family either don't like him practising Mayan culture because of their Christianity, or fear for his safety at the hands of certain Christians. "This all goes back to the '80s when they were afraid of communists. The evangelical faith in Guatemala grew up during the genocide." Unfortunately, however, the Guatemalan justice system did not. Jesús Choc Yat knew this better than most: his father had been similarly lynched by the military during the genocide. The day after Choc Yat Jr disappeared, his body was found, bearing the marks of "cruel torture".[33] As Romulo put it in San Luis, spiritual warfare is all about *doing* Christianity—and doing it against Indigenous people.

Peter Wagner saw fertile ground for strategic spiritual warfare in Latin American countries, which had seen decades of instability. He advocated a "fiercely pragmatic" approach, arguing that leaders "ought to see clearly that the end *does* justify the means."[34] Wagner believed that Christians of the Global South were leading the way when it came to the spiritual battlefield, and the idea is now finding purchase beyond his traditional mission grounds.

Brazilian megachurch leader Edir Macedo may have written a book attacking the syncretic minority faith Candomblé, but things have moved beyond words to deeds: favelas in Rio de Janeiro have seen a spate of "evangelical drug dealers" violently attacking people who practise the Afro-Brazilian religion.[35] And, as we have seen, Nigerian political and military leaders are frequently backed by or linked to pastors and churches who speak of spiritual warfare against Boko Haram, if not Muslim communities as a whole.

The global Dominionist movement is seeing many Indigenous peoples turn on their own customs, as with the death of Tata

Domingo. In 2013, Papua New Guinea's speaker of parliament attempted to "purify and sanctify" Parliament House "by destroying special carvings" symbolising the country's traditional culture, now seen by some Christians as having a demonic presence.[36] For a couple of years in the late 2010s, in Australia's remote Kimberley region, Aboriginal followers of the young Tongan-born preacher Ana Makahununiu developed the habit of setting fire to sacred artefacts representing how "Satan and his demonic beings" had been keeping Indigenous people "in bondage and slavery", according to one of her acolytes.[37]

Given that Guatemala might just be the most Pentecostal country on Earth—with an estimated 60 per cent of the country practising Pentecostalism or Charismatic Christianity—it's little wonder that it's boasted much of spiritual warfare's leadership since the death of Wagner in 2016.[38] Retired pastor Harold Caballeros, a twice-defeated presidential candidate and founder of Guatemala's supremely influential El Shaddai megachurch, is keeping the flame alive in the 'peace' era. Wagner's friend and protégé, Caballeros waged a battle against the government to build a megachurch over Mayan ruins. Wagner once said that Caballeros understands the way the "values of the kingdom of God should penetrate every level of society," and that he is "doing it right, going right to the top and taking dominion."[39]

Traditional leaders say that lynchings against them have increased in recent years. *Ajq'ij* Carlos Morán, a spiritual guide like Romulo, has said that Tata Domingo was "frowned upon" for his political stance—that is, his assertion of traditional knowledge and culture. "In the last 20 years, racism and discrimination have become more extreme with the evangelical religion," he told the press in 2020.[40]

A network of Mayan activists has taken to compiling a database of the lynchings of spiritual guides and healers, as the police rarely follow up, let alone record them. They believe that authorities only took Tata Domingo's murder seriously because there happened to be video, and because his university colleagues in the capital "made a fuss". In just one example, six months before those events in Chimay, traditional healer José Andrés López was shot twice in the head, on a main street in broad daylight, before he could perform "evil spells" on people.[41]

Just as prosperity gospel and miracle healing are most popular in places marked by an absence of social services, extrajudicial violence flourishes in unstable countries where the rule of law is absent or selectively enforced. Spiritual warfare is an alternative system of politics and justice, and one that's mandated from above. Because the worldview of spiritual warfare is at once so complex and so sweeping, it can be very opaque to those outside the movement; in the words of Virginia Garrard-Burnett, this "allows [Prophets and Apostles] to steadily expand their influence in the quest for dominion without transparency." Above all, she writes, "they move forward with the utmost confidence in the righteousness of their grand plan to restore and redeem not only their own countries, but the world itself."[42]

To date, few have been so bold as Efraín Ríos Montt in putting spiritual warfare into action on a grand scale. But the lack of state-sponsored violence in the name of the Spirit has not slowed the movement. Across the world, we are starting to see an army of individuals influenced by the doctrine, a phenomenon which has been accelerated online since the pandemic. On social media, believers are maintaining what are often second, secret lives, hunting for clues of the evil in the world and denouncing people or places as possessed.

Spiritual warfare Facebook groups, containing tens of thousands of members, are creating global networks of people posting themselves into fanaticism, and displacing anger at the real, material world. One woman posted that she was under spiritual attack after describing having to work through chronic illness.

"Diabetes and pain has crippled me, walking is more painful," she wrote, and complained how, through the stress of it all, her family were getting on each other's nerves. "Someone said maybe voodoo or a curse has been put on me."[43]

Kevin Lewis O'Neill, an anthropologist who has spent time in Guatemala City studying these modern spiritual warriors, observed this trend long before the start of Covid. After embedding at Harold Caballeros' El Shaddai, he found that the recent history of spiritual warfare shows that it is being undertaken by lone actors, launching headfirst with a "sense of solitary numbness". Their "observable battle fatigue" is giving their eyes a "1,000 yard stare", similar to that of real-life combatants.[44]

Conjuring up fears from the spirit world can become a disciplining force, keeping believers on a constant war footing in both their material and their spiritual lives. This army, whipping itself into a state of fear and frenzy online, is ripe to be exploited by the next political or religious leader in need of foot soldiers. What's happening in Guatemala is a grim warning of what that might look like.

* * *

Dr Mónica Berger de White still chokes up when she tells the story of the phone call she received that morning. The voice on the other end was telling her that her friend and colleague, Tata Domingo, had been murdered. What compounded her grief was knowing that he had been in fear for his life.

"We went out to see him a couple of weeks earlier, and he was very afraid," she told me. "He had already been accused of witchcraft, and foreigners in his hometown, working with him, could make people talk even more about what he was doing."

Bishop Mario Fiandri, representing the Catholic Church in Petén, issued a statement expressing the Church's "deep horror and rejection, indignation and shame at the lynching". He added that "what is clear is that the lynching of Tata Domingo was not a question of rejection of [his] culture", but rather, "a problem between two families." The real "version of events", as told by Chimay's parish priest and Sunday School teachers, was that the lynching occurred due to the death by illness of the father and uncle of the accused, José Pop Caal: "the family blamed Choc" for doing wrong to the man, "and that led to his lynching."[45]

People who work as spiritual guides and traditional healers are used to receiving death threats, and Tata Domingo had been no different. "We were really shocked that he was saying this, but didn't take it further," Mónica said. "We'd heard it before in other parts of the country. Even respected healers who have been in a community for a long time—all of a sudden a new religious leader comes in and starts to tell people that the Maya spirituality is the worshipping of the devil."

The medical anthropologist at the Universidad del Valle de Guatemala had worked closely with Tata Domingo for years. They were collaborating on "proving" the outcomes of traditional medicine, and protecting the community knowledge that has passed through generations, often without being written down—preserving centuries of expertise from treating people in secret, before the 1996 peace treaties gave healers the confidence to start working out in the open.

"They said that he was using his knowledge to harm people," Mónica told me, adding that many Q'eqchi' people in Petén were an internal diaspora that had fled there during the civil war: Tata Domingo's family did not have a long history in the community.

Chimay has both Pentecostal and Catholic congregations, and Mónica believes that "intolerant groups" were "punching into the [Caal] family's head that there were all these signs it was witchcraft." But he couldn't have gone "to work in the dark" as had been claimed, because he was an *Ajilonel*, a medicine man—not an *Ajq'ij*, a priest.

José Ché, secretary of the national spiritual guides' association and a former colleague of Tata Domingo, also believes there is more to his murder than a dispute between families. "The people of Chimay fear telling the truth, because the family that burned Tata Domingo are powerful in the community," he told me. "And the churches feel threatened [by Mayan spirituality] because they think that the only cure is their prayers, not our plants."

A village meeting was held after "the accident", though Mónica contends that "the family of the perpetrators" had people sign an agreement "saying that Tata Domingo was a witch, that he had been sanctioned in the past for sending illness to another person."

Church leaders then brought this document to a conciliation meeting with Mayan elders, she says: "Instead of being cordial, they went on the attack, they were disrespectful." They did not say that they were sorry for the loss of the spiritual leaders' friend and colleague. They were being aggressive and defensive.

"I don't understand why the leaders of the different churches would attack his character—there's no justification for burning anyone to death."

* * *

"You're ... they do not welcome you to church," Estuardo Galdámez told me, a little embarrassed. Estuardo was first to break the story of Tata Domingo's murder, and one of few outsiders to have visited Chimay since "the accident".

The San Luis local is a part-time reporter and part-time clown-for-hire, but there was no joking about why I was there. He was taking me out to Chimay—and had been advised in no uncertain terms that we could not arrive until after church and a village meeting had taken place. On this front, Estuardo was sympathetic towards the people of Chimay, who he said "are known for being exceptionally community-minded" and, as Indigenous Mayans, are "upset that they've been painted as savages."

We had piled into a monster 4WD borrowed from a friend, the kind that you need to navigate the undulating road between San Luis and the village—a sturdy vehicle, whose driver had even sturdier nerves. On the drive, the palm trees of a rolling semitropical landscape were the only signs of life. When we got to Chimay, as our car rolled slowly down the only road in the village, what felt like all 265 families were visibly staring at us from their front porches.

"As soon as it gets dark, everyone goes inside now," Estuardo explained. "I've been here a couple of times in the evening, and it's scary." There's also the small matter that at least one person wanted for taking part in the murder is still on the loose, while others who could be questioned are still hiding in the village. I instantly recognised the football field from the video, the vivid green church behind it.

Heads continued to turn as we rolled up to Pedro Chivajay's house at the far end of the village, close to where Tata Domingo lived. Estuardo had told me that Pedro's account of what happened tallies with other eyewitnesses he's spoken to, and Pedro and his family welcomed us with open arms. He was, to the best of my knowledge, the only direct witness willing to speak publicly about what had happened, wanting to clear his conscience of the village's collective guilt.

"Even for the people of Chimay, it was something out of reality," he began, as we sat down in the backyard. Just as Romulo had explained, Pedro spoke of the Mayan conception of the world in terms of good and evil. And he told us how, just as it had happened in San Luis decades earlier, things had begun to change around here. In the mid-2010s, he said, "people started believing in witchcraft", staging village meetings to talk about who had been doing good or bad, and whether evildoers should be kicked out, or allowed to stay. "Witchcraft is what people are most afraid of."

Like many Guatemalans before the Pentecostal surge, Pedro is both a practising Mayan priest and a Catholic, as well as a member of the Guatemalan Academy of Mayan Languages—though since the lynching, he said, he has had to hide his traditional spiritual work: "Since Tata Domingo, we are afraid to practise", as the Catholic and Pentecostal churches alike will no longer "accept" Mayan ceremonies in their midst.

"They always say in Mass not to do it, that it's evil and not accepted in the Bible," he told us. "Even the two churches are at war, and they have the same God. Put it this way: if I did a ceremony in front of my neighbours it would be fine, but the religious leaders would say I'm a witch."

Pedro said that the events leading up to "the accident" were as follows. Six months before his death, Tata Domingo had had a falling out with a neighbour, José Pop Caal, about dogs crossing property lines. Sometimes, after dark, Pedro could hear him yelling drunk into the night that "this happened because you messed with me." Shortly before Caal died, villagers say, he had warned his sons not to mess with Tata Domingo; told them that the healer could pay in the next life instead.

The day before Tata Domingo was killed, Caal's family had gone to other spiritual guides to find out if he was guilty—if he had killed Caal through witchcraft, they learned, he would still have to finish the job with a ritual in the cemetery overnight. A group set up a watch on the cemetery, which sits on a steep slope easily visible from the road. In the dark hours, someone arrived. It wasn't Tata Domingo, but a man who confessed—Mónica Berger says under torture—to working for him. The medicine man had been drinking again the night before, repeating his threats into the starry sky.

"The church bells rang at 5am," Pedro recalled. "It meant everyone in Chimay needed to come to the football field; it meant that something big was happening." Usually, the church bells ringing are a call to arms—thieves have come to the village and are stealing animals. "I never expected something like *this*."

Because of where his house is, at the back end of the village, Pedro was one of the last to arrive. He found Tata Domingo already there, as well as leaders from both the Catholic and Pentecostal churches. Local custom meant that the village had to wait until sunrise to hold a trial for Tata Domingo and the man accused of going to the cemetery to finish the job; they would also have to wait for elders from another village to arrive to help adjudicate. (Indigenous Guatemalans have some legal autonomy, but it's often murky when the state will and won't step in.)[46]

Tata Domingo Choc Ché was accused of the death of José Pop Caal by witchcraft, as well as running a spiritual standover business by going to people's houses demanding "protection" money in exchange for not cursing them. Statements were taken from townsfolk; "confessions too" from the accused, after "pushing and pressing". He is said to have confessed but said he was doing the bidding of a woman in the village. "After another discussion, he fully confessed, but I won't speak about this part," Pedro said, looking down at his clasped hands. "I was there for that minute when everything happened."

Tata Domingo, Pedro told us, was found guilty after his full confession, and asked for forgiveness. It was decided that the two men, the healer and his alleged accomplice, would be released and banished from Chimay. "And then Tata Domingo's wife slapped the dead man's widow. The sons threw gasoline on him; suddenly he was on fire."

I put it to Pedro that it was strange that there had been gasoline on hand to pour over Tata Domingo, and matches to light it with, too. Not only that, but the video of his death shows that no one in the crowd appeared to help the medicine man, not even once, as he was being incinerated in front of them. "The whole thing is surprising," Pedro replied, with a raised eyebrow. "But, you know—if you kill one, you change all."

With that, he announced that his wife insisted on feeding us leftovers from a village celebration the day before. Estuardo was feeling jumpy about the impending dusk, and wanted to get out of town—but the Chivajays had taken a risk by inviting us in, and they were determined to show the hospitality Chimay used to be renowned for.

Throughout our meal, Pedro stood at the head of the table, as though hovering over the words he was looking for.

"I'm worried about a modern Inquisition coming to Guatemala, coming for the Mayans again," he said, finally. "It's in the constitution that we can practise any religion. I would like to go to the church and say that, but I would probably be killed."

11

WE AIN'T GOIN' ROUND THE MOUNTAIN
ANOTHER SEVEN YEARS

A plump, middle-aged guy wearing a baseball cap with "WRSHP" on the front passed through the metal detector, carrying a curling wooden instrument wrapped around his arm. Not that security worried what people were carrying—the objects' owners were simply acknowledged with a nod by women wearing long skirts and polite smiles.

In rural Oklahoma, a congregation armed to the teeth isn't so unusual, but plenty of other things about House of David Ministries set this church—and its "Rabbi", Curt Landry—apart. Surrounded by farmland outside the small town of Fairland, House of David looks like a celebrity mansion, its American and Israeli flags flapping in the considerable breeze. A Messianic Jewish church in all but name, in a part of the world where Jews aren't exactly plentiful, at times it feels as though the congregation worships Israel as much as it does God.

Combining elements of the Jewish faith with evangelical, usually Pentecostal, Christianity, Messianic Judaism is often called Jews for Jesus, after one of its founding organisations. This syncretic movement first emerged in the United States in the 1960s. Today, there are an estimated "175,000 to 250,000 Messianic Jews in the US, and 350,000 worldwide", with a small minority living in Israel. Though Messianic Jews identify as "Jewish Christians", around half of those attending Messianic services in America are not ethnically Jewish.[1] These churches might follow laws of the Torah, observe Shabbat, and even undertake circumcision, but their ultimate belief that people must accept Jesus as their saviour means that they are not recognised by any of the major Jewish denominations.

Curt Landry rejects the Messianic label, saying, "We are an evangelical congregation made up of both Jew and Gentile Believers."[2] But for all intents and purposes, they're Messianics—and the vanguard of a global, highly political movement within Pentecostalism. America's heartland isn't the natural home for such a phenomenon; Messianic Judaism is more of a big-city idea, appealing to people of mixed religious heritage, or to secular Jews who have found Jesus. And western Oklahoma *definitely* isn't the kind of place you'd expect people to be worshipping the military of another nation.

Nearby Picher is a literal wasteland, officially abandoned after years of lead- and zinc-mining made it too toxic for human habitation. The nearest big town is Miami—*my-am-uh* to locals—population 13,000, and host to the longest Main Street along the once-famous Route 66.[3] The advent of the interstates means that the only bright lights on that old Mother Road today are the few medical marijuana dispensaries, breaking up the rows of closed shopfronts.

And then there's House of David. 'Rabbi' Landry, whose Facebook following is over 7,000 times more than the hundred or so worshippers who turn up in person,[4] doesn't preside over your usual Pentecostal gathering—but, then again, who does? This was Friday night, and some in the congregation had travelled hours to be here.

"Flow into Sabbath and surrender to the Holy Spirit within, where the supernatural happens, miracles and healings," Landry urged, smooth and syncretic as they come, before the house band launched into song. But this lacked the high production value of Bethel or Hillsong; and it was certainly lacking the ecstasy of Billy Summerford's snake-handling, poison-drinking congregation back at the Rock House in Alabama.

Landry, very much his own man, leading his own style of faith, summoned a group of six men, including the guy in the WRSHP baseball cap, up to the altar. At once, they raised their ceremonial *shofar* horns to the air and began blowing, as though they were lifting elephant trunks. It was then that the worship really got going.

A rowdy group of middle-aged blonde women had come up to House of David from Tulsa, about 90 minutes' drive away. They started singing and dancing along to the band and the Jewish horns, as though it were a hen night at a duelling piano bar. "We ain't goin' round the mountain another seven years!" one of them shrieked—an allusion to *She'll Be Comin' Round the Mountain,* which is derived from a plantation hymn about the Second Coming of Christ and the Rapture.

* * *

After a sad childhood growing up in Los Angeles, where he was "bitterly disappointed" with his adopted father, Curt Landry discovered the Jewish roots of his birth parents. The ministry he founded in 1996 combines signs and wonders with a quest "to be a bridge of unity and restoration between Israel and the Church."[5] Biblical justification for his mission is through "One New Man", an idea that comes from Ephesians 2:15, which hopes that Jews and Christians can come together to find peace. Only, this is a kind of peace that's very much in the eye of the beholder.

Since the 1980s, Pentecostals—along with much of the American religious right—have incorporated the nineteenth-century doctrine of dispensationalism, which gave us the idea of the Rapture, into a distinctly political understanding of the End Times (see Chapter 7).[6] As we know, Pentecostals—ever the pragmatists—have come up with an easy-to-understand, upbeat version of the sequence of events that speaks to the here and now. According to their 'victorious eschatology', true Christians will *not* secretly be raptured from the earth while everything falls apart, "but will remain here to transform and rule over it", in a "preparatory dominion" laying the ground for the Second Coming of Christ.[7]

Dispensationalism has many readings and has evolved over time, but what always remains central to it is the importance of the Nation of Israel for the Second Coming. The idea is that the Jewish people will return to Israel—the modern state means that this precondition is already underway—and that they will come to embrace Jesus as their Saviour during the Great Tribulation (when the earth will feel the wrath of God through earthquakes and wars, before Christ's return).[8]

Of course, none of this is clear in the Bible, and theologians have argued about interpretations and the order of events for centuries. But no matter the seeming complexity of the sequence preceding the End Times, and despite its irrelevance to the everyday lives of believers, this idea about the return of the Jews has become critically important to the Pentecostal faith. A 2015 study found that seven in ten American evangelicals agree that "God has a special relationship with the modern nation of Israel", while 73 per cent say that "events in Israel are part of the prophecies in the Book of Revelation."[9]

President Trump's decision to move the US embassy from Tel Aviv to Jerusalem in 2018 (followed by three countries including Guatemala) was seen as a watershed moment by Pentecostals at home and abroad.[10] For them, this diplomatically controversial move was fulfilling not merely a political promise, but a prophecy for the End of Days, in which Jews will return to the Promised Land and the Temple on the Mount will be rebuilt.

Not all Jews are so enthusiastic about the prospect of their role in the End Times, with one writer calling dispensationalist theology, and its use by politicians, "a somewhat twisted form of anti-semitism".[11] For one thing, there's the arguably offensive assumption that the Jews will 'see the light' and abandon their own faith, 'saving' themselves before it's too late; for another, there's the suspicion that Christians subscribing to this theology only see Jews as a means to an end—*the* End. American evangelicalism isn't exactly known for its long and fine tradition of good relations with Jewishness: Aimee Semple McPherson's enthusiastic backing of a protected Jewish homeland was something of an outlier in the early twentieth century, and the anti-semitic slur that Jews were "Christ-killers" continued to hold sway in evangelical circles even after the horrors of the Holocaust. The late televangelist Billy Graham was caught on tape in 1972 telling the then president, Richard Nixon, that the Jews' "stranglehold" on the media was ruining the United States.[12]

Today's Pentecostals, however, are firm 'philo-semites'; or, as *The Jerusalem Post* has called them, "the new Judaizers". This refers to a recent trend—which goes far beyond the walls of House of David—for appropriating Jewish practices and objects, in service of a shared 'Judeo-Christian' future. This belief isn't all one-way: in recent decades, some Jewish leaders have been capitalising on the spiritual authority conferred on them by Pentecostals. Orthodox Rabbi Shlomo Riskin has had a long relationship with Pentecostal preacher John Hagee and with Israel-supporting Christian organisations; he is known among other Jewish leaders for statements blurring the lines between the two faiths.[13] And Messianic Christians continue to draw on Jewish references. Ralph

Messer, for one, has a history of wrapping influential preachers, including Trump's 'spiritual advisor' Paula White, in Torah scrolls and lifting them into the air, to show kinship between the faiths.[14] It's the perfect distillation of the three waves of Pentecostalism, mixing showmanship for the fans, and a generous helping of tradition for those craving the 'authentic'.

Again we see the great Pentecostal ability to hold two seemingly contradictory ideas at once: a faith on the one hand so local and immediate, yet on the other, creating a spiritual, ideological global citizenship, with Israel—not the biblical tribe, but the modern state—as its capital. All along my travels through Pentecostalism, after health and wealth, the major recurring theme among preachers I met was a preoccupation with Israel, even though their congregations probably have far more immediate worries than peace—or victory—in the Middle East.

Right-wing protesters in Seoul waved Korean and Israeli flags; Israel-themed merchandise shops dotted the working-class suburb surrounding Solomon's Temple in São Paulo; the Light and Life Gypsy lads placed special store in their Holy Land pilgrimages; and an Assemblies of God preacher in San Luis put a spin on an End Times sermon that sounded like a series of Fox News talking points, warning about the danger of long-dead Hugo Chávez in Venezuela and the need to protect Israel.

Package tours to Israel are big business for Prophets and Apostles, particularly in the West and Korea, where they offer all-inclusive trips to reconnect with the historic roots of Christianity. Some 300,000 American evangelicals undertook the pilgrimage to Israel in 2016 alone.[15] Not long before the pandemic, I joined one such tour group at an IDF 'fantasy camp' in Gush Etzion, a Jewish settlement in the occupied Palestinian West Bank, not far from Bethlehem. Something of an amusement park for the faithful, Caliber 3, run by active members of the IDF, markets itself as "the leading Counter Terror & Security training academy in Israel".[16] It came to prominence in 2018 when Jerry Seinfeld took his family there on holiday, controversially posing for a publicity shot with the former commandos who run the camp.[17]

I joined a tour group on their expedition led by Ross Nichols, a Louisianan who doesn't identify as either Christian or Jewish, but believes that "Christianity was not the religion of Jesus, rather a religion about him." Similar to Landry, Nichols has assembled his own belief system from the religious currents of what he considers his two homelands. A self-described "ardent Zionist" who is active in the anti-Boycott Divestment Sanctions movement, his mission is to "present the Jewish State in a positive light."

Hearing Nichols in full flow, it wasn't hard to understand why some Jewish people are uncomfortable with the 'Israelite-mania' emerging from some parts of the religious right. Instead of being dehumanised with the anti-semitic tropes of old, there is an element of *super*humanising, imbuing Jewish Israelis with an almost magical quality that doesn't have much to do with them or their interests as individuals. "Every Jew is a miracle," Nichols told his flock as we milled about the gift shop, "so we are seeing not just one miracle, but miracles all over the nation of Israel."

Out on the range, we undertook a gentle warmup with commanders in full IDF kit, who issued us with fake guns and real slogans to memorise. "What is the foundation of the Israeli Defense Force!" shouted Moshe, the chiselled special forces leader. "Love!" we yelled back, "The IDF is built on morals and values!" The word 'Palestinian' wasn't used, but the identity of "the terrorists" we were pretending to hunt down went without saying. Likewise, the assertion that these "enemies" have "forfeited their right to life" went without challenge. But who has time for politics, when you've got a wooden gun and a pretend marketplace to defend?

Not exactly carrying ourselves like an elite fighting force, we milled around in the small training ground, one woman fretting about where we could eat during Shabbat, another man in a Krav Maga shirt quizzing the commandos on combat. A sudden BANG, and we were jolted from our formation by a man running at us with a knife. We scattered like bowling pins as trained soldiers crashed through our sagging lines. They took the bad guy down, and everybody cheered.

After a series of drills with air rifles, dogs and fake explosives, Moshe asked why the mostly American tour group would come here to shoot things, when they can go shooting in America any time they like.

Everybody laughed, because that was the joke. The 'fantasy' in this camp wasn't about firing a weapon or taking down a 'terrorist'; it was the modern state of Israel itself, with its walls and checkpoints, its constant state of militarism. It was the overwhelming sense of a march towards victory that would, at some point, finish here.

* * *

While many literally head to the Promised Land for their bornagain-again moment (being dunked in the Jordan River), the Pentecostals are pursuing redemption just as hard through politics. Elected in 1976, Democrat Jimmy Carter was America's first evangelical president; but today the movement—for white evangelicals, at least—is synonymous with conservatism and the Republican Party. Since Reagan brought the last of the faithful evangelicals back into active duty in the '80s, what was once only a religious identity has increasingly become a political one.

One example: if the 2020 presidential election was anything to go by, the Republican Party is fast gaining a following with Hispanic evangelicals, who voted almost 50/50 for Trump and Biden—whereas two thirds of Hispanic Catholics voted for their coreligionist Biden.[18] And it's going both ways—another emerging trend is for people to identify with a faith *based on* their politics. For Republicans, the share of self-described evangelicals who never or seldom attend church has increased 50 per cent since 2008.[19] Yet around half of Republicans still consider themselves "born-again".[20] Pentecostalism is one of the only religions holding up its end of the bargain, with nearly six in ten Spirit-led people attending church frequently—second only to Mormons.[21] Remember: evangelicalism as a whole is in decline, but Pentecostalism is on the up.[22]

There's a lot of crossover between standard white evangelicals and Pentecostals in the United States, but one key question highlights the differences, and illustrates the centre of gravity. In 2019, a survey found that 29 per cent of white evangelicals agreed that President Trump had been anointed by God; but this belief was shared by almost twice as many white Pentecostals, a full 53 per cent.[23] Long a shelter for the marginalised and the dispossessed, in an age of gross inequality, Pentecostalism is becoming synonymous with an anti-liberal worldview.

Not only is this movement a political project, but it is one that is a direct challenge to the most important issues the world is facing: climate catastrophe, mass migration, evolving social norms about gender and sexuality, skyrocketing inequality, and changing geopolitics, including the rise of China. After all, if you're trying to create the conditions for Christ to return, what are a few million parts of carbon emissions in the atmosphere? If you're convinced that you're on the right side of eternity, will you fear pushing Iran to the brink of nuclear war?

Some might call it hubris, but there's an inherent paradox here. Given the apparent ease with which Prophets and Apostles convert the already faithful, the truly great rival to Pentecostalism is the rise of the 'nones'—those of no religion. But, as the roots of the Seven Mountain Mandate show, the desire to take over the world comes precisely from knowing that they are in the minority. Pentecostals feel simultaneously triumphant about the fate of the world, but besieged by the secular culture around them.[24]

This isn't simply the story of white American conservatives, or even white Americans. The ethnic majority aren't the only ones who might be alarmed by many rich economies' loss of interest in faith communities as key social pillars—religion's decline takes away a powerful form of belonging from those who might need it most. One of the fastest-Pentecostalising groups in the United States today are Latino Catholics, both new immigrants and subsequent generations, many of whom benefit from Pentecostal churches' material and networking support with integration.[25] In addition to this draw, many undocumented migrants see faith as a form of "spiritual citizenship" that makes them a bit more American and less deportable.[26] This echoes the experiences of British Gypsies, who tend to stop travelling after conversion and become 'truly British' in the eyes of many; likewise North Korean defectors, who become more assimilated to the South if they are born-again.

Still, while recognising the genuine value of Pentecostalism to many marginalised people around the world, you can't deny that it seems to be working best of all for those already at the top. Among many who hold power, or wish to, the Holy Spirit remains a key political ally. In 2019, after a bloodless coup led by the police and army, Senator Jeanine Áñez was appointed interim president of Bolivia (via a parliamentary mechanism whose constitutional legitimacy has been questioned).[27] The triumphant Áñez walked into the presidential palace brandishing an enormous Bible. "Thank god, the Bible has returned to the Bolivian government," she said, while a group of supporters surrounding her shouted the echo, "The Bible has returned to the government!"[28]

Led by a business, political and religious elite of the country's white minority, the coup against Indigenous president Evo

Morales hadn't been a morally framed "conquest of love" like Ríos Montt's takeover of Guatemala, but a naked power grab. Many powerful figures in the country had wanted to get rid of the Indigenous-led, socialist government at any cost. Áñez herself was more or less an unknown before taking the top job, so it would be controversial to place her within a takeover conspiracy—but she certainly represented this anti-Indigenous attitude. "I dream of a Bolivia without satanic indigenous rituals," she wrote in a 2013 tweet, adding, "the city isn't made for indians, they need to go back to the countryside!"[29]

In case the message of spiritual warfare wasn't already clear, Pastor Irene Squillaci said a couple of months after the coup that the ongoing power struggle between Morales' supporters and enemies was "a battle between Good and Evil". Luis Aruquipa Carlo, an evangelical leader who heads the conservative National Christian Council, declared, "Evo's era is coming to an end. And the era of Christ is being born." Under Morales, Aruquipa said, the nation wanted to legalise abortion and gay marriage: "they wanted to legalize the satanistas!"[30] We don't know exactly how many Bolivians are Pentecostal, but it seems to be at least 10 per cent, and rapidly growing—as is the case across Latin America.[31]

The intent of the coup plotters to marry church and state was best evidenced in a stunt arranged during Áñez's presidency, organised jointly by the Ministry of Defence and the Pentecostal House of Prayer Church, where her brother, Juan Carlos, is a preacher: a convoy of vehicles driving around Santa Cruz, Bolivia's largest city, in a "day of prayer and anointing". As at House of David, traditional Jewish *shofars* were being blown in triumph.[32]

Áñez proved her position within the Spirit-led camp not only with gestures, but with policy. Early on in her brief presidency, she suspended relations with Cuba, and re-established them with

Israel.[33] A right-wing Latin American leader declaring their country pro-Israel isn't especially surprising; this classic move always serves as a strong signal to Washington that the government is on board with the United States' long, grisly programme in its backyard. But Pentecostalised worship of Israel is becoming a symbol of righteous power, and one that can be found in some unexpected places.

Drug-trafficker Álvaro Malaquias Santa Rosa, known as Peixão, controls a number of favelas in cities across Brazil. Members of his gangs have been known to terrorise those who practise traditional African religions. Peixão runs what he calls an "Israel complex" in 'his' favelas, flying Israeli flags and displaying images of the Star of David. During a 2021 raid on the kingpin's compound, police discovered a bunker containing ammunition, a bulletproof vest and a copy of the Torah. Beside a sizeable swimming pool, they found a large painting reproducing part of the city of Jerusalem. On the left side of the canvas were men who were clearly part of an army, carrying a Star of David flag. At the top of the canvas were the words "Happy is the nation whose God is the lord".[34]

The idea of the Jewish state as a beacon of Christian freedom in a troubled neighbourhood even extends as far as Myanmar, where the Kachin ethnic minority, traditionally observing a mixture of animism and Buddhism, have been heavily Pentecostalised, with many baptisms and widespread embrace of prosperity gospel. Frequent targets of state genocide, the Kachin armed insurgency is zealously pro-Israel, according to a journalist specialised in marginalised South-East Asian communities.[35]

* * *

Many Pentecostals might look to the United States for leadership, for now at least, but Israel has become the movement's totemic moral centre, epitomised by the IDF fantasy camp where foreign Pentecostals can come and act out their dreams of shooting Muslim 'terrorists' and living in a militarised, walled-up ethno-state. In other words, somehow, 'Israel' has become shorthand for a fiercely Christian worldview. And here, given the direction of travel in Israel's own politics so far this century, we have to come back to the new wave of nationalist populist movements around the world.

There's nothing new in leaders using the faith to enhance their authority, but at a fraught and divisive time in global politics, the Pentecostal vision—prizing personal experience over universal truth, and dismissing social problems as failings of faith—is being taken up by some of the most notable strongmen of the day, who are using identity to grapple with crisis, and employing politics-as-entertainment over substance. No one has defined this better than Trump, the most un-Christian of presidents: though voted out of office, he remains a figure of worship for some Pentecostals in America and beyond—and he's back on the campaign trail, with the new slogan "Save America!"[36] But the world is much bigger than the United States; and, like the Spirit-led faith itself, this Pentecostalisation of politics can be tailored to local conditions.

In the Philippines, Pastor Apollo Quiboloy, the self-proclaimed "Appointed Son of God", was a key early figure behind the strongman head of state Rodrigo Duterte, lending his private jet and helicopter during Duterte's first presidential campaign in 2016.[37] Famously, in 2019 President Duterte accepted the pastor's claim that he had stopped an earthquake by yelling at it.[38] Having been abused by a Catholic priest as a teenager,[39] Duterte has called the Pope a "son of a whore".[40] In his brash way, and although he appears not to have any strong faith himself, his rise has reflected a rapid Pentecostalisation in what was once a deeply Catholic country. Today, the Philippines appears to be on a spiritual course similar to Brazil's.

Looking at the movement's advance in the Philippines also reveals another emerging Pentecostal phenomenon. As one of the world's largest diaspora nations—with around 10 million people, or 11 per cent of the population, working overseas[41]—Filipinos abroad are taking up the faith in significant numbers, just as workers moving from the countryside to big cities have found comfort in Pentecostalism in places like São Paulo, Seoul and London. Particularly in the Gulf states, Spirit-filled faith is a way of dealing with inhumane working conditions and homesickness for Filipino and, increasingly, Subcontinental migrant workers. One Filipino preacher in Saudi Arabia, a former leader of the kingdom's first 'legal' church, told me that his family had been converted by countrymen decades earlier, the state allowing them to practise discreetly in wedding venues. Now, reforms have enabled them to start an open church—so long as they don't try converting any native Saudis.

Middle Eastern strongmen aren't joining the Pentecostal party themselves, but their small acceptance of the faith highlights their role in this right-wing, populist axis that came out of the 2010s, with the state of Israel at its centre: towards the end of the Trump administration in 2020, some Gulf states recognised Israel and began normalising diplomatic relations with the country long held up as an enemy.

In Europe, the new right is personified by Hungarian prime minister and self-described champion of "illiberal democracy" Viktor Orbán. And, yes, his rise to power was also aided by Pentecostals, in a country where there aren't many.[42] At least for now—Orbán's son, Gáspár, is now a part-time Pentecostal preacher, having been converted by a Christian American charity on a trip to Uganda. He styles himself as a hipster preacher to Hungary's largely faithless youth.[43]

Broadly speaking, the countries that used to live behind the Iron Curtain are prime conversion territory for people of the

Spirit. To date, Gáspár Orbán appears to have gone about his faith relatively quietly, eschewing interviews and serving as a Hungarian soldier, including training at Sandhurst in 2020.[44] Instead, the mantle of leading preacher in Eastern Europe is held by the unlikely figure of Sunday Adelaja, a controversial and outspoken Nigerian-born pastor. His Kyiv megachurch, the Embassy of the Blessed Kingdom of God for All Nations, is the third-largest church in Europe.[45] Adelaja runs soup kitchens and rehab centres, and has dabbled in Ukraine's contentious politics, but is perhaps most famous for allegations from his own church members that he was involved in a Ponzi scheme. (A criminal case was brought in 2009, but prosecutors haven't taken it forward.)[46]

Having been brought to the Soviet Union in its dying days as a journalism student, practising his faith in secret, Adelaja understands the role Pentecostalism can play in the modern post-Soviet state. From his home television studio, he highlighted the appeal of the movement's outlook in the current climate. "Individual Christians should get involved in politics, and promote their values—just like gay people promote their values," he said matter-of-factly. Adelaja added, "I love the Seven Mountain Mandate," pausing to note that he believes the "American version is not engaging enough." People from his church, he said proudly, occupy all seven of the mountains, from education to business. "We shouldn't worry about the end of days," he believes; "we still have a lot of work to do in the next 50 years."

A young man I spoke to who is training in the Catholic Ukrainian Church said that established churches in the country are now looking over their shoulders: "The Ukrainian Church always says that the biggest barrier for faith after the Soviet Union is practical morality, and the Pentecostals are so much better at that in a modern context." From Romanian Gypsies to the son of illiberalism's regional champion, the success of Spirit-led faith in the old Eastern Bloc hasn't gone unnoticed, and it has even reached into the former Motherland itself.

Pentecostal churches in Russia expanded by up to 25 per cent a year in the 1990s, to the point where there are now believed to be at least 1 million believers in the country. One sociologist even estimates that the faith could speak to "a plurality of Russians by mid-century."[47] Vladimir Putin, who might be called the godfather of the internationalist-nationalist right, draws a lot of his power from alliance with the Orthodox Church, but he hasn't put up the same barriers to Pentecostals as he has with other Christian sects like Jehovah's Witnesses.[48] Hillsong already has a strong presence in Moscow and the Ukrainian capital Kyiv, repeating the story of capturing an aspirational, upwardly mobile class. It's unlikely that Pentecostals will become the dominant form of Christianity in Russia as they have elsewhere, but it is highly probable that the Orthodox Church will begin to take on Pentecostal practices if it feels it is losing its flock, as we've seen elsewhere.

Many in the movement still see China as the great frontier—it has been this way since the very beginning, when Agnes Ozman thought that the Holy Spirit had given her the gift of speaking and writing in Chinese. Not only are there over a billion potential souls to be saved, but in the 2020s, China's 'spiritual marketplace' also represents the potential to dramatically change the course of history. In a reshaping geopolitical landscape, with America leading the charge against a rising China, we can expect to see Pentecostals leading the 'moral' case against the growing power and influence of the nation often called the "godless communists".

Instead of dreamy ideas about language gifts and setting sail for distant lands, today's Pentecostals are transnational, highly organised and well-connected. It's widely agreed now that we've moved well past the End of History, that period in the 1990s after the fall of communism, when many believed that there was no longer any serious competition to secular, liberal democracies with market economies. In terms of what comes next, dogmatic beliefs with practical applications are bound to be a successful recipe.

* * *

Like a magnet pulling iron filings, Pentecostalism is becoming *the* authentic representation of Christianity in the world today. In spite of its fundamentalist beliefs, the movement has already shown itself to be the future of Christian faith with its uncanny ability to stay in lockstep with the social zeitgeist. Even if denominations are refusing the label, or even shedding it, in substance an awful lot of Christian churches are becoming more Pentecostal in order to survive.[49] Hell, we've even seen Islamic and Jewish groups trying to look more like them. Equally, it can be said that, in many places, what might otherwise have been secular forms of belief are aligning with Pentecostalism too, as we've seen in the movement's convergence with the QAnon and Stop the Steal conspiracies.

Of course, it's unlikely that the faith's spectacular growth will continue forever. The zeal of the convert is an important thing, and the rising numbers of those born into the faith, not having had the same experience of the miraculous and of transformed personal circumstances, might drop out.[50] But certainly, in the parts of the world growing most quickly, Pentecostalism is, if it is not already, likely to become the dominant Christian faith—as one researcher put it, "Catholicism without priests".[51]

Taken together, the chapters of this book reveal a personalised faith that accommodates something far more mystical and individual; a worldview that appeals to 'spiritual, not religious' self-help types, yet remains distinctly political; a religious practice that fits into modern lifestyles, indulging in feel-good concerts and social media's dopamine surges, but also speaks to the outlook of extreme right-wing nativists and Christian fundamentalists who just want to go back—to an imagined past that was pure.

Towards the end of my journey through the universe of third-wave Pentecostalism, I was coming to the conclusion that the movement had become more earthly than biblical; a belief system to help believers navigate the real world, very different from the son of freed slaves and his friends stamping and screaming in a Los Angeles church, praying for salvation and fearing the End Times were upon them.

And then I came across Shannon Nuszen.

The daughter of a Texas Assemblies of God preacher and a mother who attended 'Rabbi' Curt Landry's House of David in Oklahoma, Nuszen converted to Judaism and moved to Israel in 2015—to the West Bank settlement of Gush Etzion in fact, where she trains at the IDF fantasy camp. A devout Orthodox Jew, she assured me that we hadn't been brought into each other's orbit by coincidence.

Nuszen calls herself a "missionary awareness consultant"; her calling is to further Jewish causes, both in Israel and abroad. But, as her parentage indicates, she took a slightly long and winding road to get to this point.

After being raised in the Assemblies of God and the United Pentecostal Church, Nuszen had found a Messianic Jewish congregation, which she says differed from these Pentecostal churches only in name. Here, it was clear that it was necessary to save the Jews ahead of the End Times. "The Great Commission is to preach the Gospel to the whole world. But the Jewish people, specifically, play a very important role—it's they who trigger the Second Coming of Jesus."

This was how Nuszen found herself, in the mid-2000s, as an undercover Pentecostal missionary with a Messianic Jewish congregation in Texas, infiltrating Houston synagogues to try and convert practising Jews to Jesus. "If you're out in the open, you're not very successful," Nuszen told me from her home in the settlement. "The only way to convert Jewish people is if they don't feel threatened, and because they feel they are seeing a friendly face." She worked her way into these communities, establishing relationships and connections; and, eventually, a conversation about faith would come up. That was the moment when she could explain that she believed a little differently. "I didn't instigate these conversations, so they wouldn't feel like I was proselytising, but it was my intention all along to lead them down that path so that they would ask," she explained.

But, in the end, it was Shannon herself who 'saw the light'. While studying the Jewish faith in order to become a better missionary among Jews, she encountered Tovia Singer, an American-born Orthodox rabbi who has studied the Pentecostal movement closely, and had a theological argument to counter all of Nuszen's claims. Struck by "the obvious agenda to all of the mistranslations" of Jewish texts into Christian prophecies, Nuszen began her conversion. Now, she and Rabbi Singer are working together to investigate and unmask Christian missionaries posing as Jews like she did—a problem Singer tells me is "rampant" in Israel itself.

"The Pentecostal movement is much more keyed into [the Second Coming] than other Christians," he said. "They believe that we're living in the End Times right now, that the Holy Spirit is moving. They're amped up on Jewish salvation, believing that this conversion triggers the Second Coming. Others believe it too, but Pentecostals believe that Spirit is speaking through them in an unprecedented way—and they're living it now."

In the spring of 2021, Singer and Nuszen had had enough, and began a campaign to unmask sleeper-cell missionaries working in Israel. They started with Rabbi Michael Elkohen, better known as Mike Elk, a high-ranking Orthodox figure who ran a rabbinical training school. After studying religion at a Christian college in Pennsylvania, Elk appears to have come to the Pentecostal faith, worshipping at a branch of the Vineyard church started by John Wimber, before moving to a "Messianic synagogue". Elk divorced his first wife in 2004, and appears to have figured out a loophole that could give him official recognition as a Jew. According to *The Jewish Chronicle*, which extensively verified Nuszen's and Singer's investigation, Elk had convinced his ex-wife to pose as a Jew when they married, which had led to them being granted a Jewish divorce. This had allowed Elk to receive Israeli citizenship and emigrate. The *JC* actually discovered that the 'rabbi' had already been found out once—back in 2014, when he confessed to rabbinical authorities that he was in the pay of an evangelical ministry; he had claimed to "repent", the paper reported, but simply moved neighbourhoods to continue his double life.[52]

This wasn't a one-off crazy story: Rabbi Singer says that Christians finding ways to claim Jewish identity is becoming commonplace. "There are people you can pay off," he told me. "Because you need to get a letter from a rabbi saying that you're Jewish, there are rabbis who have been bribed [or] lied to." Following the scandal that erupted in Israel after his unmasking, Elk fled the country,[53] but not before Singer and Nuszen began exposing other members of the "cell": a further ten "fake Jews" they believed were operating in Israel and the United States under Elk's leadership.

"You can't get funding in Israel for missionary activity, so the money has to come from North America, Australia, South Korea," Singer explained. "The way that we're able to catch them is when they produce YouTube videos telling their supporters what they're doing." The year before, an Israeli regulator had ordered the global evangelical station God TV to come off air, accusing it of deviating from its licence to serve a Christian audience, instead proselytising to Jews. (The broadcaster denied this, but complied.)[54]

Singer fears that replacement theology, the belief that Christians have superseded Jews as God's chosen people, is still

bubbling away under the surface of these activities. And, sometimes, above the surface—in August 2017, on the eve of the
far-right, pro-Trump 'Unite the Right' rally in Charlottesville,
Virginia, young men marched through the streets, shouting,
"Jews will not replace us!"[55]

Rabbi Singer believes that the movement to infiltrate and convert Jews is significant, and won't be slowing down any time
soon. Israel might be an all-important ideal for many Pentecostals
in their drive to build the "Kingdom Now", but so long as Jews
fail to accept Christ, nothing can save them. If he's right, then in
spite of its modern trappings, the global Pentecostal movement
hasn't moved as far as we might think from its apocalyptic vision
in those first days at Azusa Street. It's just that now, it's about
laying the path for God's rule, rather than fearing His wrath.

Seen in this light, the modern Pentecostals' command of
twenty-first-century media, politics and secular culture isn't so
much a new, soft image, but a formidable armoury for what
Singer believes is still the key to the movement: even today, it's
all about being able to *do God's stuff*. "Mainline Christianity is
falling away and losing people, and the fundamentalists are stepping in," Singer sighed. "The charismatic movement really hit a
perfect nerve—God is speaking through you—that's where
they've been extremely successful, riding what appears to be two
polar opposite views."

William J. Seymour believed that "Pentecostal power, when
you sum it all up, is just more of God's love."[56] But in reality,
today's Pentecostals have come to see the Holy Spirit not only as
the form of God's presence in their lives, but as the means of
God's empowerment.[57] They have bought into the ultimate
Pentecostal promise of a victorious life—both here and now, *and*
ever after. But today's believers have also bought into the same
principle that led Seymour to fast and study for days, in the hope
of speaking tongues: the Pentecostal idea of faith as a transac-

tion. These chosen people, who have the Spirit moving through them, have to *use* that Spirit; they have to *work* for the ultimate promise to be fulfilled.

And when you're called to war, passive faith is no longer an option.

NOTES

PREFACE

1. Richard Vijgen & Bregtje van der Haak, "Pentecostalism: Massive Global Growth Under the Radar", Pulitzer Center, 9 March 2015, https://pulitzercenter.org/stories/pentecostalism-massive-global-growth-under-radar [accessed 5/6/2021]; Isabelle V. Barker, "Engendering Charismatic Economies: Pentecostalism, Global Political Economy, and the Crisis of Social Reproduction", paper delivered at the 2005 Annual Meeting of the American Political Science Association, 1–4 September 2012, p. 2, https://web.archive.org/web/20131217004703/http://citation.allacademic.com/meta/p_mla_apa_research_citation/0/3/9/8/7/pages39879/p39879–1.php [accessed 14/6/2021].
2. *Atlas of Pentecostalism*, an online database funded by the Pulitzer Center and developed by Richard Vijgen & Bregtje van der Haak, has it at 574.953 million as of 14 June 2021: http://www.atlasofpentecostalism.net [accessed 5/6/2021]; the Pew Center has 584 million as of December 2011: Pew Forum on Religion and Public Life, "Global Christianity: A Report on the Size and Distribution of the World's Christian Population", December 2011, p. 17, available at https://www.pewforum.org/2011/12/19/global-christianity-exec/ [accessed 14/6/2021]; *Christianity Today* had 644 million as of May 2020: Daniel Silliman, "Have Pentecostals Outgrown Their Name?", *Christianity Today*, 29 May 2020, https://www.christianitytoday.com/news/2020/may/holy-spirit-empowered-christian-global-pentecostal-study.html [accessed 14/6/2021].
3. Vijgen & van der Haak, *Atlas of Pentecostalism*.
4. Silliman, "Have Pentecostals Outgrown Their Name?"; Aaron Earls, "10 Key Trends in Global Christianity for 2017", Lifeway Research, https://lifewayresearch.com/2016/12/12/10-key-trends-in-global-christianity-for-2017/ [accessed 14/6/2021].

5. Vijgen & van der Haak, *Atlas of Pentecostalism*.
6. Ryan Burge, "Think US evangelicals are dying out? Well, define evangelicalism...", *The Conversation*, 26 January 2021, https://theconversation.com/think-us-evangelicals-are-dying-out-well-define-evangelicalism-152640 [accessed 5/7/2021].
7. *The Economist*, "Africa's population will double by 2050", 28 March 2020, https://www.economist.com/special-report/2020/03/26/africas-population-will-double-by-2050 [accessed 11/6/2021].

1. THE LAST VOMIT OF SATAN

1. Allan Heaton Anderson, *An Introduction to Pentecostalism*, 2nd edn (Cambridge: Cambridge University Press, 2013), p. 38.
2. *Christianity Today*, "Phoebe Palmer: Mother of the holiness movement", n.d., https://www.christianitytoday.com/history/people/moversandshakers/phoebe-palmer.html [accessed 5/6/2021].
3. Grant Wacker, *Heaven Below: Early Pentecostals and American Culture* (Cambridge, MA: Harvard University Press, 2001), p. 10.
4. Ibid., p. 114.
5. Ibid., p. 6.
6. Jonathan B. Root, *A People's Religion: The Populist Impulse in Early Kansas Pentecostalism, 1901–1904*, MA thesis, Kansas State University, 2009, p. 38, https://core.ac.uk/download/pdf/5165399.pdf [accessed 5/6/2021].
7. *The Topeka Capital-Journal*, "Ministry revitalizes historic building", 2 April 2011, https://www.cjonline.com/article/20110402/news/304029873 [accessed 11/6/2021].
8. *Revival Library*, "Charles Fox Parham (1873–1929)", n.d., https://www.revival-library.org/revival_heroes/20th_century/parham_charles_fox.shtml [accessed 7/6/2021].
9. Anderson, *Introduction to Pentecostalism*, pp. 21–2.
10. New International Version Bible, 1 Corinthians 12:8–10.
11. *Revival Library*, "Charles Fox Parham".
12. Gastón Espinosa, *William J. Seymour and the Origins of Global Pentecostalism: A Biography and Documentary History* (Durham, NC: Duke University Press, 2014), p. 46.
13. Ibid., p. 69.
14. Ibid.
15. Ibid., p. 40.
16. Cecil M. Robeck Jr, *The Azusa Street Mission and Revival: The Birth of the Global Pentecostal Movement* (Nashville, TN: Thomas Nelson, 2006) p. 9.

17. Ibid., p. 12.
18. Ibid., p. 6.
19. Espinosa, *Origins*, p. 205.
20. Randall H. Balmer, *Encyclopedia of Evangelicalism* (Waco, TX: Baylor University Press, 2004), p. 391.
21. Robeck Jr, *Azusa Street*, p. 270.
22. *Time*, "Religion: McPherson v. Voliva", 16 September 1929, http://content. time.com/time/magazine/article/0,9171,737880,00.html [accessed 7/6/2021].
23. Daniel Long, "The Parhamite Killings", *The Messed Up Church*, 9 June 2019, https://www.themessedupchurch.com/blog/the-parhamite-killings [accessed 7/6/2021].
24. Wacker, *Heaven Below*, p. 16.
25. Robeck Jr, *Azusa Street*, p. 35.
26. Wacker, *Heaven Below*, p. 19.
27. Marshall Trimble, "Aimee Semple McPherson Part I", *True West*, December 2017, https://truewestmagazine.com/article/aimee-semple-mcpherson-part-i/ [accessed 7/6/2021].
28. Wacker, *Heaven Below*, p. 33.
29. Naomi Grimley, "The mysterious disappearance of a celebrity preacher", BBC News, 25 November 2014, https://www.bbc.com/news/magazine-30148022 [accessed 14/6/2021].
30. Gilbert King, "The Incredible Disappearing Evangelist", *Smithsonian Magazine*, 17 June 2013, https://www.smithsonianmag.com/history/the-incredible-disappearing-evangelist-572829/ [accessed 11/6/2021].
31. Gary Krist, "Aimee Semple McPherson: The L.A. evangelist who built the world's first megachurch", *Los Angeles Times*, 24 June 2018, https://www.latimes.com/opinion/op-ed/la-oe-krist-aimee-semple-mcpherson-20180624-story.html [accessed 7/6/2021].

2. I JUST SING LIKE THEY DO BACK HOME

1. Associated Press, "'Alabama Snake' to tell story of snake-handling preacher", 5 December 2020, https://apnews.com/article/alabama-birmingham-scottsboro-3ce9bc1b417f527741d67de2531da09b [accessed 7/6/2021].
2. Jessica Diaz-Hurtado, "Forebears: Sister Rosetta Tharpe, The Godmother Of Rock 'N' Roll", NPR, 24 August 2017, https://www.npr.org/2017/08/24/544226085/forebears-sister-rosetta-tharpe-the-godmother-of-rock-n-roll [accessed 10/6/2021].
3. Randall J. Stephens, *The Devil's Music: How Christians Inspired, Condemned, and Embraced Rock 'n' Roll* (Cambridge, MA: Harvard University Press, 2018), p. 37.

4. Bruce Warren & Alex Lewis, "Sister Rosetta Tharpe Gets Her Day In The Rock & Roll Hall Of Fame", NPR, 12 April 2018, https://www.npr.org/sections/world-cafe/2018/04/12/601808069/sister-rosetta-tharpe-gets-her-day-in-the-rock-roll-hall-of-fame [accessed 7/6/2021].

5. Melissa Ruggieri, "Sister Rosetta Tharpe: Singer influenced key rock 'n' roll figures", *The Atlanta Journal-Constitution*, 9 May 2020, https://www.ajc.com/entertainment/music/sister-rosetta-tharpe-singer-influenced-key-rock-roll-figures/UTzkpIsRNvvenWoaTGamtM/ [accessed 7/6/2021].

6. Stephens, *Devil's Music*, p. 39.

7. Ibid., p. 40.

8. Richard Riss, "The Latter Rain Movement of 1948 and the Mid-Twentieth Century Evangelical Awakening", *Pneuma* 4.1, 1 January 1982, p. 35.

9. David Di Sabatino (dir.), *Frisbee: The Life and Death of a Hippie Preacher*, Jester Media, 2005.

10. *Christianity Today*, "Wimber's Wonders", 9 February 1998, https://www.christianitytoday.com/ct/1998/february9/8t2015.html [accesssed 14/6/2021].

11. Donald Kammer, "The Perplexing Power Of John Wimber's Power Encounters", *Churchman*, 106.1, p. 46, available at https://churchsociety.org/docs/churchman/106/Cman_106_1_Kammer.pdf [accessed 8/6/2021].

12. John Wimber & Kevin Springer, *Power Evangelism* (Delight, AR: Gospel Light Publications, 2009), p. 14.

13. Ibid., p. 77.

14. Vineyard Church Mombasa, "Doing the Stuff", YouTube, 25 January 2013, https://www.youtube.com/watch?v=U7wLM77curg [accessed 15/6/2021].

15. Di Sabatino, *Frisbee*.

16. Ibid.

17. John Dart & Bonnie Hayes, "Renowned Pastor Wimber Dies at 63", *Los Angeles Times*, 18 November 1997, https://www.latimes.com/archives/la-xpm-1997-nov-18-me-55098-story.html [accessed 7/6/2021].

18. Some scholars call this the third wave, but I have used the 'second wave' definition—for ease of reference, and because I believe that there is a clear delineation between the charismatic wave and the neo-charismatic wave.

19. T.M. Luhrmann, "Blinded by the Right? How hippie Christians begat evangelical conservatives", *Harper's Magazine*, April 2013, https://harpers.org/archive/2013/04/blinded-by-the-right/ [accessed 7/6/2021].

20. Brad Christerson & Richard Flory, *The Rise of Network Christianity: How Independent Leaders Are Changing the Religious Landscape* (New York, NY: Oxford University Press, 2017), pp. 20–1.

21. Andrew McCarron, "The year Bob Dylan was born again: a timeline", *OUPblog*,

21 January 2017, https://blog.oup.com/2017/01/bob-dylan-christianity/ [accessed 8/6/2021].

22. Allan Heaton Anderson, *An Introduction to Pentecostalism*, 2nd edn (Cambridge: Cambridge University Press, 2013), p. 79.

23. Elisha Fieldstadt, "Founder of Hillsong Church says he had concerns about disgraced former pastor Carl Lentz for years", NBC News, 19 May 2021, https://www.nbcnews.com/news/us-news/founder-hillsong-church-says-he-had-concerns-about-disgraced-former-n1267842 [accessed 11/6/2021].

24. Hillsong Australia, "Hillsong Church Annual Report 2019", June 2020, https://issuu.com/hillsong/docs/hillsong_annual_report_2019?fr=sMzU3Yj E5MzkzNDg [accessed 8/6/2021].

25. Christerson & Flory, *Network Christianity*, p. 106.

26. Keith Caulfield, "P!nk's 'Hurts 2B Human' Album Debuts at No. 1 on Billboard 200 Chart", Billboard, 6 May 2019, https://www.billboard.com/articles/columns/chart-beat/8510202/pink-hurts-2b-human-album-debuts-number-1-billboard-200-chart [accessed 14/6/2021].

27. Kelsey McKinney, "How Hillsong Church conquered the music industry in God's name", *The Fader*, 11 October 2018, https://www.thefader.com/2018/10/11/hillsong-church-worship-songs-music-industry [accessed 8/6/2021].

28. Hillsong Channel tweet, 24 January 2020, https://twitter.com/hillsongchannel/status/1220712990493769730 [accessed 8/6/2021].

29. Hillsong Australia, "Annual Report 2019", p. 87.

30. Author interview with Professor Scott Thumma, 20 July 2020.

31. McKinney, "How Hillsong Church conquered the music industry".

32. John Elder, "Ten wary of false idols—and rivals", *The Age*, 7 October 2007, https://www.theage.com.au/entertainment/ten-wary-of-false-idols-and-rivals-20071007-ge5zq3.html [accessed 8/6/2021].

33. Michael Giltz, "American Idol 'Shout to the Lord' Controversy and Results", *Huffington Post*, 10 April 2008, https://www.huffpost.com/entry/emamericanidolem-jesus-c_b_96176 [accessed 8/6/2021].

34. New International Version Bible, Colossians 3:16.

35. New International Version Bible, Revelation 14:3.

36. Chris Graham, "Hillsong On Marriage Equality: How To Dog Whistle Hate Without Even Really Trying", *New Matilda*, 20 August 2017, https://newmatilda.com/2017/08/20/hillsong-church-on-marriage-equality-how-to-dog-whistle-hate-without-even-really-trying/ [accessed 8/6/2021].

37. Rachel DeSantis, "Hillsong Founder Says Carl Lentz Had Multiple 'Significant' Affairs in Leaked Audio: Report", *People*, 4 December 2020, https://people.com/human-interest/hillsong-founder-leaked-audio-carl-lentz-affairs-report/ [accessed 8/6/2021].

38. Fergus Hunter et al., "Hillsong pastor Brian Houston charged for allegedly concealing child sexual abuse by his father", *The Sydney Morning Herald*, 5 August 2021, https://www.smh.com.au/national/nsw/hillsong-pastor-brian-houston-charged-for-allegedly-concealing-child-sexual-abuse-by-his-father-20210805-p58g7z.html [accessed 19/8/2021].

3. IF GOD MESSES WITH ME, HE'S DEAD

1. Author interview with Chanyang Ju (trans. Grace Moon), 29 January 2021.

3. Pew Research Center, "Historical Overview of Pentecostalism in South Korea", 5 October 2006, https://www.pewforum.org/2006/10/05/historical-overview-of-pentecostalism-in-south-korea/ [accessed 8/6/2021]; Center for International Affairs, Academy of Korean Studies, "Geography of Korea: Population Growth", http://cefia.aks.ac.kr:84/index.php?title=GK:2.1.1_Population_Growth#.282.29_Population_during_the_Japanese_occupation_period_.281910.E2.80.931945.29 [accessed 8/6/2021].

4. Grant Wacker, *Heaven Below: Early Pentecostals and American Culture* (Cambridge, MA: Harvard University Press, 2001), p. 192.

5. Dave Hazzan, "Christianity and Korea: How did the religion become so apparently prevalent in South Korea?", *The Diplomat*, 7 April 2016, https://thediplomat.com/2016/04/christianity-and-korea/ [accessed 8/6/2021].

6. James H. Grayson, *Korea: A Religious History* (London: Routledge, 2002), p. 174.

7. B.R. Myers, *The Cleanest Race: How North Koreans See Themselves—And Why It Matters* (Brooklyn, NY: Melville House, 2011), p. 176.

8. Hazzan, "Christianity and Korea".

9. Matthew Bell, "The biggest megachurch on Earth and South Korea's 'crisis of evangelism'", Public Radio International, *The World*, 1 May 2017, https://www.pri.org/stories/2017–05–01/biggest-megachurch-earth-facing-crisis-evangelism [accessed 8/6/2021]; Andrew Johnson, "A Crisis of Integrity in Seoul, the Megachurch Capital of the World", Center for Religion and Civic Culture, 9 February 2016, https://crcc.usc.edu/a-crisis-of-integrity-in-seoul-the-megachurch-capital-of-the-world/ [accessed 8/6/2021].

10. BBC News, "South Korean balloons: Plans to stop people sending cross-border messages", 4 June 2020, https://www.bbc.com/news/world-asia-52917029 [accessed 15/6/2021].

11. Robert R. King, "Number of North Korean Defectors Drops to Lowest Level in Two Decades", Center for Strategic & International Studies, 27 January 2021, https://www.csis.org/analysis/number-north-korean-defectors-drops-lowest-level-two-decades [accessed 8/6/2021].

12. Men are more likely to flee for political reasons, such as problems in the mil-

itary hierarchy, but the vast majority of North Korean defectors are women. Wikipedia cites South Korea's Unification Ministry on this: Wikipedia, "North Korean defectors", last edited 11 June 2021, https://en.wikipedia.org/wiki/North_Korean_defectors#Demographics [accessed 11/6/2021].

13. Myers, *Cleanest Race*, p. 16.
14. Author interview with Professor Jin-Heon Jung, 1 April 2020.
15. Myers, *Cleanest Race*, p. 51.
16. Wikipedia, "North Korean defectors".
17. Interview with Chanyang Ju.
18. Interview with Jin-Heon Jung.
19. Ibid.
20. Myers, *Cleanest Race*, p. 76.
21. Ibid.
22. Daniel Goodkind & Loraine West, "The North Korean Famine and Its Demographic Impact", *Population and Development Review* 27.2, 2001, pp. 219–38.
23. Victor Cha, *The Impossible State: North Korea, Past and Future* (New York, NY: Ecco, 2012), p. 425.
24. Nadja Sayej, "Defector TV: the North Korean escapees who sparked a reality show craze", *The Guardian*, 13 April 2016, https://www.theguardian.com/tv-and-radio/2016/apr/13/defector-tv-the-north-korean-escapees-who-sparked-a-reality-show-craze [accessed 8/6/2021].
25. Liat Clark, "Believing in God can trigger the same reward regions of the brain as taking drugs", *Wired*, 30 November 2016, https://www.wired.co.uk/article/mormons-experience-religion-like-drug-takers-feel-highs-neuroscientists-say [accessed 8/6/2021].
26. Allan Anderson et al. (eds), *Studying Global Pentecostalism: Theories and Methods* (Berkeley, CA: University of California Press), p. 96.
27. That said, the number of supporters for reunification is dropping, particularly among younger people, who prefer peaceful coexistence.
28. Jin-Heon Jung, "The post-division (Christian) citizenship: the Christian encounters of North Korean migrants and South Korean Protestant Church (completed)", Max Planck Institute for the Study of Religious and Ethnic Diversity, n.d., https://www.mmg.mpg.de/266382/the-post-division-christian-citizenship [accessed 8/6/2021].
29. Sarah Eunkyung Chee, "Borders of Belonging: Nationalism, North Korean Defectors, and the Spiritual Project for a Unified Korea", DPhil thesis, University of California Santa Cruz, December 2015, p. 132, https://escholarship.org/uc/item/7200m3ft [accessed 14/6/2021].
30. Author interview with Yoseb Shin, translated by Grace Moon, 20 February 2021.

31. Barbara Demick, *Nothing to Envy: Ordinary Lives in North Korea* (New York, NY: Spiegel & Grau, 2009), p. 460.

32. Bell, "The biggest megachurch on Earth".

33. J.Y. Lee, "Korean Megachurches Debate If Pastors' Kids Can Inherit Pulpits", *Christianity Today*, 12 July 2019, https://www.christianitytoday.com/news/2019/july/myungsung-presbyterian-church-korea-pck-pastoral-succession.html [accessed 29/6/2021].

34. BBC News, "South Korean pastor Lee Jae-rock jailed for raping followers", 22 November 2018, https://www.bbc.com/news/world-asia-46299239 [accessed 21/6/2021].

35. Bell, "The biggest megachurch on Earth".

36. Mt King, "A CCK Pastor just threatened God 'Don't mess with me God. If God messes with me, he's dead.'", YouTube, 23 December 2019, https://www.youtube.com/watch?v=wdyWUBzqkMg [accessed 10/6/2021].

37. Lee Yong-pil, "Jeon Kwang-hoon: 'The only thing that can blow homosexuality and shogunate in one shot is the Christian Liberal Party': Feast of Fake News—CCK 'Christian Leader' Forum, 'People who lack the Juche idea take control of the Blue House'" (in Korean), *News & Joy*, 23 May 2019, https://www.newsnjoy.or.kr/news/articleView.html?idxno=223661 [accessed 29/6/2021].

38. Yoon Won-sup, "Muslim Community Gets New Recognition", *Korea Times*, archived, n.d., https://web.archive.org/web/20170613124702/http://www.islamkorea.com/english/articlean2.html [accessed 8/6/2021].

39. *New Straits Times*, "S. Korea jails pastor linked to Covid-19 resurgence", 9 September 2020, https://www.nst.com.my/world/region/2020/09/623143/s-korea-jails-pastor-linked-covid-19-resurgence [accessed 8/6/2021].

40. Ock Hyun-ju, "Potential clusters of COVID-19 virus emerge outside Daegu", *The Korea Herald*, 25 February 2020, http://www.koreaherald.com/view.php?ud=20200225000788 [accessed 8/6/2021].

41. Michael Breen, *The Koreans: Who They Are, What They Want, Where Their Future Lies* (New York, NY: St. Martin's, 2004), p. 115; author interview with Dr Sung-gun Kim, 24 May 2019.

42. Martin Farrer et al., "Coronavirus: South Korea to test 200,000 sect members as pandemic fears hit markets", *The Guardian*, 25 February 2020, https://www.theguardian.com/world/2020/feb/25/coronavirus-south-korea-to-test-200000-sect-members-as-pandemic-fears-hit-markets [accessed 21/6/2021].

4. THE FATHER, THE SONS AND THE HOLY MESS

1. Pastor Anderson Do Carmo, Instagram post, 20 May 2019, https://www.instagram.com/p/Bxq5ALCD952/ [accessed 15/6/2021].

2. Marina Lang, "Pastor killed in RJ founded church with deputy wife and adopted 51 children" (in Portuguese), UOL, 17 June 2019, https://noticias.uol.com. br/cotidiano/ultimas-noticias/2019/06/17/pastor-morto-no-rj-fundou-igreja-com-esposa-deputada-e-adotou-51-criancas.htm?cmpid=copiaecola [accessed 12/6/2021].

3. Maria Martha Bruno, "Congresswoman, evangelical, community leader—and murderer?", *The Brazilian Report*, 20 July 2019, https://brazilian.report/power/2019/07/20/flordelis-congresswoman-evangelical-community-leader-murderer/ [accessed 12/6/2021].

4. *O Globo*, "The family that Flordelis formed was considered a model of love and solidarity" (in Portuguese), 24 August 2020, https://g1.globo.com/jornal-nacional/noticia/2020/08/24/familia-que-flordelis-formou-era-considerada-modelo-de-amor-e-solidariedade.ghtml [accessed 12/6/2021].

5. *O Globo*, "Flordelis case has fight over money, betrayal, possible poisoning and arrests" (in Portuguese), 24 August 2020, https://ultimosegundo.ig.com.br/brasil/2020–08–24/caso-flordelis-tem-briga-por-dinheiro-traicao-possivel-en-venenamento-e-prisoes.html [accessed 12/6/2021].

6. Carolina Heringer, "How Anderson do Carmo transformed Flordelis into a celebrity" (in Portuguese), *Globo Era*, 22 August 2019, https://epoca.globo. com/brasil/como-anderson-do-carmo-transformou-flordelis-em-celebri-dade-23894431 [accessed 12/6/2021].

7. Plataforma, "Brazilian deputy had sex with her husband hours before ordering his death", 2 September 2020, https://www.plataformamedia.com/en/2020/09/02/brazilian-deputy-had-sex-with-her-husband-hours-before-ordering-his-death/ [accessed 12/6/2021].

8. Jon Lee Anderson, "The Murder Scandalizing Brazil's Evangelical Church", *The New Yorker*, 7 June 2021, https://www.newyorker.com/magazine/2021/06/14/the-murder-scandalizing-brazils-evangelical-church [accessed 14/6/2021].

9. C.H. Gardiner, "Husband of Brazilian Federal Deputy Assassinated", C.H. Gardiner website, n.d., https://chgardiner.com/husband-of-brazilian-fed-eral-deputy-assassinated- [accessed 12/6/2021].

10. Alexis Schwartz, "Congresswoman, Gospel Singer, Murder Suspect: The Wild Story of Flordelis", *MEL*, April 2021, https://melmagazine.com/en-us/story/congresswoman-gospel-singer-murder-suspect-the-wild-story-of-flordelis [accessed 12/6/2021].

11. Raquel Zanatta Coutinho & André Braz Golgher, "The changing landscape of religious affiliation in Brazil between 1980 and 2010: age, period, and cohort perspectives", *Revista Brasileira de Estudos de População*, 31.1, 2014.

12. Eduardo Campos Lima, "As evangelicals gain, Catholics on verge of losing

majority in Brazil", *National Catholic Reporter*, 5 February 2020, https://www.ncronline.org/news/parish/evangelicals-gain-catholics-verge-losing-majority-brazil [accessed 21/6/2021]; IGBE Brazil, "2010 Census: number of Catholics falls and that of Evangelicals, Spiritists and those without religion increases" (in Portuguese), 29 June 2012, https://agenciadenoticias.ibge.gov.br/agencia-sala-de-imprensa/2013-agencia-de-noticias/releases/14244-asi-censo-2010-numero-de-catolicos-cai-e-aumenta-o-de-evangelicos-espiritas-e-sem-religiao [accessed 21/6/2021].

13. Alex Cuadros, *Brazillionaires: Wealth, Power, Decadence, and Hope in an American Country* (London: Profile Books, 2016), p. 118.

14. Kate Bowler, *Blessed: A History of the American Prosperity Gospel* (New York, NY: Oxford University Press, 2013), p. 45.

15. Ibid., p. 137.

16. Ibid., p. 133.

17. Ibid., p. 234.

18. Ibid., p. 303.

19. Bishop Edir Macedo official website, "Official inauguration of the Temple of Solomon", 2014, https://blogs.universal.org/bispomacedo/en/timeline-of-bishop/official-inauguration-of-the-temple-of-solomon/ [accessed 12/6/2021].

20. Sarah Pulliam Bailey, "How the prosperity gospel is sparking a major change in predominantly Catholic Brazil", *The Washington Post*, 31 October 2017, https://www.washingtonpost.com/local/social-issues/forget-the-germans-this-is-where-the-protestant-reformation-debates-are-happening-now/2017/10/29/7723af30-b807-11e7-be94-fabb0f1e9ffb_story.html [accessed 12/6/2021].

21. UN, *2019 Revision of World Population Prospects*, cited by Macrotrends, "Sao Paulo, Brazil Metro Area Population 1950–2021", n.d., https://www.macrotrends.net/cities/20287/sao-paulo/population [accessed 21/6/2021].

22. Allan Heaton Anderson, *An Introduction to Pentecostalism*, 2nd edn (Cambridge: Cambridge University Press, 2013), p. 63. For more on the bad blood between the Pope and El Verbo, see Russell Watson, "John Paul Goes To War", *Newsweek*, 2 November 1996, https://www.newsweek.com/john-paul-goes-war-179730 [accessed 12/7/2021].

23. Cuadros, *Brazillionaires*, p. 262.

24. Ibid., pp. 280–1; Tom Phillips, "Brazil charges church leaders with embezzling millions from poor", *The Guardian*, 13 September 2011, https://www.theguardian.com/world/2011/sep/13/brazil-church-embezzling-millions-poor [accessed 22/6/2021].

25. Anthony Faiola & Marina Lopes, "This Brazilian pastor said he was saving souls. Police say he ran a slave-labor ring", *The Washington Post*, 14 April 2018, https://www.washingtonpost.com/world/the_americas/this-brazilian-pastor-

said-he-was-saving-souls-police-say-he-ran-a-slave-labor-ring-/2018/04/14/184c87fe-230d-11e8-946c-9420060cb7bd_story.html [accessed 21/6/2021].

26. Anderson, "The Murder Scandalizing Brazil's Evangelical Church".

27. *Forum*, "Universal Church relaunches a book that treats Afro-Brazilian religions as 'demonic'" (in Portuguese), 5 August 2019, https://revistaforum.com.br/brasil/igreja-universal-relanca-livro-que-trata-religioes-afro-brasileiras-como-demoniacas/ [accessed 12/6/2021].

28. Juan Fernandez Gonzalez, "Globo telenovelas draw 50% of Brazilian viewers", Rapid TV News, 15 September 2017, https://www.rapidtvnews.com/2017091548835/globo-telenovelas-draw-50-of-brazilian-viewers.html#axzz6aku5lcHd [accessed 12/6/2021].

29. Cuadros, *Brazillionaires*, p. 212.

30. Bruno, "Congresswoman, evangelical".

31. Anderson, "The Murder Scandalizing Brazil's Evangelical Church".

32. Heringer, "How Anderson transformed Flordelis".

33. Tom Phillips, "Brazilian evangelical politician accused of masterminding husband's 'barbaric' murder", *The Guardian*, 24 August 2020, https://www.theguardian.com/world/2020/aug/24/flordelis-case-brazil-evangelical-preacher-politician-accusations [accessed 12/6/2021].

34. *O Globo*, "Flordelis case: Two years after death of pastor, recalling family plots with fighting over money, reports of sexual abuse and suspected poisoning" (in Portuguese), 16 June 2021, [accessed 22/6/2021].

35. Heringer, "How Anderson do Carmo transformed Flordelis".

36. iG, "Flordelis received prophecy of the death of a pastor, but disdained: 'Dog prophetess'" (in Portuguese), 27 June 2019, https://ultimosegundo.ig.com.br/politica/2019–06–27/flordelis-recebeu-profecia-da-morte-de-pastor-mas-desdenhou-profetiza-do-cao.html [accessed 12/6/2021].

37. *O Globo*, "The family that Flordelis formed was considered a model of love and solidarity" (in Portuguese), 24 August 2020, https://g1.globo.com/jornal-nacional/noticia/2020/08/24/familia-que-flordelis-formou-era-considerada-modelo-de-amor-e-solidariedade.ghtml [accessed 12/6/2021].

38. Carolina Heringer, "Casa de Flordelis had secret rituals with nudity, sex and even blood, reveals witness" (in Portuguese), *Globo Extra*, 22 June 2020, https://extra.globo.com/casos-de-policia/casa-de-flordelis-tinha-rituais-secretos-com-nudez-sexo-ate-sangue-revela-testemunha-rv1-1-24491691.html [accessed 12/6/2021].

39. Carolina Heringer, "Flordelis' son tells police his mother had a baseball bat 'for hitting others'", *Globo Extra*, 17 June 2020, https://extra.globo.com/casos-de-policia/filho-de-flordelis-diz-policia-que-mae-tinha-taco-de-beisebol-para-bater-nos-outros-24482977.html [accessed 18/6/2021].

40. O Globo, "The family that Flordelis formed".
41. Vianne Burog, "Brazilian Evangelical Congresswoman Masterminded Husband's Brutal Murder, Police Says", *Latin Times*, 25 August 2020, https://www.latintimes.com/brazilian-evangelical-congresswoman-masterminded-husbands-brutal-murder-police-says-461120#:~:text=Nunes%20concluded%20that%20about%2020,been%20arrested%20for%20the%20crime [accessed 12/6/2021].
42. Rodrigo Viga Gaier & Gram Slattery, "Former Brazil congresswoman goes to jail on charges of killing husband", Reuters, 14 August 2021, https://www.reuters.com/world/americas/former-brazil-congresswoman-goes-jail-charges-killing-husband-2021-08-14/ [accessed 20/8/2021].
43. *O Globo*, "Flordelis case".
44. BBC News, "Flordelis de Souza: Brazilian MP accused of ordering husband's murder", 24 August 2020, https://www.bbc.co.uk/news/world-latin-america-53895457 [accessed 12/6/2021],
45. *Hora do Povo*, "It has to be said" (in Portuguese), 9 September 2020, https://horadopovo.com.br/tem-que-ser-dito/ [accessed 12/6/2021].
46. Author interview with Professor Andrew Chesnut, 19 October 2020.
47. Claudia Zilla, "Evangelicals and Politics in Brazil: The Relevance of Religious Change in Latin America", Stiftung Wissenschaft und Politik (SWP), Research Paper 2020/RP 01, 17 January 2020, https://www.swp-berlin.org/10.18449/2020RP01/#en-d37459e405 [accessed 12/6/2021].
48. Francisco Costa et al., "Stop Suffering! Economic Downturns and Pentecostal Upsurge", EPGE Escola Brasileira de Economia e Finanças, Paper No. 815, December 2019, p. 20, http://bibliotecadigital.fgv.br/dspace/bitstream/handle/10438/28596/fgv-epge-ensaio-economico-815.pdf;jsessionid=C525C5E0BD40556A28EAB7ED81CEE696?sequence=1 [accessed 21/6/2021].
49. Gustavo Ribeiro, "Lula's plan to get the evangelical vote", *The Brazilian Report*, 13 January 2020, https://brazilian.report/newsletters/brazil-weekly/2020/01/13/lula-workers-party-bidding-evangelical-voters/ [accessed 12/6/2021].

5. THE BIGGER THE PROPHECY, THE BIGGER THE POCKET

1. Allan Heaton Anderson, *An Introduction to Pentecostalism*, 2nd edn (Cambridge: Cambridge University Press, 2013), p. 121.
2. Ibid., pp. 127–8.
3. Ibid., p. 54.
4. Ibid., pp. 43–5.
5. Barry Morton, "The Big Con: John Alexander Dowie and the Spread of Zionist Christianity in Southern Africa", paper presented at the University of Leiden,

African Studies Center, 20 June 2013, https://www.academia.edu/6779053/ The_Big_Con_John_Alexander_Dowie_and_the_Spread_of_Zionist_ Christianity_in_Southern_Africa_Paper_Presented_at_the [accessed 13/6/2021].

6. Allan Heaton Anderson, *Spirit-Filled World: Religious Dis/Continuity in African Pentecostalism* (London: Palgrave Macmillan, 2018), p. 52.

7. Barry Morton, "Yes, John G Lake was a con man: a response to Marius Nel", *Studia Historiae Ecclesiasticae* 43.2, 2017, http://www.scielo.org.za/scielo. php?script=sci_arttext&pid=S1017–04992017000200002 [accessed 12/6/2021].

8. Cecil M. Robeck Jr, *The Azusa Street Mission and Revival: The Birth of the Global Pentecostal Movement* (Nashville, TN: Thomas Nelson, 2006), p. 12.

9. Solomon Kgatle, *The Fourth Pentecostal Wave in South Africa: A Critical Engagement* (Oxford: Routledge, 2020), p. 24.

10. Ibid., p. 26.

11. Abram Mashego, "Bushiri empire crashes—state looks to seize assets including luxury cars, private jet", *City Press*, 4 February 2019, https://www.news24. com/citypress/news/bushiri-empire-crashes-state-looks-to-seize-assets-including-luxury-cars-private-jet-20190203 [accessed 21/6/2021]; Lily Kuo, "Malawian pastor defends buying a third private jet by saying, 'I am what God says. I was born a winner'", *Quartz Africa*, 8 January 2016, https://qz.com/ africa/589558/malawian-pastor-defends-buying-a-third-private-jet-by-saying-i-am-what-god-says-i-was-born-a-winner/ [accessed 21/6/2021].

12. Reuters, "Malawi court frees pastor wanted in South Africa for fraud, money-laundering", 19 November 2020, https://www.reuters.com/article/malawi-safrica-bushiri/malawi-court-frees-pastor-wanted-in-south-africa-for-fraud-money-laundering-idINKBN27Z2MJ [accessed 21/6/2021].

13. BBC News, "Shepherd Bushiri: Preacher flees South Africa ahead of fraud trial", 15 November 2020, https://www.bbc.com/news/world-africa-54949819 [accessed 13/6/2021].

14. Sam Matthew, "Video: It's a miracle (that anyone takes this preacher seriously): Zimbabwe prophet's attempt to prove he can 'walk on air' falls flat thanks to one rather obvious giveaway", *MailOnline*, 1 October 2015, https://www.dailymail.co.uk/video/news/video-1218290/Christian-preacher-Shepherd-Bushiri-walks-air.html [accessed 13/6/2021].

15. Shepherd Bushiri, *Prophetic Codes* (Pretoria: SB Publishers, 2018), p. v.

16. Cara Anna, "Post-apartheid South Africa is world's most unequal country", AP, 7 May 2019, https://apnews.com/article/nelson-mandela-elections-south-africa-international-news-johannesburg-a1cd5ebc5ed24a7088d970d30bb04ba1 [accessed 13/6/2021].

17. Kgatle, *Fourth Pentecostal Wave in South Africa*, p. 25.

18. *The Citizen*, "Pastor Lesego 'cooks' Mpumalanga man", 10 August 2015, https://

citizen.co.za/news/south-africa/445285/pastor-lesego-cooks-mpumalanga-man/ [accessed 29/6/2021].

19. Nehanda Radio, "We are the Church of Horror—Pastor Penuel Mnguni", 26 May 2015, https://nehandaradio.com/2015/05/26/we-are-the-church-of-horror-pastor-penuel-mnguni/ [accessed 29/6/2021].

20. Inemesit Udodiong, "SA pastor tells church members to masturbate, they obey! [PHOTO]", *Pulse*, 26 January 2017, https://www.pulse.ng/communities/religion/penuel-mnguni-sa-pastor-tells-church-members-to-masturbate-they-obey-photo/7w70fe3 [accessed 29/6/2021].

21. BBC News, "The men who claim to be Africa's 'miracle workers'", 27 November 2016, https://www.bbc.com/news/world-africa-38063882 [accessed 18/6/2021].

22. God's Voice International Ministry, Facebook post, 20 November 2016, https://www.facebook.com/Lethebo/posts/821196644690136 [accessed 21/6/2021].

23. BBC News, "South Africa's 'Doom Pastor' found guilty of assault", 9 February 2018, https://www.bbc.co.uk/news/world-africa-43002701 [accessed 29/6/2021].

24. Khaya Koko, "Prophet slapped with lawsuit for resurrection hoax", IOL, 26 February 2019, https://www.iol.co.za/the-star/news/prophet-slapped-with-lawsuit-for-resurrection-hoax-19511570 [accessed 21/6/2021].

25. CBN, "Daniel: Raised from the Dead", n.d., https://www1.cbn.com/700club/daniel-raised-dead [accessed 13/6/2021].

26. Karl Maier, "Planned Christian Revival Sparks Riots in Nigeria", *The Washington Post*, 20 October 1991, https://www.washingtonpost.com/archive/politics/1991/10/20/planned-christian-revival-sparks-riots-in-nigeria/c5023a4a-08c9-45d2-bfcf-667bfaec89cb/ [accessed 21/6/2021].

27. Heidi Baker & Rolland Baker, "Back from the Dead", Iris Global, 14 January 2002, https://www.irisglobal.org/newsletters/back-from-the-dead [accessed 13/6/2021].

28. Author interview with Professor Candy Gunther Brown, 18 November 2020.

29. Candy Gunther Brown et al., "Study of the Therapeutic Effects of Proximal Intercessory Prayer (STEPP) on Auditory and Visual Impairments in Rural Mozambique", *Southern Medical Journal* X.XX, 2010, p. 2.

30. Ibid., p. 3.

6. DO YOU KNOW THE ONE ABOUT THE GOOD SAMARITAN?

1. David Child, "In historic first, Roma included as ethnicity on UK census", Al Jazeera, 19 March 2021, https://www.aljazeera.com/features/2021/3/19/hold-uk-roma-census-2021 [accessed 18/6/2021].

2. Bishop Dr Joe Aldred, "Pentecostalism in Britain today: Making up for failures of the past", LSE Blog, 25 November 2016, https://blogs.lse.ac.uk/africaatlse/2016/11/25/pentecostalism-in-britain-today-making-up-for-failures-of-the-past/ [accessed 13/6/2021].

3. Katharine Quarmby, *Romani Pilgrims: Europe's New Moral Force* (eBook: Newsweek Insights, 2014), quoted in Sarah Hughes, "How Tyson Fury's words shine a light on Traveller faith", *The Guardian*, 13 December 2015, https://www.theguardian.com/sport/2015/dec/13/tyson-fury-traveller-faith [accessed 13/6/2021].

4. Susan Nadathur, "Waiting on Dibel: The Growth of Pentecostalism among Spanish Gypsies", Missio Nexus, 1 April 2011, https://missionexus.org/waiting-on-dibel-the-growth-of-pentecostalism-among-spanish-gypsies/ [accessed 13/6/2021].

5. René Zanellato, "Gypsy And Traveler International Evangelical Fellowship Report 2017: Worldwide Gypsy Work", n.d. (supplied by report author), p. 4.

6. Ibid.

7. Ian Hancock, *The Historiography of the Holocaust* (New York, NY: Palgrave Macmillan, 2004), pp. 383–96, available at https://web.archive.org/web/20110928102756/http://www.radoc.net/radoc.php?doc=art_e_holocaust_porrajmos&lang=en&articles= [accessed 13/6/2021].

8. United States Holocaust Memorial Museum, "Classification System In Nazi Concentration Camps", Holocaust Encyclopedia, n.d., https://encyclopedia.ushmm.org/content/en/article/classification-system-in-nazi-concentration-camps [accessed 13/6/2021].

9. René Zanellato, "An Amazing Story Woven With Miracles", n.d. (supplied by report author), p. 1.

10. Movements blog, "Gypsy Faith", 16 January 2007, https://www.movements.net/blog/2007/01/15/gypsies-find-christ.html [accessed 13/6/2021].

11. Association Protestante des Amis des Tziganes, "The Gypsy Evangelical Mission in France", *Musée virtuel du protestantisme*, n.d., https://museeprotestant.org/en/notice/la-mission-evangelique-tzigane-de-france/ [accessed 13/6/2021].

12. Magdalena Slavkova, "'Singing and Dancing in the Spirit'. Gypsy Pentecostal Music and Musicians", *Axis Mundi Journal of Religious Studies*, January 2012, p. 39, https://www.researchgate.net/publication/306103107_'Singing_and_Dancing_in_the_Spirit'_Gypsy_Pentecostal_Music_and_Musicians/link/5e0f6843a6fdcc283755ef06/download [accessed 13/6/2021].

13. Richard Wike et al., "European Public Opinion Three Decades After The Fall Of Communism: 6. Minority Groups", Pew Research Center, 14 October 2019, https://www.pewresearch.org/global/2019/10/14/minority-groups/ [accessed 13/6/2021].

14. René Zanellato, "Romania or the history of the sufferings of a people", 2002 (supplied by report author), p. 1.
15. Stephen Hunt, "A history of Pentecostalism in Britain", LSE blog, 21 November 2016, https://blogs.lse.ac.uk/religionglobalsociety/2016/11/a-history-of-pente-costalism-in-britain/#:-:text=Today%2C%20however%2C%20it%20might%20be,17%2C000%20Pentecostal%20churches%20in%20the [accessed 13/6/2021]; Peter Brierley, "Churches Outnumber Pubs in the UK", *Christianity Today*, 28 May 2019, https://www.christianitytoday.com/news/2019/may/churches-outnumber-pubs-in-uk-london-attendance-pentecostal.html [accessed 13/6/2021].
16. Brierley, "Churches Outnumber Pubs".
17. Uebert Angel, Facebook post, 28 May 2019 (since deleted), https://www.facebook.com/ProphetUebertAngel/posts/2644788085532556?comment_id=2644790178865680&comment_tracking=%7B%22tn%22%3A%22R%22%7D [viewed by author April 2021].
18. Kristi Severance, "France's Expulsion of Roma Migrants: A Test Case for Europe", Migration Policy Institute, 21 October 2010, https://www.migra-tionpolicy.org/article/frances-expulsion-roma-migrants-test-case-europe [accessed 13/6/2021].
19. *The Economist*, "Britain's Gypsies and travellers demand justice", 23 July 2020, https://www.economist.com/britain/2020/07/23/britains-gypsies-and-travel-lers-demand-justice [accessed 13/6/2021]. The 2011 census recorded 58,000 Gypsies and Travellers, but officials have noted that the real population is likely to be 200,000 or even 300,000 strong.
20. Patrick Barkham, "Gypsy groups report the Sun to the police", *The Guardian*, 10 March 2005, https://www.theguardian.com/media/2005/mar/10/pressand-publishing.localgovernment [accessed 13/6/2021].
21. Rachel Shields, "No blacks, no dogs, no Gypsies", *The Independent*, 23 October 2011, https://www.independent.co.uk/news/uk/home-news/no-blacks-no-dogs-no-gypsies-860873.html [accessed 13/6/2021].
22. "Who is a gypsy? Britain's new definition is causing problems", *The Economist*, 11 January 2018, https://www.economist.com/britain/2018/01/11/who-is-a-gypsy-britains-new-definition-is-causing-problems [accessed 13/6/2021].
23. Shields, "No blacks, no dogs, no Gypsies".
24. Jane Dalton, "Tories accused of 'criminalising Gypsies and protecting illegal fox-hunting' under crackdown on trespass", *The Independent*, 30 November 2019, https://www.independent.co.uk/news/uk/politics/general-election-boris-johnson-trespass-law-gypsies-travellers-fox-hunting-manifesto-a9227511.html [accessed 13/6/2021].
25. HC Deb 2 July 2020, vol 678, col 525, https://hansard.parliament.uk/

Commons/2020-07-02/debates/c92800b3-b3fc-4dc5-a72f-67ec8e
60498a/CommonsChamber [accessed 29/6/2021].

26. Jessica Murray, "Blanket bans on camping by Gypsies and Travellers ruled illegal at high court", *The Guardian*, 12 May 2021, https://www.theguardian.com/world/2021/may/12/blanket-bans-on-camping-by-gypsies-and-travellers-ruled-at-high-court [accessed 13/6/2021].

27. Matthew Parris, "It's time we stopped pandering to Travellers", *The Times*, 15 May 2021, https://www.thetimes.co.uk/article/its-time-we-stopped-pandering-to-travellers-2slbdvbvp [accessed 13/6/2021].

28. Sophie Hemery, "UK Gypsies and Travellers—a community under pressure", *Equal Times*, 7 April 2016, https://www.equaltimes.org/uk-gypsies-and-travellers-a?lang=en#.YGD2H2RKjt0 [accessed 13/6/2021].

29. Steven Horne, "The 'Good Samaritan' Retold: Gypsies And Jesus", *Travellers' Times*, 11 April 2016, https://www.travellerstimes.org.uk/features/good-samaritan-retold-gypsies-and-jesus [accessed 13/6/2021].

7. A COMPANY TOWN

1. Brad Christerson & Richard Flory, *The Rise of Network Christianity: How Independent Leaders Are Changing the Religious Landscape* (New York, NY: Oxford University Press, 2017), p. 14.

2. Bethel Pray, Facebook post, 8 April 2020, https://www.facebook.com/groups/BethelPRAY/permalink/3914422495242036/ [accessed 24/6/2021].

3. Bethel, "Healed of Stage Four Cancer!", *Bethel Testimonies*, 8 February 2007, https://www.bethel.com/testimonies/healed-of-stage-four-cancer/ [accessed 23/6/2021].

4. Leonardo Blair, "Bethel Church pastor Beni Johnson says she's felt 'so much peace' despite cancer diagnosis", *Christian Today*, 17 August 2018, https://www.christiantoday.com/article/bethel-church-pastor-beni-johnson-says-shes-felt-so-much-peace-despite-cancer-diagnosis/130230.htm [accessed 29/6/2021].

5. Annelise Pierce, "The Really Big Business of Bethel Church: Part 3—Known for Its Generosity", A News Cafe, 30 September 2019, https://anewscafe.com/2019/09/30/redding/the-really-big-business-of-bethel-church-part-3-an-evangelical-disneyland-known-for-its-generosity/ [accessed 23/6/2021].

6. Bethel Redding, "Want to Work at Bethel?", n.d., https://apply.workable.com/bethel-church-of-redding/j/C47B331772/?utm_campaign=google_jobs_apply&utm_source=google_jobs_apply&utm_medium=organic [accessed 23/6/2021].

7. Bethel School of Supernatural Ministry, "BSSM On-Campus 2021–2022 Finance Packet", 31 March 2021, https://bssm.net/wp-content/uploads/2021/05/2021-2022-BSSM-Finance-Packet-03–31–2021.pdf [accessed 23/6/2021].

8. Lauren Smiley, "The True Story of the Antifa Invasion of Forks, Washington", *Wired*, 10 August 2020, https://www.wired.com/story/antifa-social-media-rumor-forks-washington/ [accessed 22/6/2021].

9. Bill Johnson & Randy Clark, *Healing Plugged: Conversations and Insights from Two Veteran Healing Leaders* (Bloomington, IN: Chosen Books, 2012), p. 32.

10. "Bill Johnson: On Earth As It Is in Heaven", CBN, n.d., https://www1.cbn.com/700club/bill-johnson-earth-it-heaven [accessed 14/6/2021].

11. Martin Trench, "Victorious Eschatology: a simple summary", website post, n.d., https://martintrench.com/victorious-eschatology-a-simple-summary/ [accessed 22/6/2021].

12. Os Hillman, "Loren Cunningham Original Vision of 7 Mountains Strategy", YouTube, 2007 interview, https://www.youtube.com/watch?v=iOrLz_RdOjQ [accessed 22/6/2021].

13. Lance Wallnau & Bill Johnson, *Invading Babylon: The 7 Mountain Mandate* (Shippensburg, PA: Destiny Image, 2013), p. 23.

14. Kris Vallotton, "Are You Believing This Destructive Lie About the End of the World?", blog post, 10 May 2019, https://www.krisvallotton.com/created-stalk-darkness [accessed 22/6/2021].

15. Author interview with Professor André Gagné, 21 May 2020.

16. C. Peter Wagner, *Praying with Power: How to Pray Effectively and Hear Clearly from God* (Shippensburg, PA: Destiny Image, 1997), p. 208.

17. Frederick Clarkson, "Project Blitz by Any Other Name", Political Research Associates, 7 November 2019, https://www.politicalresearch.org/2019/11/07/project-blitz-any-other-name [accessed 23/6/2021].

18. Jamie Seidel, "The 'Seven Mountains' conspiracy", *The Advertiser*, 8 January 2019, https://www.adelaidenow.com.au/news/world/the-seven-mountains-revelation/news-story/be825c6262f5e764a3c2cbd385442702 [accessed 23/6/2021].

19. See Changed Movement website: https://changedmovement.com/ [accessed 23/6/2021].

20. Annelise Pierce, "The Really Big Business of Bethel Church, Part 1: Show us the Money!", A News Cafe, 13 May 2019, https://anewscafe.com/2019/05/13/redding/the-really-big-business-of-bethel-church-part-1-show-us-the-money/ [accessed 23/6/2021].

21. Andy Mason, "Heaven in Business", Bethel Ministries, n.d., https://www.bethel.com/ministries/heaven-in-business/ [accessed 23/6/2021].

22. Nathan Solis, "City Council accepts Bethel donation for police unit", *Record Searchlight*, n.d., https://eu.redding.com/story/news/local/2017/04/18/city-council-address-bethel-offer-fund-redding-police-unit/100626478/ [accessed 23/6/2021].

23. Sean Longoria, "Bethel Church offers to give Redding $25,000 for police drones", *Record Searchlight*, n.d., https://eu.redding.com/story/news/local/

2017/12/15/bethel-church-offers-give-redding-25-000-police-drones/
954147001/ [accessed 29/6/2021].

24. A News Cafe, "Environmental Group Poses Questions to Redding City Council Candidates: Part 1—Julie Winter", 2 October 2020, https://anewscafe.
com/2020/10/02/redding/shasta-environmental-alliance-poses-questions-to-redding-city-council-candidate-part-1-julie-winterto-julie-winter/ [accessed 29/6/2021].

25. Ashley Gardner, "COVID-19 cases tied to Bethel double as a leader criticizes mask policies", KRCR, 14 October 2020, https://krcrtv.com/news/local/covid-19-cases-tied-to-bethel-double-as-a-leader-criticizes-mask-policies [accessed 27/6/2021]. Though this doesn't seem to be echoed in local reporting or county statements, the *LA Times* put the cases at "more than 300": Hailey Branson-Potts & Anita Chabria, "God, masks and Trump: What a coronavirus outbreak at a California church says about the election", *LA Times*, 1 November 2020, https://www.latimes.com/california/story/2020–11–01/god-masks-and-trump-what-a-coronavirus-outbreak-at-a-california-church-reveals-about-the-election [accessed 29/6/2021].

26. Bethel, "Glory Cloud at Bethel Church", YouTube, 19 December 2011, https://www.youtube.com/watch?v=lvJMPccZR2Y&t=66s [accessed 23/6/2021].

27. Doni Chamberlain, "Bethel Church: Supernatural COVID-Spreading, Plus a Viral Vacation Video", A News Cafe, 13 October 2020, https://anewscafe.
com/2020/10/13/redding/bethel-church-supernatural-covid-spreading-and-a-viral-vacation-video/ [accessed 24/6/2021].

28. Raideragent, "Bethel Church Soaking up the 'anointing' of dead men, or Grave Sucking", YouTube, 9 December 2011, https://www.youtube.com/watch?v=LrHPTs8cLls&t=18s [accessed 23/6/2021].

29. Kris Vallotton, Facebook post, 18 May 2015, https://www.facebook.com/kvministries/posts/ive-been-asked-what-i-think-about-grave-sucking-several-times-lately-personally-/10152893202998741/ [accessed 23/6/2021].

30. Bethel, "The Power of Soaking", *Bethel Testimonies*, 31 January 2006, https://www.bethel.com/testimonies/the-power-of-soaking/ [accessed 23/6/2021].

31. Damon Arthur, "UPDATE: Bethel pastor Johnson addresses attempts to resurrect child", *Record Searchlight*, 17 December 2019, https://www.redding.
com/story/news/2019/12/17/bethel-family-seeks-bring-daughter-back-life-through-prayer-song-and-praise/2676273001/ [accessed 23/6/2021].

32. The Dead Raising Team, "Our Director", n.d., http://deadraisingteam.com/our-director/ [accessed 23/6/2021].

33. Caleb Parke, "Pastors, worship leaders pray for Trump in Oval Office amid impeachment fight", Fox News, 11 December 2019, https://www.foxnews.com/

politics/pastors-worship-leaders-pray-for-trump-in-oval-office-amid-impeach-ment-fight [accessed 23/6/2021].

34. Wallnau & Johnson, *Invading Babylon*, p. 65.

35. Lance Wallnau, Facebook livestream, 9 July 2020, https://www.facebook.com/watch/live/?v=1488876877985599&ref=watch_permalink   [accessed 24/6/2021].

36. Robert Leslie, "We went inside the Tennessee church whose Trump-revering pastor combines politics with Christian nationalism", *Insider*, 26 April 2021, https://www.insider.com/patriot-church-pastor-ken-peters-knoxville-tennes-see-trump-2021–4 [accessed 23/6/2021].

37. Charisma News, Facebook post, 5 January 2021, https://www.facebook.com/116056801813862/posts/3611633078922866 [accessed 24/6/2021].

38. Andrea Salcedo, "A Florida man admitted storming the Capitol, feds say. Then he told the FBI his pastor had come with him.", *The Washington Post*, 25 June 2021, https://www.washingtonpost.com/nation/2021/06/25/cusick-capitol-riot-pastor-melbourne-florida/ [accessed 29/6/2021].

39. LocalPrayers, "Global Outreach Ministries", n.d., https://www.localprayers.com/US/Melbourne/1608746089402018/Global-Outreach-Ministries [accessed 5/7/2021].

40. Bethel Church, Redding, Facebook post, 14 January 2021, https://www.face-book.com/156375031823/photos/a.160110206823/10157948479466824/ [accessed 23/6/2021].

41. E.g. Beni Johnson (benij5), Instagram post, 1 December 2020, https://www.instagram.com/p/CIRj2D0hN0I/ [accessed 29/6/2021]; 5 January 2021, https://www.instagram.com/p/CJrWfbyBIcC/ [accessed 29/6/2021]; 7 January 2021, https://www.instagram.com/p/CJwS2aGhGqX/ [accessed 24/6/2021].

42. *Wondering Eagle*, "Beni Johnson Joined Proud Boys and Other Militia/Terrorist Groups to Protest in Sacramento, California on January 6, 2021", 18 March 2021, https://wonderingeagle.wordpress.com/2021/03/18/beni-johnson-joined-proud-boys-and-other-militia-terrorist-groups-to-protest-in-sacramento-cal-ifornia-on-january-6-2021/ [accessed 24/6/2021].

43. Casey Sanchez, "'Arming' for Armageddon: Militant Joel's Army Followers Seek Theocracy", Southern Poverty Law Center, intelligence report, Fall 2008, archived at https://web.archive.org/web/20080901214431/http://www.splcen-ter.org/intel/intelreport/article.jsp?aid=964 [accessed 23/6/2021].

44. Joel's Army/QAnon links https://twitter.com/profagagne/status/116220236 4918607872

45. Steve Rabey, "Charis Bible College graduate entered U.S. Capitol during Jan. 6 attack", *The Gazette*, 23 February 2021, https://gazette.com/pikespeakcou-

rier/charis-bible-college-graduate-entered-u-s-capitol-during-jan-6-attack/article_824d8a80-7635-11eb-853f-83865a73aea5.html [accessed 23/6/2021].

46. Resist Programming, Twitter thread, 18 January 2021, https://twitter.com/RzstProgramming/status/1351010261633740800 [accessed 29/6/2021]. Ethridge can be seen confirming he is inside the Capitol in the thread reply posted at 3:35am ("While inside the Captiol building...").

47. John Fea, "It appears we have a direct connection between Seven Mountain Dominionism and the insurrection on the U.S. Capitol.", *Current*, 7 February 2021, https://currentpub.com/2021/02/07/it-appears-we-may-have-a-direct-connection-between-seven-mountain-dominionism-and-the-insurrection-on-the-u-s-capitol/ [accessed 23/6/2021].

48. Seidel, "The 'Seven Mountains' conspiracy".

49. Rabey, "Charis Bible College graduate entered U.S. Capitol".

50. Ibid.

51. Ashton Pittman, "The 'End Times' Are Here, Mississippi Elections Chief Says, Calling For Christian Leaders to Heed the Signs", Mississippi Free Press, 6 May 2021, https://www.mississippifreepress.org/11852/the-end-times-are-here-mississippi-elections-chief-says-calling-for-christian-leaders-to-heed-the-signs/ [accessed 6/7/2021].

8. FULLY CURSED AND ABUNDANTLY BLESSED

1. M. Insa Nolte et al., "Inter-religious relations in Yorubaland, Nigeria: corpus methods and anthropological survey data", *Corpora* 13:1, April 2019, pp. 27–64.

2. Nimi Wariboko, "Pentecostalism in Africa", Oxford Research Encyclopedias, 26 October 2017, https://oxfordre.com/africanhistory/view/10.1093/acrefore/9780190277734.001.0001/acrefore-9780190277734-e-120 [accessed 27/6/2021].

3. Yemisi Adegoke, "Nigerians debate giving 10% of their income to the church", BBC News, 19 April 2018, https://www.bbc.com/news/world-africa-43286733 [accessed 3/7/2021].

4. Nduka Orjinmo, "Enoch Adeboye sexism row: Why the Nigerian pastor is so popular", BBC News, 12 August 2020, https://www.bbc.com/news/world-africa-53488921 [accessed 27/6/2021].

5. Leonardo Blair, "Pastor E.A. Adeboye Tells Members Don't Give Offering If They Are Unsure of Salvation", *The Christian Post*, 10 December 2015, https://www.christianpost.com/news/pastor-e-a-adeboye-tells-members-dont-give-offering-unsure-salvation-heaven-newsweek.html [accessed 24/6/2021].

6. Ebenezer Obadare, "The Muslim response to the Pentecostal surge in Nigeria:

Prayer and the rise of charismatic Islam", *Journal of Religious and Political Practice* 2.1, 2016, pp. 75–91.

7. Kelechi Chika Ubaku, Amaechi Alex Ugwuja, "Pentecostalism And The Dwindling State Of Igbo Language: An Appraisal" (Proceedings of 86th The IIER International Conference, Johannesburg, South Africa, 9–10 November 2016), p. 26, https://www.edouniversity.edu.ng/oerrepository/articles/pente-costalism_and_the_dwindling_state_of_igbo_language_an_appraisal.pdf [accessed 5/7/2021].

8. Author interview with Professor Olufemi Vaughan, 21 December 2020.

9. Henry A. Kissinger, "Memorandum for the President", 28 January 1969, State Department, *Foreign Relations, 1969–1976, Volume E-5, Documents on Africa, 1969–1972*, https://2001–2009.state.gov/r/pa/ho/frus/nixon/e5/55258.htm [accessed 28/6/2021].

10. World Peace Foundation, "Nigeria: Civil war", Mass Atrocity Endings project, Tufts University, 7 August 2015, https://sites.tufts.edu/atrocityendings/2015/08/07/nigeria-civil-war/ [accessed 5/7/2021].

11. UN Department of Public Information, "World population projected to reach 9.8 billion in 2050, and 11.2 billion in 2100—says UN", UN Sustainable Development Goals, 21 June 2021, https://www.un.org/en/development/desa/population/events/pdf/other/21/21June_FINAL%20PRESS%20RELEASE_WPP17.pdf [accessed 28/6/2021].

12. Author interview with Professor Ebenezer Obadare, 27 January 2021.

13. Apostle Suleman website, "Apostle Johnson Suleman", n.d., https://www.apos-tlesuleman.org/omega-fire-ministries/apostle-johnson-suleman [accessed 5/7/2021].

14. Apostle Suleman website, "Omega Fire Ministries", n.d., https://www.apos-tlesuleman.org/omega-fire-ministries-1 [accessed 25/6/2021].

15. Nicholas Ibekwe, "Popular Nigerian preacher tells church members to kill Fulani herdsmen", *Premium Times*, 23 January 2017, https://www.premiumtimesng.com/news/more-news/221305-popular-nigerian-preacher-tells-church-members-kill-fulani-herdsmen.html [accessed 25/6/2021]; SaharaTV, "Nigerian priest Apostle Johnson Suleiman [sic] urge his followers to kill Fulani herds-man", YouTube, 22 January 2017, https://www.youtube.com/watch?v=mwF CwpVeHwI [accessed 28/6/2021].

16. *Vanguard*, "DSS invitation to me in order, says Apostle Suleman", 30 January 2017, https://www.vanguardngr.com/2017/01/dss-invitation-order-says-apos-tle-suleman/ [accessed 25/6/2021].

17. Ibekwe, "Popular Nigerian preacher".

18. Emmanuel Sadi, "Apostle Suleman says gay people are possessed by a demon from hell and lists other reasons for gayness.", *The Rustin Times*, 31 August

2018, https://therustintimes.com/2018/08/31/apostle-suleman-says-gay-people-are-possessed-by-a-demon-from-hell-and-lists-other-reasons-for-gayness/ [accessed 25/6/2021].

19. Fikayo Olowolagba, "How Buhari govt is frustrating freedom of speech—Apostle Suleman", *Daily Post*, 11 October 2019, https://dailypost.ng/2019/10/11/buhari-govt-frustrating-freedom-speech-apostle-suleman/ [accessed 5/7/2021].

20. Fikayo Olowolagba, "Oyedepo's curse on Fulani herdsmen stirs reaction", *Daily Post*, 9 August 2019, https://dailypost.ng/2019/08/09/oyedepos-curse-fulani-herdsmen-stirs-reaction/ [accessed 5/7/2021].

21. Collins Nnabuife, "Killer Herdsmen: Why Christians Must Defend Themselves—CAN Gen Sec, Asake", *Nigerian Tribune*, 28 January 2018, https://tribuneonlineng.com/killer-herdsmen-christians-must-defend-can-gen-sec-asake/ [accessed 25/6/2021].

22. BBC News, "Nigeria's Boko Haram crisis: Maiduguri rocket attack kills 10", 24 February 2021, https://www.bbc.com/news/world-africa-56184033#:-:text=The%20Boko%20Haram%20insurgency%2C%20which,million%20in%20north%2Dea stern%20Nigeria [accessed 25/6/2021].

23. Gwladys Fouche, "Millions at risk from African famine worsened by Boko Haram: U.N.", Reuters, 24 February 2017, https://www.reuters.com/article/us-nigeria-famine/millions-at-risk-from-african-famine-worsened-by-boko-haram-u-n-idUSKBN1631F3 [accessed 25/6/2021].

24. *Vanguard*, "Boko Haram ressurects [sic], declares total Jihad", 14 August 2009, https://www.vanguardngr.com/2009/08/boko-haram-ressurects-declares-total-jihad/ [accessed 25/6/2021]. My emphasis.

25. John Campbell & Asch Harwood, "Boko Haram's Deadly Impact", Council on Foreign Relations, 20 August 2018, https://www.cfr.org/article/boko-harams-deadly-impact [accessed 25/6/2021].

26. Sulaimon Salau, "NASFAT condemns kidnap, pray for quick return of Kankara students", *The Guardian* of Nigeria, 18 December 2020, https://guardian.ng/features/friday-worship/nasfat-condemns-kidnap-pray-for-quick-return-of-kankara-students/ [accessed 25/6/2021].

27. Interview with Olufemi Vaughan; Alexander Thurston, "Interactions Between Northern Nigeria and the Arab World in the Twentieth Century", MA thesis, Georgetown University, April 2009, p. 35, https://repository.library.george-town.edu/bitstream/handle/10822/552835/thurstonalexander.pdf?sequence=1 [accessed 5/7/2021].

28. Author interview with Professor Ebenezer Obadare, 30 June 2020.

29. Brian Larkin & Birgit Meyer, "Pentecostalism, Islam & Culture: New Religious Movements in West Africa", in Emmanuel K. Akyeampong (ed.), *Themes in*

West Africa's History, 2006, pp. 286–312. Chapter summary available at https://www.cambridge.org/core/books/themes-in-west-africas-history/pentecostalism-islam-culture-new-religious-movements-in-west-africa/65388F6E383222716C9F0A5124BBCBE5 [accessed 25/6/2021].

30. Ruth Marshall, "Destroying arguments and captivating thoughts: Spiritual warfare prayer as global praxis", *Journal of Religious and Political Practice* 2.1, 2016, pp. 92–113.

31. Mark Juergensmeyer, *Global Rebellion: Religious Challenges to the Secular State, from Christian Militias to al Qaeda* (Berkeley/Los Angeles, CA: University of California Press, 2009), p. 33.

32. Achille Mbembe & Sarah Nuttall's phrase, cited in David Pratten, "The Precariousness of Prebendalism", in Wale Adebanwi & Ebenezer Obadare (eds), *Democracy and Prebendalism in Nigeria* (New York, NY: Palgrave Macmillan), p. 244.

33. William Hansen, "Fear dominates the lives of Nigerians: the consequences are dire", *The Conversation*, 2 November 2020, https://theconversation.com/fear-dominates-the-lives-of-nigerians-the-consequences-are-dire-148321 [accessed 25/6/2021].

34. Ima Jackson-Obot, "What makes Nigerians in diaspora so successful", *Financial Times*, 29 October 2020, https://www.ft.com/content/ca39b445-442a-4845-a07c-0f5dae5f3460 [accessed 5/7/2021]; Molly Fosco, "The Most Successful Ethnic Group in the U.S. May Surprise You", OZY, 7 June 2018, https://www.ozy.com/around-the-world/the-most-successful-ethnic-group-in-the-u-s-may-surprise-you/86885/ [accessed 5/7/2021].

35. Richard Wike et al., "1. Little trust in Trump's handling of international affairs", Pew Research Center, 8 January 2020, https://www.pewresearch.org/global/2020/01/08/little-trust-in-trumps-handling-of-international-affairs/ [accessed 25/6/2021].

36. Gallup, "Can the U.S. Shake Its Image Problem? Rating World Leaders: 2020", 2020, https://www.gallup.com/analytics/315803/rating-world-leaders-2020.aspx?thank-you-report-form=1 [accessed 28/6/2021].

37. Damaris Parsitau, "African Evangelicals and President Trump", *The Elephant*, 20 November 2020, https://www.theelephant.info/long-reads/2020/11/20/african-evangelicals-and-president-trump/ [accessed 5/7/2021].

38. BBC News, "Nigeria protests: President Buhari says 69 killed in unrest", 23 October 2020, https://www.bbc.com/news/world-africa-54666368 [accessed 28/6/2021].

39. Ebenezer Obadare, *Pentecostal Republic: Religion and the Struggle for State Power in Nigeria*, African Arguments series (Chicago, IL: University of Chicago Press, 2018), pp. 34, 153.

40. Patrick Egwu, "Christian Victims in Nigeria Fear Future Attacks", *Foreign Policy*, 9 October 2020, https://foreignpolicy.com/2020/10/09/christian-victims-in-nigeria-fear-future-attacks/ [accessed 5/7/2021]; Amnesty International, "NIGERIA: Government failings leave rural communities at the mercy of gunmen", 24 August 2020, https://www.amnesty.org/en/latest/news/2020/08/nigeria-government-failings-leave-rural-communities-at-the-mercy-of-gunmen-1/ [accessed 5/7/2021].

41. Sahara Reporters, "Buhari Calls Pastor Adeboye To Seek His Blessing Before Announcing Osinbajo As Running Mate", 17 December 2014, http://sahara-reporters.com/2014/12/17/buhari-calls-pastor-adeboye-seek-his-blessing-announcing-osinbajo-running-mate [accessed 25/6/2021].

42. Olusegun Obasanjo, "Full text of Obasanjo's open letter to Buhari", *The Guardian* of Nigeria, 15 July 2019, https://guardian.ng/features/full-text-of-obasanjos-open-letter-to-buhari// [accessed 25/6/2021].

43. *The Guardian* of Nigeria, "Osinbajo disagrees with bleak view of Nigeria's history", 1 October 2020, https://guardian.ng/news/nigeria/national/osinbajo-disagrees-with-bleak-view-of-nigerias-history/ [accessed 29/6/2021].

44. Ruth Marshall, *Political Spiritualities: The Pentecostal Revolution in Nigeria* (Chicago, IL: University of Chicago Press, 2009).

9. NOT YOUR GRANDMOTHER'S CHURCH

1. Gary Cartwright, "The Last Posse", *Texas Monthly*, March 1998, https://www.texasmonthly.com/articles/the-last-posse/ [accessed 29/6/2021].

2. The National Institute of Justice, "An Overview of John Schools in the United States: Summary Based Upon Research from the Study, 'A National Assessment of Prostitution and Sex Trafficking Demand Reduction Efforts'", 7 January 2013, p. 4, https://demand-forum.org/wp-content/uploads/2012/01/John-School-Overview-from-National-Assessment.pdf [accessed 6/7/2021]; author interview with Michael Shively, 24 August 2018.

3. Couch & Russell Financial Group, "For Tax Year 2019: Bartimaeus Ministries", 2020, https://static1.squarespace.com/static/524dd7d1e4b0cf883cfba8db/t/5fc6ac1d3c02f22b9df90831/160685 [accessed 29/6/2021].

4. World Population Review, "Black Population By State 2021", 2021, https://worldpopulationreview.com/state-rankings/black-population-by-state [accessed 5/7/2021]. This website uses 2018 US Census estimates.

5. Pew Research Center, "The New Face of Global Christianity: The Emergence of 'Progressive Pentecostalism'", 12 April 2006, https://www.pewforum.org/2006/04/12/the-new-face-of-global-christianity-the-emergence-of-progressive-pentecostalism/ [accessed 5/7/2021].

6. Tax records for 2019 available via Open990, "Equip and Empower Ministries Inc", last updated 17 June 2021, https://www.open990.org/org/421582446/equip-and-empower-ministries-inc/ [accessed 25/6/2021].

7. The A21 Campaign Inc, "Return of Organization Exempt From Income Tax", IRS Form 990 (2019), https://pdf.guidestar.org/PDF_Images/2019/263/442/2019–263442008–202012769349300906–9.pdf?_gl=1*1e7kmy3*_ga*MTQ1MDI4ODc5OC4xNjI0NjE1MzI4*_ga_0H865XH5JK*MTYyNTQyOTQ2Ni4yLjEuMTYyNTQyOTQ4OS4w*_ga_5W8PXYYGBX*MTYyNTQyOTQ2Ni4yLjEuMTYyNTQyOTQ4OS4w&ga=2.154319096.1551513571.1625429467-1450288798.1624615328 [accessed 5/7/2021].

8. Gabby Orr, "Pence income: No bounce from Marlon Bundo", *Politico*, 16 May 2019, https://www.politico.com/story/2019/05/16/mike-pence-pet-bunny-1329384 [accessed 25/6/2021].

9. Michael Lowe, "Texas Penal Code Amended to Address Human Sex Trafficking Over the Internet" DallasJustice.com, 16 August 2019, https://www.dallasjustice.com/new-texas-sex-crimes-the-online-prostitution-laws-effective-september-1-2019/ [accessed 25/6/2021].

10. Tarpley Hitt, "Inside Exodus Cry: The Shady Evangelical Group With Trump Ties Waging War on Pornhub", *The Daily Beast*, 16 October 2020, https://www.thedailybeast.com/inside-exodus-cry-the-shady-evangelical-group-with-trump-ties-waging-war-on-pornhub [accessed 25/6/2021].

11. Jason Hanna, "How police spent months taking down a spa where Robert Kraft is accused of paying for sex", CNN, 16 March 2019, https://edition.cnn.com/2019/03/15/us/robert-kraft-florida-day-spa-investigation/index.html [accessed 5/7/2021].

12. Elizabeth Nolan Brown, "Florida Masseuse Ordered to Pay $31,573 After 'Soliciting' Robert Kraft To 'Commit Prostitution'", *Reason*, 2 December 2020, https://reason.com/2020/12/02/florida-masseuse-ordered-to-pay-31573-after-soliciting-robert-kraft-to-commit-prostitution/ [accessed 25/6/2021].

13. Rachel Lovell, "Mug Shots: The Public Shaming of 'Johns'", *re/search* blog, DePaul University, 18 May 2012, https://ssrcdepaul.wordpress.com/2012/05/18/mug-shots-part1/ [accessed 6/7/2021]: "Not surprisingly, most arrests occur on the West and South Sides", whose populations are generally lower-income and Black; and she remarks that arrests "based on pure suspicion not probable cause only take place in black and brown communities."

14. Rachel Lovell, "Mug Shots: Transgender 'Johns'", *re/search* blog, DePaul University, 31 May 2012, https://ssrcdepaul.wordpress.com/2012/05/31/mug-shots-part2/ [accessed 6/7/2021].

15. C. Eugene Emery Jr., "Does becoming a prostitute mean you've only got about

7 years to live?", PolitiFact, 31 May 2015, https://www.politifact.com/fact-checks/2015/may/31/rebecca-quigley/does-becoming-prostitute-mean-youve-only-got-about/ [accessed 25/6/2021].

16. Joshua Fechter, "Sheriff: 20 'weird sickos' arrested in Central Texas child solicitation sting", *San Antonio Express-News*, 6 November 2014, https://www.mysanantonio.com/news/local/article/20-arrested-in-Central-Texas-underage-sex-sting-5875593.php [accessed 25/6/2021].

17. WBUR, "15% Of Americans Believe QAnon Theory, Poll Says", 31 May 2021, https://www.wbur.org/hereandnow/2021/05/31/qanon-poll-americans-religion [accessed 30/6/2021].

18. Jason Springs, https://contendingmodernities.nd.edu/theorizing-modernities/qanon-evangelical-apocalypse/

19. Author interview with Travis View (pseudonym), researcher on QAnon, 11 September 2020.

20. Cecilia Saixue Watt, "The QAnon orphans: people who have lost loved ones to conspiracy theories", *The Guardian*, 23 September 2020, https://www.theguardian.com/us-news/2020/sep/23/qanon-conspiracy-theories-loved-ones [accessed 25/6/2021].

10. SIN TODAY, REPENT TOMORROW

1. Sonia Pérez D., "Guatemala: demands for justice for lynching of Mayan [spiritual] leader" (in Spanish), AP, 10 June 2020, https://apnews.com/article/d2ee2955905c6d3e8f8485b55f052cfe [accessed 27/6/2021].

2. Sonia Pérez D., "Guatemala: several detained for lynching of spiritual leader" (in Spanish), AP, 10 June 2020, https://apnews.com/article/19096384185a68aee617c16b2200780f [accessed 27/6/2021].

3. Julio Román, "Three sentenced to 20 years for their crime against Domingo Choc Che, lynched and accused of witchcraft" (in Spanish), *Prensa Libre*, 24 June 2021, https://www.prensalibre.com/ciudades/peten/condenan-a-20-anos-de-carcel-a-tres-personas-por-el-crimen-contra-domingo-choc-che-quien-fue-linchado-acusado-de-brujeria-breaking/ [accessed 6/7/2021].

4. DesInformémonos, "The murderer of Don Domingo Choc Che speaks" (in Spanish), 9 June 2020, https://desinformemonos.org/habla-el-asesino-de-don-domingo-choc-che/ [accessed 28/6/2021].

5. David de la Garza, "The Xibalba: Mysteries Of The Mayan Underworld", Blog Xcaret, 21 October 2016, https://blog.xcaret.com/en/the-xibalba-mysteries-of-the-mayan-underworld/ [accessed 28/6/2021].

6. Quimy De León et al., "What was the cause of the crime against Domingo Choc Che Aj Ilonel?" (in Spanish), *Prensa Comunitaria*, 9 June 2020, https://www.

prensacomunitaria.org/2020/06/cual-fue-la-causa-del-crimen-contra-domingo-choc-che-aj-ilonel2/ [accessed 28/6/2021]. Thanks to my fixer, José Mazariegos, for explaining the denominational breakdown.

7. Sonia Pérez D., "Guatemala: several detained".

8. Richard H. Immerman, *The CIA in Guatemala: The Foreign Policy of Intervention* (Austin, TX: University of Texas Press, 1982), p. 87.

9. Reuters, "TIMELINE: Latin American earthquakes since 1970", 16 August 2007, https://www.reuters.com/article/us-peru-earthquake-factbox/timeline-latin-american-earthquakes-since-1970-idUSN1633320120070816 [accessed 28/6/2021]; Worldometer, "Guatemala Population", using data from the UN Department of Economic and Social Affairs, Population Division, n.d., https://www.worldometers.info/world-population/guatemala-population/ [accessed 1/7/2021].

10. Virginia Garrard-Burnett, *Terror in the Land of the Holy Spirit: Guatemala under General Efraín Ríos Montt, 1982–1983* (New York, NY: Oxford University Press, 2010), p. 55.

11. Phil Gunson, "Gen Efraín Ríos Montt obituary", *The Guardian*, 2 April 2018, https://www.theguardian.com/world/2018/apr/02/gen-efrain-rios-montt-obituary [accessed 28/6/2021].

12. Garrard-Burnett, *Terror*, p. 57.

13. Jeffrey J. Carmel, "Guatemala coup seems to please most of country", *The Christian Science Monitor*, 19 April 1982, https://www.csmonitor.com/1982/0419/041942.html [accessed 6/7/2021].

14. Garrard-Burnett, *Terror*, pp. 56–7.

15. Sara Diamond, *Spiritual Warfare: The Politics of the Christian Right* (Boston, MA: South End Press, 1989), p. 165.

16. Garrard-Burnett, *Terror*, p. 59.

17. Gunson, "Gen Efraín Ríos Montt obituary".

18. Garrard-Burnett, *Terror*, p. 3.

19. Diamond, *Spiritual Warfare*, p. 166.

20. Garrard-Burnett, *Terror*, p. 6.

21. Ibid., p. 7.

22. Ibid., p. 72.

23. Ibid., p. 88.

24. "Guatemalan Vows to Aid Democracy", *New York Times*, 6 December 1982, https://www.nytimes.com/1982/12/06/world/no-headline-080267.html [accessed 28/6/2021].

25. Garrard-Burnett, *Terror*, p. 128.

26. Stephanie M. Huezo, "The Murdered Churchwomen in El Salvador", Origins

blog, Ohio State University, December 2020, https://origins.osu.edu/mile-stones/murdered-churchwomen-el-salvador [accessed 4/7/2021].

27. Carol Glatz, "Vatican statistics show continued growth in number of Catholics worldwide", *National Catholic Reporter*, 26 March 2021, https://www.ncron-line.org/news/vatican/vatican-statistics-show-continued-growth-number-cath-olics-worldwide [accessed 6/7/2021].

28. Garrard-Burnett, *Terror*, pp. 101, 140.

29. Ibid., p. 11.

30. Kevin Lewis O'Neill, *City of God: Christian Citizenship in Postwar Guatemala* (Berkeley/Los Angeles, CA: University of California Press, 2009), p. 56.

31. Garrard-Burnett, *Terror*, p. 6.

32. Connor Yearsley, "The Murder of Guatemalan Maya Spiritual Guide Jesús Choc Yat", *HerbalGram: The Journal of the American Botanical Council* 130, Summer 2021, p. 39.

33. Gilberto Escobar, "Mayan spiritual guide murdered in Quiché; authorities are unaware of the case" (in Spanish), *Prensa Comunitaria*, https://www.prensa-comunitaria.org/2021/01/asesinan-a-guia-espiritual-maya-en-quiche-y-auto-ridades-desconocen-del-caso/# [accessed 6/7/2021].

34. C. Peter Wagner, *Your Church Can Grow: Seven Vital Signs of a Healthy Church* (Eugene, OR: Wipf & Stock Publishers, 1998), pp. 160–1. Emphasis in orig-inal.

35. Robert Muggah, "Evangelical gangs in Rio de Janeiro wage 'holy war' on Afro-Brazilian faiths", *The Conversation*, 16 December 2019, https://theconversa-tion.com/evangelical-gangs-in-rio-de-janeiro-wage-holy-war-on-afro-brazil-ian-faiths-128679 [accessed 6/7/2021].

36. Thomas Strong, "Becoming Witches: Sight, Sin, and Social Change in the Eastern Highlands of Papua New Guinea", in Knut Rio et al. (eds), *Pentecostalism And Witchcraft: Spiritual Warfare in Africa and Melanesia* (Boston, MA: Palgrave Macmillan, 2017), p. 74.

37. Erin Parke, "The Christian converts who are setting fire to sacred Aboriginal objects", ABC News, 19 September 2019, https://www.abc.net.au/news/2019–09–20/the-christian-converts-who-are-setting-fire-to-sacred-aborigi-nal/11527402 [accessed 28/6/2021].

38. Pew Research Center, "Spirit and Power—A 10-Country Survey of Pentecostals", 5 October 2006, https://www.pewforum.org/2006/10/05/spirit-and-power/ [accessed 28/6/2021].

39. *Church & State Magazine*, "Pentecostal Candidate Seeks 'Dominion' Over Guatemala", March 2007, https://www.au.org/church-state/march-2007-church-state/people-events/pentecostal-candidate-seeks-dominion-over [accessed 28/6/2021].

40. Quimy De León et al., "What was the cause of the crime against Domingo Choc Che Aj Ilonel?"

41. Ibid.

42. Virginia Garrard, "Hidden in Plain Sight: Dominion Theology, Spiritual Warfare, and Violence in Latin America", *Religions* 11.12, 2020, p. 648.

43. Post in the Spiritual Warfare and Tactics Squad—SWATS Friends Facebook group, 10 April 2021. The group has over 20,000 members at the time of writing.

44. O'Neill, *City of God*, p. 89.

45. *Prensa Libre*, "Catholic Church of Petén denies that Domingo Choc's lynching was due to cultural and religious differences" (in Spanish), 10 June 2020, https://www.prensalibre.com/ciudades/peten/iglesia-catolica-de-peten-niega-que-linchamiento-de-domingo-choc-haya-sido-por-diferencias-culturales-y-religiosas/ [accessed 2/7/2021].

46. Rachel Sieder, "The judiciary and indigenous rights in Guatemala", *International Journal of Constitutional Law* 5.2, 2007, pp. 211–41.

11. WE AIN'T GOIN' ROUND THE MOUNTAIN ANOTHER SEVEN YEARS

1. Ingrid Anderson, "Why the history of messianic Judaism is so fraught and complicated", *The Conversation*, 13 November 2018, https://theconversation.com/why-the-history-of-messianic-judaism-is-so-fraught-and-complicated-106143 [accessed 2/7/2021].

2. Curt Landry Ministries, "One New Man Terminology", n.d., https://www.curtlandry.com/one-new-man-terminology/#.YORMZhNKh3m [accessed 6/7/2021].

3. Visit Miami, Oklahoma, "Route 66", n.d., http://www.visitmiamiok.com/map/ [accessed 2/7/2021].

4. Curt Landry Ministries, Facebook page, https://www.facebook.com/curtlandryministries/ [accessed 5/7/2021].

5. Curt Landry Ministries, "The Love of a Good Father", 16 March 2017, https://www.curtlandry.com/the-love-of-a-good-father/#.YOLllhOA4TU [accessed 5/7/2021]; Idem, "Curt Landry's Personal Testimony", n.d., https://www.curtlandry.com/curt-landry/#.YN3ucROA79E [accessed 2/7/2021].

6. Trevor O'Reggio, "The Rise of the New Apostolic Reformation and its Implication for Adventist Eschatology", *Andrews University Faculty Publications*, Paper 25, January 2012, p. 140, https://digitalcommons.andrews.edu/cgi/viewcontent.cgi?article=1024&context=church-history-pubs [accessed 1/7/2021].

7. Ibid., p. 141.

8. Michael J. Vlach, "Dispensational Theology", n.d., The Gospel Coalition,

https://www.thegospelcoalition.org/essay/dispensational-theology/ [accessed 5/7/2021].

9. Bob Smietana, "American Evangelicals Stand Behind Israel", Lifeway Research, 14 July 2015, https://lifewayresearch.com/2015/07/14/american-evangelicals-stand-behind-israel/ [accessed 30/6/2021].

10. Ilan Ben Zion, "Honduras opens embassy in Jerusalem, 4th country to do so", AP, 24 June 2021, https://apnews.com/article/donald-trump-jerusalem-honduras-middle-east-religion-49d8f0a908d2a0bf16830071e2c6f5f0 [accessed 6/7/2021].

11. Nancy LeTourneau, "A More Twisted Form of Anti-Semitism", *Washington Monthly*, 12 February 2019, https://washingtonmonthly.com/2019/02/12/a-more-twisted-form-of-anti-semitism/ [accessed 30/6/2021].

12. BBC News, "Graham regrets Jewish slur", 2 March 2002, http://news.bbc.co.uk/2/hi/americas/1850077.stm [accessed 5/7/2021].

13. Michael Schulson, "How an Orthodox Rabbi Became an Unlikely Ally of the Christian Right", Religion & Politics project, 14 February 2017, https://religionandpolitics.org/2017/02/14/how-an-orthodox-rabbi-became-an-unlikely-ally-of-the-christian-right/ [accessed 26/8/2021].

14. Dan Hummel, "The new Judaizers", *The Jerusalem Post*, 10 March 2018, https://www.jpost.com/magazine/the-new-judaizers-540415 [accessed 30/6/2021].

15. Ibid.

16. Caliber 3, "About", n.d., https://www.caliber3range.com/about [accessed 5/7/2021].

17. Yaakov Schwartz, "Seinfeld under fire over visit to West Bank 'military camp'", *The Times of Israel*, 11 January 2018, https://www.timesofisrael.com/seinfeld-under-fire-over-visit-to-west-bank-military-camp/ [accessed 12/7/2021].

18. Ryan Burge Twitter thread reply, 29 March 2021, 20:40, https://twitter.com/ryanburge/status/1376620219163148304 [accessed 5/7/2021]. Overall, I am indebted in this section of the chapter to the surveys and data analysis of Dr Burge, who is Assistant Professor of Political Science at Eastern Illinois University, specialising in the intersection between religiosity and political behaviour.

19. Ryan Burge Twitter thread reply, 30 March 2021, 17:14, https://twitter.com/ryanburge/status/1376930893152026624 [accessed 12/7/2021].

20. Ryan Burge tweet, 5 March 2021, https://twitter.com/ryanburge/status/1367878917885984768 [accessed 12/7/2021].

21. Ryan Burge tweet, 19 April 2018, https://twitter.com/ryanburge/status/987006158698401798 [accessed 5/7/2021].

22. Ryan Burge, "Think US evangelicals are dying out? Well, define evangelicalism...", *The Conversation*, 26 January 2021, https://theconversation.com/think-

us-evangelicals-are-dying-out-well-define-evangelicalism-152640 [accessed 5/7/2021].

23. Ryan Burge, "How many Americans believe Trump is anointed by God?", Religion News Service, 25 November 2019, https://religionnews.com/2019/11/25/how-many-americans-believe-trump-is-anointed-by-god/ [accessed 5/7/2021].

24. The Religious Studies Project podcast, "Understanding Evangelical Opposition to Climate Action", 12 April 2021, https://www.religiousstudiesproject.com/podcast/understanding-evangelical-opposition-to-climate-action/ [accessed 5/7/2021].

25. Sonya Geis, "Latino Catholics Increasingly Drawn To Pentecostalism, Shift Among Immigrants Could Affect Politics", *The Washington Post*, 30 April 2006, https://www.washingtonpost.com/archive/politics/2006/04/30/latino-catholics-increasingly-drawn-to-pentecostalism-span-classbankheadshift-among-immigrants-could-affect-politicsspan/29f93822-89b5-4d13-b6b5-e0a2e6f32cce/ [accessed 5/7/2021].

26. Melissa Guzman Garcia, "Spiritual Citizenship: Immigrant Religious Participation and the Management of Deportability", *International Migration Review* 52.2, 2018, pp. 404–29.

27. Jo Tuckman & Dan Collyns, "Bolivia: Jeanine Añez claims presidency after ousting of Evo Morales", *The Guardian*, 13 November 2019, https://www.theguardian.com/world/2019/nov/12/evo-morales-arrives-mexico-bolivia-power-vacuum [accessed 6/7/2021].

28. OpenDemocracy, "The bible makes a comeback in Bolivia with Jeanine Añez", 20 November 2019, https://www.opendemocracy.net/en/democraciaabierta/qui%C3%A9n-es-jeanine-a%C3%B1ez-y-por-qu%C3%A9-desprecia-los-pueblos-ind%C3%ADgenas-de-bolivia-en/ [accessed 5/7/2021].

29. Ibid.

30. Tom Phillips, "'Satan, be gone!': Bolivian Christians claim credit for ousting Evo Morales", *The Guardian*, 27 January 2020, https://www.theguardian.com/world/2020/jan/27/bolivian-christians-evo-morales-indigenous-catholic-protestant [accessed 5/7/2021].

31. Patricia Robertson, "The Rise of Pentecostalism in Latin America: A Study of Conversion, Politics, and the Dark Secrets within Contemporary Bolivia", undergraduate thesis, University of Calgary, April 2007, p. 19, https://www.researchgate.net/publication/290446247_The_Rise_of_Pentecostalism_in_Latin_America_A_Study_of_Conversion_Politics_and_the_Dark_Secrets_within_Contemporary_Bolivia [accessed 6/7/2021].

32. Fabiola Gutiérrez (trans. Liam Anderson), "Pious, assertive, and 'mother of all Bolivians': The political narrative of President Jeanine Áñez", Global Voices,

10 August 2020, https://globalvoices.org/2020/08/10/pious-assertive-and-mother-of-all-bolivians-the-expensive-political-narrative-of-president-jeanine-anez/ [accessed 5/7/2021].

33. TeleSUR/MP, "Bolivia De Facto Govt Reestablishes Diplomatic Ties With Israel", TeleSUR English, 4 February 2020, https://www.telesurenglish.net/news/Bolivia-De-Facto-Govt-Reestablishes-Diplomatic-Ties-With-Israel-20200204–0011.html [accessed 5/7/2021].

34. Caroline Heringer, "Evangelical and drug dealer who created 'Israel Complex' in Rio's favelas painted the city of Jerusalem on wall of his house" (in Portuguese), *O Globo*, 16 April 2021, https://oglobo.globo.com/rio/evangelico-traficante-que-criou-complexo-de-israel-em-favelas-do-rio-pintou-cidade-de-jerusalem-no-muro-de-casa-24974398 [accessed 5/7/2021].

35. *Radio War Nerd*, episode 271, "Burma's Ethnic Militias", 7 March 2021, 1:51–2, https://podcastaddict.com/episode/120065263 [accessed 5/7/2021].

36. David Smith, "'He's not a quitter': faithful out in force as Trump gets back to the campaign trail", *The Guardian*, 27 June 2021, https://www.theguardian.com/us-news/2021/jun/27/hes-not-a-quitter-faithful-out-in-force-as-trump-gets-back-to-the-campaign-trail [accessed 6/7/2021].

37. Kenny Hodgart, "The Messiah friend of President Duterte", *Asia Times*, 7 October 2016, https://asiatimes.com/2016/10/messiah-friend-president-duterte-2/ [accessed 6/7/2021].

38. Darryl John Esguerra, "Duterte says he believes Quiboloy stopped Mindanao quake", *Philippine Daily Inquirer*, 22 November 2019, https://newsinfo.inquirer.net/1193444/duterte-says-he-believes-quiboloy-stopped-mindanao-quake#ixzz6tHNueVTY [accessed 30/6/2021].

39. Benjamin Kentish, "Philippines president Rodrigo Duterte reveals he was abused by priest as a child", *The Independent*, 18 October 2016, https://www.independent.co.uk/news/world/asia/philippines-duterte-war-on-drugs-sexual-abuse-crackdown-human-rights-a7366941.html [accessed 12/7/2021].

40. Matt Payton, "Philippine's [sic] President-elect calling Pope Francis a son of a whore 'was just banter', says campaign team", *The Independent*, 13 May 2016, https://www.independent.co.uk/news/world/asia/philippine-s-president-elect-rodrigo-duterte-says-calling-pope-francis-son-whore-was-just-banter-a7028891.html [accessed 12/7/2021].

41. Ritchel Mendiola, "DFA Pays Tribute To Overseas Filipinos On Migrant Workers' Day", *Asian Journal*, 10 June 2020, https://www.asianjournal.com/world/dfa-pays-tribute-to-overseas-filipinos-on-migrant-workers-day/ [accessed 5/7/2021].

42. Pew Research Center, "Religious Belief and National Belonging in Central and Eastern Europe", 10 May 2017, https://www.pewforum.org/2017/05/10/reli-

gious-belief-and-national-belonging-in-central-and-eastern-europe/ [accessed 5/7/2021]. Most of the 13 per cent of Hungarians identified here as Protestant are Lutherans, bunched together with other non-Pentecostal Protestants.

43. Dariusz Kalan, "How Viktor Orbán's Son Found God Instead Of Politics", OZY, 30 October 2019, https://www.ozy.com/news-and-politics/how-viktor-orbans-son-found-god-instead-of-politics/97175/ [accessed 5/7/2021].

44. John Woods, "PM Orbán's son graduated from British RMA Sandhurst—Hungary paid his tuition fee", *Daily News Hungary*, 15 January 2021, https://dailynewshungary.com/pm-orbans-son-graduated-from-british-rma-sandhurst-hungary-paid-his-tuition-fee/ [accessed 5/6/2021].

45. Jeremy Weber, "Will Europe's Third-Largest Church Punish Pastor for Multiple Affairs?", *Christianity Today*, 17 May 2016, https://www.christianitytoday.com/news/2016/may/will-embassy-of-god-punish-sunday-adelaja-multiple-affairs.html [accessed 5/7/2021].

46. Clifford J. Levy, "An Evangelical Preacher's Message Catches Fire in Ukraine", *The New York Times*, 22 April 2011, https://www.nytimes.com/2011/04/23/world/europe/23kiev.html [accessed 5/7/2021].

47. John L. Allen Jr., "If demography is destiny, Pentecostals are the ecumenical future", *National Catholic Reporter*, 28 January 2008, https://www.ncronline.org/news/if-demography-destiny-pentecostals-are-ecumenical-future [accessed 30/6/2021].

48. Human Rights Watch, "Russia: Escalating Persecution of Jehovah's Witnesses", 9 January 2020, https://www.hrw.org/news/2020/01/09/russia-escalating-persecution-jehovahs-witnesses [accessed 6/7/2021].

49. Adelle M. Banks, "Poll Says Many Pentecostals Don't Speak in Tongues", Religion News Service, 6 October 2006, https://religionnews.com/2006/10/06/poll-says-many-pentecostals-dont-speak-in-tongues/ [accessed 30/6/2021].

50. Allen Jr., "If demography is destiny".

51. Ibid.

52. Jake Wallis Simons & Jonathan Sacerdoti, "EXCLUSIVE: Unmasked, the Christian missionary who went undercover in Jerusalem as an Orthodox rabbi", *The Jewish Chronicle*, 6 May 2021, https://www.thejc.com/news/israel/exclusive-unmasked-the-christian-missionary-who-went-undercover-as-an-orthodox-rabbi-1.516346 [accessed 5/7/2021].

53. Jonathan Sacerdoti, "EXCLUSIVE: Remove body of undercover missionary from Jewish cemetery, say rabbinical chiefs", *The Jewish Chronicle*, 2 June 2021, https://www.thejc.com/news/israel/remove-body-of-undercover-missionary-from-jewish-cemetery-say-rabbinical-chiefs-1.517289 [accessed 5/7/2021].

54. Paul Goldman & Saphora Smith, "Israel orders evangelical Christian media network God TV to take channel off air", NBC News, 29 June 2020, https://

www.nbcnews.com/news/world/israel-orders-evangelical-christian-media-network-god-tv-take-channel-n1232403 [accessed 5/7/2021].

55. Mykal McEldowney, "What Charlottesville Changed", *Politico*, 12 August 2018, https://www.politico.com/magazine/story/2018/08/12/charlottesville-anniversary-supremacists-protests-dc-virginia-219353/ [accessed 5/7/2021].

56. Krista Blankenburg, "The Forgotten Story of the Black Man Who Invented Pentacostalism [sic]", *Relevant*, 23 February 2018, https://www.relevantmagazine.com/faith/forgotten-story-black-man-invented-pentacostalism/ [accessed 5/7/2021].

57. Allan Heaton Anderson, *Spirit-Filled World: Religious Dis/Continuity in African Pentecostalism* (London: Palgrave Macmillan, 2018), p. 244.

INDEX

INDEX

INDEX

INDEX

INDEX

INDEX

INDEX

INDEX

INDEX

INDEX

INDEX

INDEX

INDEX

INDEX

INDEX

INDEX

INDEX

INDEX

INDEX

INDEX

September 11 attacks (2001), 63
slavery in, 4, 9, 10
snake-handling churches, 25–9, 36
South Korea, relations with, 48, 64
Stop The Steal movement (2021), 162–6, 256
sundown towns, 26
televangelism in, 18, 19, 73, 76
Trump administration (2017–21), *see* Trump, Donald
Unite the Right rally (2017), 261
Vineyard Movement, 36
World War I (1914–18), 20
World War II (1939–45), 21
Zionist Church, 98–9
Universal Church of the Kingdom of God, 78–82, 83, 131, 149
University of Michigan, 211
University of South Africa, 113
Uspantán, Quiché, 229

Valle, Angelina, 215
Vallotton, Kris, 153, 159
Vanderbloemen, William, 160–61
Vatican, 172, 221
Vaughan, Olufemi, 175, 183, 189
Venezuela, 246
Verbo, El, 222–3, 224, 227
Vie et Lumière, 124, 127, 135
Vineyard Movement, 36
Vladivostok, Russia, 59
Voliva, Wilbur Glenn, 98

Wacker, Grant, 18, 19

Waco, Texas, xiv, 195–203, 205, 209, 211, 212
Wagner, Charles Peter, 37, 38, 151, 153–4, 190, 220, 230, 231
Wailing Wall, Jerusalem, 126
Wallnau, Lance, 152, 155, 160, 162, 164, 165
Washington Post, The, 162
Watson, Michael, 165
waves, *see* Pentecostal waves
Wesley, John, 4
West Bank, Palestine, 246
White, Paula, 246
Wigglesworth, Smith, 101–2, 159
Wild Torch, 201
Williams, Ken, 155
Wimber, John, 29, 33–8, 40, 151, 153, 220, 222, 259
Windrush generation (1948–70), 132
Winners Chapel International, 180–81, 186
Winter, Julie, 157
Wommack, Andrew, 164
Woning, Elizabeth, 155–6
Word, The, 222–3, 224, 227
World War I (1914–18), 20
World War II (1939–45), 21, 47
Wynette, Tammy, 31

Yalu River, 51
Yeouido Island, Seoul, 62
Yoido Full Gospel Church, 61–3, 65, 149
Yoruba people, 168, 175, 176, 189

INDEX